# The Paper Dragon

# The Paper Dragon

*An Account of the China Wars, 1840-1900*

## John Selby

FREDERICK A. PRAEGER, Publishers
New York · Washington

BOOKS THAT MATTER

Published in the United States of America in 1968
by Frederick A. Praeger, Inc., Publishers
111 Fourth Avenue, New York, N.Y. 10003

© 1968, in England, by John Selby

Library of Congress Catalog Card Number: 68-30678

Printed in Great Britain

# Contents

# Illustrations and Maps

## MAPS

# Acknowledgements

During a recent visit to the Far East, I stayed for a few weeks in Hong Kong, the start of so many of the operations described in this book; and while there I was indebted to Mr I. W. Hughes, Head of the Extra-Mural Department of Hong Kong University, for his help. Mr and Mrs Hughes did everything possible to make the visit a profitable one, among other things inviting members of the World Press in Hong Kong and the heads of the Arts Faculties of the University to a conversazione for my benefit.

I also want to thank Mr Loren Fessler of *Time* for presenting me with his book on China, and for putting his vast experience at my disposal by allowing me to pick his brains while I tried to eat Chinese fare with chopsticks as his guest.

Canon E. W. L. Martin, now of St John's College, Hong Kong, and formerly headmaster of Stanley School, was most kind to me during my stay, and I am very grateful for his help.

He drove me in his car all over Hong Kong Island, the Kowloon Peninsula and the New Territories. In the neighbourhood of his old school at Stanley, we saw some of the multitude of memorial headstones on the island to the soldiers of British regiments who died there of disease during the China Wars. Chusan and Hong Kong were then most unhealthy, and more soldiers died of fever in the camps on these two islands off the coast of China than were killed in the fighting. It is something of a paradox that Hong Kong and the Stanley area in particular, is now a health resort.

In Japan I was entertained by the Superintendent and Officers of the Defence Academy at Oharadai, Yokosuka, and wish to thank them for their kindness and help in my research on the relief force sent to Peking in 1900.

A*

## Acknowledgements

At home, I wish to thank Mr King of the Ministry of Defence Library (Central and Army) for putting the benefit of his wide knowledge at my disposal, and to Mr Davis and the rest of his staff for their assistance on many occasions. I also want to thank the staff of the British Museum, the Public Record Office and Hove Public Library for their help. I am indebted to Mr Paris and Mr W. Y. Carman and the staff of the National Army Museum for advice on the illustrations; and to Lieut-Colonel L. H. Yates and Major Melia of the Prince Consort Library, Aldershot and Lieut-Colonel G. A. Shepperd and the staff of the RMA Sandhurst Library, Mr Cresswell of the University Library Cambridge and Dr M. I. Scott of its China Room, for their help. Finally I wish to thank Messrs Matheson & Co. for permitting me to quote from material in their archives and Professor Franz Michael and the University of Washington Press for allowing me to quote from *The Taiping Rebellion*.

# 1 The First China War, 1839-42

' An important event happened on 2 March 1841. Major-General Sir Hugh Gough arrived off Canton from Madras to assume command of all the land forces, by order of the Governor-General of India. The arrival of a general of acknowledged bravery and distinction was a subject of much congratulation, and was looked upon as likely to lead to energetic and decisive steps;' thus wrote Captain Hall of the *Nemesis*, then in China waters.

By this time China had been in conflict with Britain and the West for several years. It started in 1757 when an Imperial edict drastically changed the arrangements which allowed foreign vessels to trade at several Chinese ports and confined them to Canton. There were other irksome restrictions as well. Europeans were not allowed to live in the Chinese part of Canton; they were confined to the suburbs, and neither women nor arms could be brought to their trading factories.

Such trade as was allowed was also, in the opinion of the foreign merchants, over-regulated. The Superintendency of the Customs at Canton was a Court appointment and usually given to a Manchu relative of the Emperor. Customs dues were paid into the National Exchequer, but the Superintendent – Hai Kwan-pu was his official designation, or ' Hoppo ' to the British – was not salaried. He was expected to pay himself from his takings. Indeed, he had to purchase the appointment which (with the squeezes he could make on the foreign traders) was one of the most lucrative in the Empire. In 1804, the then Hoppo's takings were estimated at £200,000 a year. Under the Hoppo there were Tide-Waiters or officials on the spot to give chops or permits to traders, and a body of contractors known as the Co-Hong appointed by the Hoppo through whom the foreign merchants had to buy and sell, and who took their own squeeze in the process. For the privilege of conducting the foreign trade of Canton and making sure the foreign merchants in the factories obeyed the various regulations, the Co-Hong contractors, in addition to buying their posts in the same way as the Hoppo, were subject to further squeezes from him. Nevertheless, Howqua, the leading merchant of the Co-Hong at this time, was clever enough, in spite of a long course of exactions, to amass a fortune reputed to equal five millions sterling. Such men as the long-faced, white bearded Howqua were well liked by the foreign traders and had a reputation for fair dealing within the limits of the system. Howqua is said to have invested some of his own money in the American firm of Russell & Co., and to have been a most courteous host when he invited English and American merchants to chopstick dinners of birds' nest soup, plovers' eggs, sharks' fins, roasted snails and other delicacies, accompanied by wines prepared from rice, green peas and various fruits. At the end of such dinners he would send out coolies with large lanterns to escort his guests back to the factories.

Two others matters, however, rankled with the British and other foreigners even more. The Chinese insisted on trying foreigners under Chinese law; and, believing all foreign countries inferior to China, they refused to open proper diplomatic relations. This meant, as regards Britain, that attempts to establish ambassadors at Peking always failed, and that her representatives were compelled to deal with erratic local dignitaries. In the period about to be described, these local officials were the famous Lin[1] and Kishen. Also, by the 1830s the Emperor would not receive political emissaries at all. Although the British and the Chinese had traded with each other for centuries there was no British minister at the Imperial Court, and the Imperial Government had no representative in London. Britain had made two attempts to establish ambassadors in Peking. In 1792, Lord Macartney, bringing £13,000 worth of presents for the Emperor, managed to obtain an audience, but his refusal to kow-tow nullified any chance of further negotiation. All he achieved was the inscription of Great Britain on the list of tribute-bearing dependencies and

---

[1] Lin Tse-hsü, the commissioner appointed by the Emperor, to suppress the opium trade, was famous enough to appear in Madame Tussauds' Waxworks in 1845.

the notification of a visit from a ' barbarian ' envoy – ' barbarian ' being the Chinese term for all foreigners.

Lord Amherst fared even worse in 1816. Macartney at least saw the Emperor Chien-lung, a shrewd old man who had been on the throne for nearly sixty years, and who had brought Manchu power to its highest point in Chinese history. But Amherst had to admit defeat without even seeing the Emperor Chia-ching who had succeeded Chien-lung.

The kow-tow was again the cause of the trouble, and one wonders why our plenipotentiaries were so firm in refusing this obeisance which, though servile, was nevertheless customary in China. It was practised by the Emperor himself to the Gods, and by all the mandarins (officials) of the Emperor to their overlord. The kow-tow consisted of a series of triple kneelings, bowing the head three times to the ground each time, and making the ninefold prostration which was too much for our pompous British ambassadors. But Commissioner Lin is recorded as turning his body and kow-towing every evening in the direction of Peking. He even bowed to the reports he sent to the Emperor: ' At the Hour of the Rat (*11 p.m.*) I bowed to my report and despatched it to Peking by relay-post.'

The ending of the East India Company's monopoly in 1763 produced no improvement in trading conditions. Rather the reverse. Without the tactful Company agents to smooth matters, things became worse for everyone. Then in 1836, the Imperial Government appointed Lin commissioner in Canton, and trouble for the British really began.

Lin was given the task of stopping the opium trade which had long been a bone of contention between the British and the Imperial Government. At this time the traders had set up a depot on the island of Lintin in the mouth of the Canton River from which smugglers and others took supplies at their own risk into China. Some traders also sent ships to sell opium northwards up the coast in the so-called Coast Trade. Chinese officials and even the Chinese anti-smuggling fleet were agreeable to allow opium to come into China for a personal consideration.

There was a huge demand for opium in China, and its sale helped the finances of the East India Company, which almost monopolized its production, the Government of India, who collected revenue from its sale, and Britain's balance of payments to China. Before the sale of opium, China's products of rhubarb (a valuable laxative), tea and silk were worth more than the bales of longcloth and Bombay cotton which the British traders offered to China; and silver had to be sent into China to make up the difference. With the development of imported opium from India, this state of affairs was reversed. Silver now came out of China to make up the Chinese trade gap. But there is no doubt that the Emperor, his senior officials and the newly appointed Commissioner Lin were wholeheartedly determined to end the opium trade on humanitarian grounds as well as for its economic disadvantage to China. There is also no doubt that the measures Lin took had considerable effect.

The three most important firms engaged in the China trade at this time were Jardine, Matheson & Co., their rivals Thomas Dent & Co., and the American firm of Russell & Co., already mentioned. The letters of James Matheson of the first of these firms paint a clear picture of the position at Canton before the arrival of General Gough for the stronger prosecution of hostilities in the last years of the First China War of 1839-42. Matheson makes little comment on the moral principles involved, but shows himself as a realist anxious that peaceful trade should be allowed again. His correspondents in the letters quoted are his principals in London, William Jardine and John Abel Smith, and his firm's representatives in India and Manila, Charles Lyall, F. W. Henderson and the Parsee Iamsetjee Iejeebhoy. His correspondence from January 1838 to March 1841, when Gough arrived, shows – if only from his constant reference to it – the importance of opium. But such other articles as bales of longcloth, Bombay cotton, Madras and Bengal staple, cornelians, camlets and piecegoods are also referred to. He indicates the corruption in the pre-war period in all articles of trade: 'The Tide-Waiter in front of the Creek factory has been in the habit of soliciting foreigners to land various articles at his Chop (*permit*) House under his protection and pay him a certain sum for his silence and assistance. Cornelians, camlets, piecegoods and even opium have been so landed for the last twelve months.'[1] Then he shows the result of Lin's activities to stop the opium trade: 'In consequence of severe Imperial edicts lately received from Pekin, the dealers are in such a state of panic that it is impossible to sell

[1] This chapter is based on material in the Jardine Matheson Archives.

a single chest on any terms; so that we are obliged to trust to Namo and Chincheu Bays (Coast Trade) for running off our remaining stocks.' Also: ' Should the same rigid persecution be continued for twelve months the consumption would not be more than one third of the average consumption for the last three years; but I cannot fancy the local authorities in the more turbulent districts to preserve it for many months without creating a general spirit of discontent. Report says this has already been the case in some provinces, but it wants confirmation. In the vicinity of Canton there has been no relaxation and petty seizures are made every day . . .' Then, ' Nothing doing in the drug – the trade is not likely to be long *entirely stopped* but the consumption will be very much limited and prices with you must rule extremely low.' Jardine trusts that the Chinese people will not stand for the cessation of the trade and reports hopefully: ' The public are much exasperated against the Viceroy and abusive placards are posted on the gate of his palace, night after night; but no general remonstrance has yet been made nor is there any appearance of outrage. In the more Northern provinces remonstrances have been made to good effect.'

On the ending of the East India Company's monopoly of the Chinese Trade the British Government had appointed a Chief Superintendent of Trade in China to deal with the Hoppo and the Co-Hong in the place of the East India Company's agents. The first of these superintendents was Lord Napier, and at the time of the First China War Captain Elliot occupied this position. Captain Elliot had a most difficult task to carry out. He was required by the Foreign Secretary, Lord Palmerston, to ' communicate with the Chinese officials on terms of absolute equality, and to abolish unconditionally the existing usage of approaching through the Hong merchants.' The Chinese Emperor and the Chinese officials had never been willing to consent to this. They thought all other countries inferior to the Celestial Empire. They would not allow foreigners to trade with them except on their own restrictive terms, and they only allowed communications to be made in the form of servile petitions through the Co-Hong. They would not consider any diplomatic representation and insisted on foreigners being tried in Chinese courts. Short of a miracle Captain Elliot had no chance of achieving anything. Only armed force could gain these aims. Although the coming war was called the opium war, it was in fact fought in the name of freer trade, diplomatic equality with China and extraterritoriality.

Lin's actions soon brought war near. He demanded the surrender of 20,000 chests of British-owned opium, and to enforce this he surrounded the foreign merchants' warehouses and quarters at Canton and ordered their Chinese servants to leave their masters. Then after the siege of the factories the opium was handed over and destroyed by Lin. Such pressure and inconvenience to the traders was hard to put up with even by those who believed that the opium trade should not be allowed to continue, and those who lost chests of the valuable commodity demanded compensation.

But worse was to follow. In the past merchants and their families had been based on Portuguese Macao and for the short permitted season had been allowed to occupy and trade from their factories in the suburbs of Canton. On 7 July 1839, however, an incident at Kowloon ended this. A party of British and American sailors went ashore to a small village on the Kowloon side of Hong Kong anchorage. After a heavy drinking bout they found they could get no more liquor in the village, and they showed their displeasure by attacking its inhabitants. During the fighting a Chinese called Lin Wei-shi was killed. Lin the Viceroy ordered Captain Elliot to hand over the murderer. But since the case of the gunner of *Lady Hughes* in 1784 it had become a cardinal principle never to surrender an Englishman to Chinese justice. The gunner had been ordered to fire a saluting gun, and in doing so inadvertently killed a Chinese boatman who was alongside. The Chinese threatened to stop trade if he were not delivered up to them for trial. Rather than risk a stoppage the East India Company handed him over, and after a secret trial he was strangled. Although this had happened over fifty years previously, it still rankled. The Chinese declared that blood for blood was the law, but it was considered an undying disgrace that the Company had allowed it.

Elliot knew that the Chinese would demand the culprit and tried offering sums of money to the family of the deceased, to the local mandarins and for general distribution in the village. This did no good. Lin's success over the confiscation of the opium had led him to think that he could force the British to recognize

Chinese courts. He demanded that the guilty seaman be delivered up.

Meanwhile Elliot put six of the rioters on trial before a court of his own. A certain Tom Tidder, a boatswain, was charged with the murder and acquitted, but five of the men were convicted of rioting and sentenced to terms of imprisonment and fines. This by no means satisfied Lin, and as it was obvious that Elliot would not hand over the murderer, the Commissioner moved with a body of troops on Portuguese Macao, which although it remained basically Chinese property, high dignitaries and troops from China had never before entered.

The Portuguese were not to be relied upon. They had never been really friendly with their British rivals, and their naval and military forces were meagre. To safeguard British subjects nominally in his charge, Captain Elliot moved them all, men, women and children, in a number of small vessels to the anchorage at Hong Kong.

The British merchants had commodious houses in Macao, set along the ridge commanding lovely views. Here they had lived in the greatest comfort, waited on by many servants – who had begun to leave as Lin approached. It was a great shock for such people to be told, in the hottest month of the year, to abandon their luxurious homes at a moment's notice to live a crowded life on shipboard in Hong Kong anchorage. *The Chinese Repository* thus sums up the scene: ' Men, women and children, all alike were hurried from their residences, to seek a secure retreat on board their ships. This was their only peaceful course. Most of them proceeded straight to Hong Kong . . . the little fleet, consisting of small boats, schooners and lorchas, crowded with passengers, presented an affecting spectacle as it moved slowly away from the harbour. But we forbear to speculate on what will be the consequences of this memorable event.' The consequence was, in fact, war.

The British traders were incensed now. They had been driven from their factories at Canton, and even from their main base in Macao. Their opium had been confiscated without compensation, although Captain Elliot hoped to get some monetary payment either from the Home Government or the Chinese authorities. But worst of all their legitimate trade was at a standstill. However, one of the most important of the British merchants, Mr

William Jardine, was now in London and appealing direct to Lord Palmerston, the Foreign Secretary, to help the British traders in China. Palmerston, ever ready to give his support to the British anywhere in the world, by threats or by gunboats, was soon to take action.

He sent a formal ultimatum to the Imperial Government demanding the restoration of the confiscated goods or their monetary equivalent, and security for future British trade. ' In making these demands,' Palmerston said, ' I do not dispute China's right to prohibit opium imports. The Queen of England,' he explained, ' wished her subjects in foreign countries to obey the laws of those countries, but Her Majesty could not allow them to be treated with violence, and when wrong was done to them, she would see they obtained redress.'

The Chinese made no response, and war followed, at first a ' phony ' war – begun even before Palmerston's ultimatum – of minor naval engagements like the battles of Chuenpi and Anson Bay interspersed with periods of peace during which Captain Elliot made vain efforts to negotiate. Finally came the larger scale operations employing a considerable land force under General Gough.

The original military plan for the operations against China was for a British force to seize the off-shore island of Chusan, and with this pawn to make demands direct on the Chinese Government at Peking. The first force numbered fifteen men-of-war, five armed steamers, including the famous iron paddle steamer *Nemesis,* and five transports carrying 4,000 men. British troops landed on Chusan and captured its chief town Tinghai without difficulty; but this did not have much effect on the authorities at Peking, and as a next step Captain Elliot went with some ships to Taku at the mouth of the Peiho to try to establish communications with Peking. Meanwhile, to put more pressure on China, the rest of the fleet blockaded Canton, Amoy, Ningpo and the mouth of the Yangtze. The approach of a British force so near the capital as Taku in the Province of Chihli in which Peking lay worried the Emperor enough for him to allow a mandarin from Taku to receive Palmerston's despatch and to begin negotiations. Kishen, the Governor-General of Chihli was China's representative. Unlike Lin, Kishen was conciliatory in every way and even ordered an officer to supply the British ships lying off Taku with provisions. But his instructions were to try to get the British back to Canton to negotiate. The gist of his orders was that should foreigners wish to pursue legitimate trade they should proceed to Canton to request the privilege there. 'All foreign trade should be confined to Canton and no new ports were to be opened.'

At the conference Kishen treated Captain Elliot with great courtesy but dared not make any concessions particularly when Elliot demanded an indemnity for the opium destroyed by Lin. He did, however, on the Emperor's instructions, indicate that should the British require to resume legitimate trade, provided they returned to Canton, Chinese officials would open fresh negotiations there. Kishen in fact laboured indefatigably at the conference to persuade the British to move south to Canton to reopen negotiations, and after many uncertainties his tact at last won the day, for back the vacillating Captain Elliot went. But, the Imperial Court was so distressed at the fall of Tinghai and the landing on Chusan that they had grown sceptical of the strong policy of Commissioner Lin. Accordingly, on 28 September 1840, he was dismissed and sent into exile. He was replaced in the south by the more tolerant Kishen from Chihli whose view apparently was that the Chinese were too weak to oppose the British with military action with any chance of success.

In the series of parleys which followed in the south, the British demanded an indemnity for the opium, and the Chinese asked for the restoration of Tinghai. The British replied that if they received some other port like Hong Kong, they would return Tinghai to the Chinese. In January 1841, horrified at the extent of the British demands, the Chinese broke off negotiations. Captain Elliot replied by ordering the seizure of the forts of Chuenpi and Tycock, guarding the narrow waterway up to Canton. The British fleet accomplished this in a few hours, killing 500 Chinese in the process at the expense of 38 British wounded.

Facing now what he thought was a hopeless situation, Kishen concluded on 20 January the Chuenpi Convention, which, among other things, ceded the island and harbour of Hong Kong to the British Crown in exchange for Tinghai, reopened trade at Canton and offered an indemnity of six million dollars.

All seemed well, when, somewhat strangely, the Chuenpi Convention was repudiated by both sides. China's concessions under the Convention, although insufficient to satisfy the British Government, were nevertheless too drastic for the Imperial Court at Peking. Kishen who was responsible for the unhappy convention was now in his turn dismissed. He left Canton on 12 March to await his trial in Peking.

After this, in the pattern of the previous months, hostilities were begun and suspended several times until finally a full scale attack was mounted on Canton under General Gough assisted by the navy under Captain Senhouse. Captain Elliot, although soon to be dismissed himself for his part in the abortive Chuenpi Convention, was still in overall control for this final assault on Canton, and again showed himself so varied in his decisions as to be, in Gough's words, ' as whimsical as a shuttlecock '; Elliot even allowed the ransoming of Canton before Gough had completed its capture.

Lin had shown himself a stubborn patriot, too inflexible to succeed in stamping out the opium trade without upsetting the legitimate trade of foreigners. Kishen had been just the opposite; fearful of the power and might of Britain, he had been too tolerant to British demands for his masters at Peking. What of Captain Elliot, who for so long, and so patiently, had attempted to restore trading facilities for his country's merchants as well as normal diplomatic relations with China? History seems to have been a shade unfair on him. The correspondence of James Matheson from November 1840 to May 1841 shows that Palmerston's instructions to Captain Elliot were for operations to be more in the ' nature of communications than hostilities ' and Captain Elliot in fact carried out these instructions to the best of his ability. A letter to John Abel Smith of London, dated 25 June 1840, Macao, says: ' I believe there is no doubt their destination is Chusan after taking possession of which the plenipotentiaries (Captain Elliot and the admiral commanding the fleet) will probably seek to open a communication with Peking before attempting further hostilities. This tallies with Lord Palmerston's declaration in Parliament that the proposed operations will be more in the way of " communications " than hostilities. Before the arrival of the fleet it was fully intended to take the Bogue Forts (Chuenpi and Tycock at the mouth of the narrow channel leading up to Canton called the Bogue, or Bocca Tigris), but I rather think the instructions from home do not countenance this;

and should they be taken hereafter, which I much doubt unless the Chinese should provoke us to it by their aggressions, it will be on the Admiral's own responsibility. This forbearance is a very general disappointment to everyone from our chief downwards. And all seem to think it will tend with the smallness of

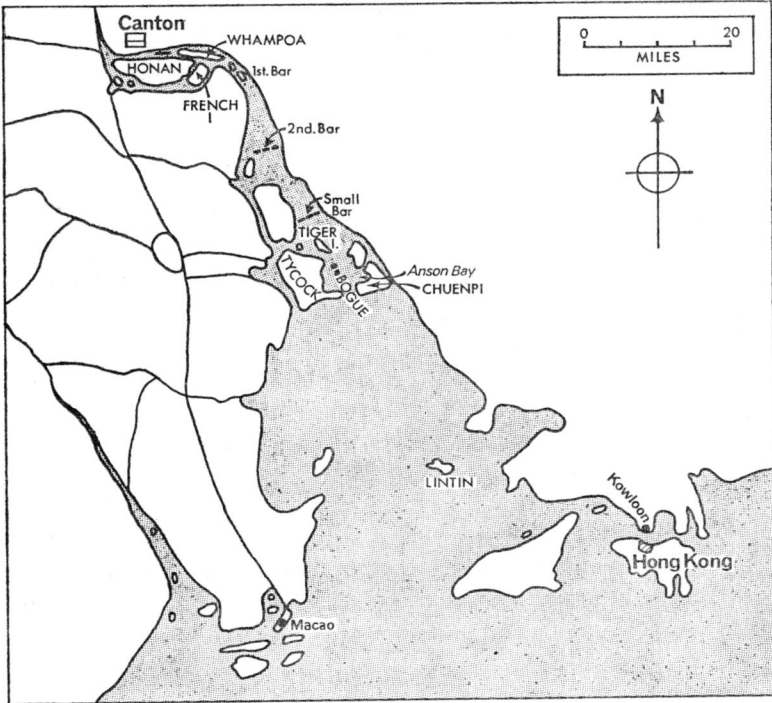

Map 1   Canton estuary

the force (only 5,000 men) greatly to protract a final settlement which would have been far more hopeful from a bolder and more sudden course of action that would have taken the authorities by surprise and rendered them panic struck by a signal display of the power of British Arms. By the plan which to all appearances is proposed to be adopted they will have time to recover from their alarm and to exercise their well known ingenuity in getting

the better of us by wily negotiations. In short we look forward
to its being a very long-winded affair, and I am now by no means
so confident as before in the expectation I expected of Trade being
practicable on the Coast, which was entirely based on the sup-
position (no longer probable) that the Authorities would be so
paralysed as to be unable to prevent their people from dealing
with us. Still such is Elliot's eagerness for Trade and so great his
boasting and self gratulation on what he has already done in this
way (no thanks to him!) that I am convinced Trade he *will* have
at all hazards.'

This shows Matheson mocking at Captain Elliot's efforts, but
extracts from later letters indicate that he is more sympathetic to
what Elliot is trying to do for them than their rivals Dent & Co.

A letter of 21 November 1840 to F. W. Henderson of Bombay
reads: 'A few days will develop whether negotiation *alone* without some fighting will bring about a settlement . . . Patna and
Malwi opium may now be quoted at about $430 a chest but I
fear we shall not be able to obtain as much for your goods . . .
while I am writing I learn the Admiral and Captain Elliot have
gone to the Bogue in the *Queen*.'

On 23 November 1840 he writes to Charles Lyall of Calcutta:
' It seems plain enough they (Peking) have come to the conclusion that peace is their wiser course. He (Captain Elliot) thinks
that their aim will now be directed to test the minimum concessions which will satisfy us, thereunto we shall probably have
difficulties and it may be a little fighting . . . In all this I entirely
agree with Captain Elliot but he and I differ as to time. He ex-
pects an early adjustment of differences and renewal of trade
will happen soon – in which I cannot agree with him.'

On 18 January 1841, to F. W. Henderson again, Matheson
writes: ' I have much pleasure in informing you that Captain
Elliot has at length *actually come to a settlement* with the
Chinese;' and to William Jardine in London on 22 January, presumably about the same shortlived settlement and others' reaction
to it, ' I really believe had it been ever so favourable it would
have been impossible to please the cankered minds of some of
our neighbours under the influence of Dent & Co. who are at
violent animosity with Elliot;' but on 19 February ' You will
perceive from our accompanying circular that to all appearances
hostilities are about to recommence to my great regret and dis-

22

gust.' To Iamsetjee Iejeebhoy of Bombay on 26 February, 'I do not think we have enough force to take possession of Canton even after the arrival of the troops expected from Chusan . . . We have occurred a heavy expense to obtain the service of the *Folkestone* (a remarkable sailer) for conveying the present news to you and our mutual friends in England.'

Finally, when a more vigorous phase in the hostilities was about to begin, Matheson wrote to James Adam Smith of Manila, on 20 March, 'I believe our leading officials are now convinced that the petty warfare we have been hitherto pursuing will not answer, and the Commodore is just starting for Calcutta in the *Queen* steamer to persuade the Governor-General to send on more troops.'

By the time of the assault on Canton more troops had arrived which, together with the men from Chusan and the naval force available, produced a total of nearly 2,400[1] for Gough to use for the landing. On 24 May 1841, Captain Elliot decided to employ with more vigour 'the final argument of kings' and the attack on Canton began.

THE RANSOM OF CANTON

Canton was no easy place to reach in order to assault. Many navigable waterways led to it, but for vessels of some draught there were bars and reefs which could only be crossed at high water, and shallows which had to be avoided. Fortunately, armed paddle steamers like *Nemesis* needed such little water (four or five feet) that they could go almost anywhere, and Gough's final plan made full use of this valuable ship. According to its captain: 'the channel through which our forces were now to advance upon

---

[1] The total British force in the Far East including the naval ratings was probably over 5,000 by this time, although many of the original soldiers had died of disease in the unhealthy camps on Chusan. Between 13 July and 31 December 1840, the 49th Regiment of Foot had 142 deaths, the 26th Regiment had 238 deaths and the 18th Regiment, who had a healthier situation on a hill, escaped more lightly with 52 deaths (*Regimental History of the Royal Berkshire Regiment*, i, 121). Hong Kong was not much healthier at that time, and on the return of the troops there after the 'Ransom of Canton' many of the participants in the campaign, including Captain Senhouse, died. But it is said that exposure to the great heat in the fields before Canton may have laid the seeds of the disease that killed these men.

Canton . . . runs southward of French Island towards the Macao passage (*see map*) . . . and is a safe and deep passage for vessels drawing sixteen feet of water up to the city of Canton (from the Bogue), except two bars which it required high water to pass.' This meant that fairly large warships could approach Canton and bombard its guarding forts – which they did to some effect. But for the transport of troops a very strange approach was worked out by General Gough and Captain Senhouse after they 'went up in person to make a careful reconnaissance': after the 26th Regiment, some of the Madras artillery and some sappers and miners had been sent to the Factories in the south-west suburbs of Canton outside its encircling walls, the main force[1] was put on board *Nemesis* or in boats in tow of *Nemesis*. This was a more numerous flotilla than any steamer had yet towed. It moved first by the route already mentioned and then right round the west of Canton by water to land at Tsing-poo. The main assault on Canton was to come from the rear.

The 26th Regiment under Major Pratt landed at the Factories without incident before five o'clock on 24 May, and at once began to strengthen the post. The Chinese had fled from the neighbourhood, but in the midst of the ruins of the Factories were discovered some Americans who had imprudently remained behind when the British and others had evacuated the Factories – reoccupied again for the very short period of the Chuenpi Convention. One of the Americans, Mr Coolidge, described what happened at the Factories after the other merchants left, when pillage became the order of the day, and the Chinese mob took away all that could be moved and destroyed everything that could not. The account in the Chinese Repository based on Mr Coolidge's description reads:

During the whole day the same mad scene of destruction was continued; and whatever still defied the hands of the mob was at length made to yield to the consuming power of fire. Not all the thirteen Hongs (factories), however, were visited with this terrible pillage.

Towards the close of day, when the work of destruction was nearly

[1] The main force consisted of: Lt-Col Morris' Brigade, The 49th Regiment. The 37th Madras Native Infantry and a company of the Bengal Volunteers, 647; Captain Knowles' Artillery Brigade, Royal Artillery, Madras Artillery and Sappers and Miners, 417; Captain Bourchier's Naval Brigade, 430; and Major-General Burrell's Brigade, 18th Royal Irish Regiment and the Royal Marines, 901.

24

completed, down came, at length, the prefect of the city in person, attended by a large party of police. He now succeeded in driving away the main body of the mob, and then gave charge of the Factories to the Hong merchants, to whom all the buildings belonged, and who took possession of the little that remained, with the assistance of a number of their own hired labourers armed for the occasion.

Mr Coolidge was taken prisoner, after being in great danger of being cut down, and was, with many insults, carried into the heart of the city.

As he was marched along, he passed several bodies of soldiers and coolies, or day-labourers, hurrying down towards the Factories, and dragging guns along with them. As soon as he came near the headquarters of the Tartar general, the crowd and movement increased; officers of every grade, grooms and messengers on horseback, hurrying to and fro, executioners and city-guards, together with strange troops from distant provinces, in every variety of costume – these were huddled together and jostled in the greatest bustle and confusion.

After some delay, he was carried, with every possible insult, before the criminal judge, and there, to his horror, he discovered several of his countrymen, who had been wounded and captured as they were trying to escape in a boat down the river. The sufferings and indignities they now underwent were extreme; nor did their assertion that they were Americans prove of much service for them, for they were told that, in that case, they ' ought to speak a different language and wear a different dress '.

It is very certain, however, that the Chinese generally at Canton know perfectly well the difference between an American and an Englishman. But, on the other hand, when an Englishman gets into trouble there, he most commonly declares himself to be an American; and how could the Chinese prove that he is not so? But the national distinction is perfectly well defined, even in their own language; the American being called the ' people of the flowery flag ', from the number of stars on it, while the English are known as the ' red people or red-haired people ', an appellation originally applied to the Dutch traders.

The American prisoners remained in the condition he described, exposed to every possible suffering in the common prison for nearly two days, when they were at length turned out, and carried in chairs to the ruined Factories, where they were planted among the ruins just as if they had been portions of the marble statue which had been destroyed. It was just at this time that our troops landed, and of course every attention was paid to the unhappy sufferers; and as Mr

Coolidge observes, 'I cannot tell you with what feelings of good-will we looked upon every one of those red-coats.'

As soon as the 26th Regiment had landed at the Factories in the south-west suburbs, naval action in the reach to the south-east of Canton began on the island forts of Dutch Folly and French Folly, the shore batteries and the arsenal on the opposite shore.

The first action was fought by vessels which turned back after coming through the Macao passage. Dutch Folly was found to be un-armed, but *Atalanta* went aground on a reef off Dutch Folly and re-mained so for several days before she was put off with difficulty. The next objective was a heavy sand battery ashore having – it was dis-covered later – huge guns of 10.5-inch diameter. This was taken by a naval landing party in three boats with great gallantry, but was the only gain in the neighbourhood before dark, during which the Chinese retaliated by drifting down fire-rafts against the British ships, but these were towed clear without doing much mischief.

Captain Herbert with boats from some of the larger naval vessels attempted to approach Canton from Whampoa, up the narrow north-ern passage, but they were stopped by shots from French Folly which could not be attacked in force until the following morning, 25 May. French Folly fort was then bombarded by guns in seized junks and by the guns of two warships, after which a naval landing party stormed it gallantly. In the fort were as many as 64 guns, four being 10.5-inch. By this time the whole of the river defences were in British hands. In the naval bombardment of the forts and shore batteries, a great many naval shot were thrown into the suburbs all about above and below the batteries. During the cannonading, a fire broke out, which destroyed many poor and a few valuable houses.

Meanwhile, Gough's expedition had been making progress be-hind Canton. The Chinese system of land warfare had not yet been experienced, and it was in fact the first time that European troops were to undertake operations in China beyond the cover of ships. The Chinese had been known to declare that if they could get the British away from their ships, they would be able to win. They soon found it was not so.

This was the first time a British General had commanded in China, and Gough was determined that his men should behave well and conduct themselves chivalrously. 'Great Britain,' he said, ' had gained as much fame by her clemency and forbearance as by the gallantry of her troops. An enemy in arms is always a legitimate foe; but, the unarmed or the supplicant for mercy, of whatever country or whatever colour, a true soldier will always spare.' He was insistent on good order and discipline, and in his General Order No. 1 he wrote: 'The nature of the position to be carried, and the probable necessity of subdividing the force with separate columns of attack which may be through the town and suburbs, make it the more necessary to enforce the most rigid discipline, and to guard against any man leaving the ranks upon any pretence whatever. The man who does so will most probably be cut off; but even should he escape his name should be branded as a disgrace to his corps.' In the event, Gough had no need to complain that his orders were not obeyed. As will be seen, his troops were not even tempted by some supplies of samshoo[1] which came to hand, and samshoo was a drink to which the British soldier and sailor in China was sorely addicted.

On board *Nemesis* were the 49th Regiment together with General Gough, Captain Senhouse and Captain Elliot. As she had advanced up river, numerous boats from the ships were picked up until there were nearly eighty of them hanging on behind each other and following in the wake of the long low steamer. ' It was altogether an animated scene. The numerous flags, the motley appearance of the boats, the glitter of arms and accoutrements and the various uniforms of the men, produced a very exciting spectacle. Had the Chinese not been already panic struck by the lessons they had so recently received, they might have occasioned great annoyance, and perhaps loss, to our troops, exposed as they were in boats, by firing on them from the banks of the river, in places where they would have been themselves under cover. No opposition of any kind, however, was offered.'

By dusk, *Nemesis* and its fleet, under the charge of Captain Hall, reached Tsing-poo, where General Gough was the first to land and go off with a small escort to reconnoitre. By this time it was too late in the day to do more than land the 49th Regiment. This was easily effected as they could walk ashore directly

---

[1] 'The liquor which is given to sailors on entering most of the shops which they are wont to frequent in Canton, and which is frequently conveyed to them either openly or secretly at Whampoa, is a rare dose, composed often of alcohol, tobacco juice, sugar and arsenic. The liquor which contains the alcohol and which constitutes the principal part of the dose, is literally and very properly called ho-tsew, "fire liquor". Its effects, with the substances mixed with it are awful; when taken in considerable quantities it not only destroys the reason and senses of the man, but at intervals, it throws him into the most frightful paroxysms of rage.' (*C.R.* II, 423).

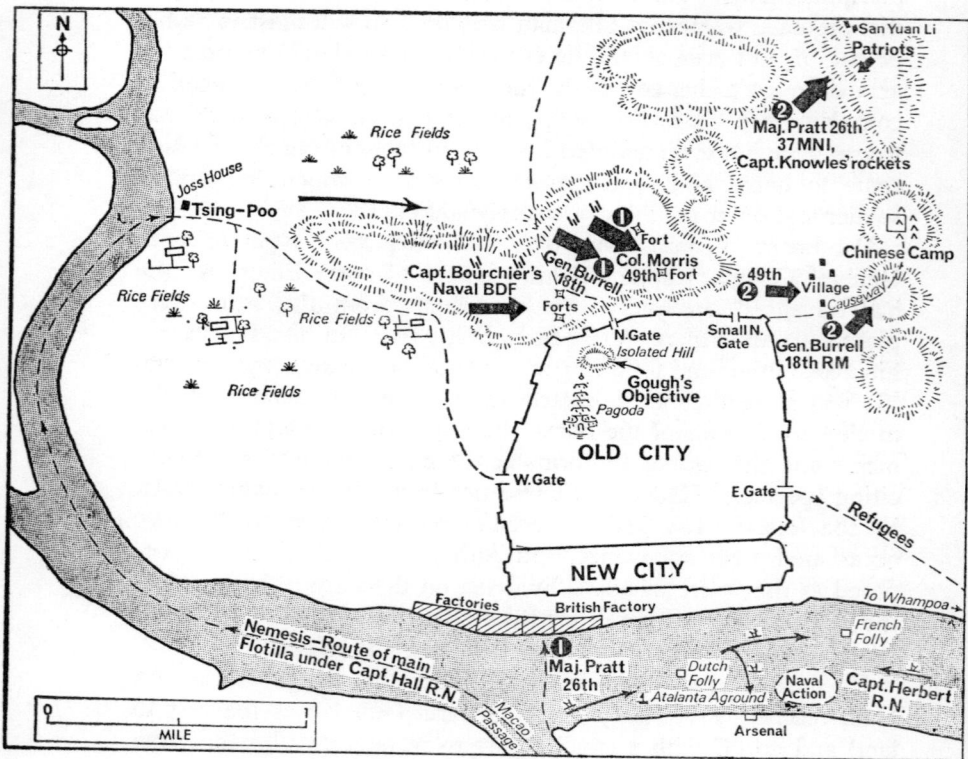

Map 2   Gough's attack on Canton

out of the flatbottomed steamer, without the necessity of using boats or causing any delay whatever. During the rest of the evening of 24 May and into the night, the guns, ammunition and stores were also landed, but the rest of the force did not disembark until the following morning.

As soon as the 49th were landed they took possession of a large temple, or so-called joss-house, near the landing place. This remained a fortified post throughout the operation, manned by a mixed force from the 49th, 18th and Madras Native Infantry. This was just as well, for on one occasion the Chinese attempted to cut the force's communications by advancing on the landing place at Tsing-poo.

General Gough's task was a formidable one, for Canton was a well defended city with high walls. From the direction from which the main British force was approaching, a ridge ran up towards Canton and along, and a short distance from, the northern walls. An isolated hill from this chain lay within the city itself, and this dominating mound became Gough's objective. By its occupation he thought he could control the whole town without resorting to clearing it street by street. On either side of the ridge away from the town were rich green gardens and rice fields, with here and there a clump of trees or a small village or the country house of one of the wealthier inhabitants of the city. Further off to the north-east it was hillier.

Where the ridge reached the city's north wall, it was crowned by two pairs of forts: two off the north-west corner and two in front of the centre of the north wall. All these features are shown on the map.

The direct approach from the landing place at Tsing-poo towards the guarding forts was a difficult one for the guns of Gough's force, and two of the 12-pounder howitzers and two of the 9-pounder guns were not got into position on the heights, in order to bombard Canton and its outlying forts, until the next day. Two 12-pounders and two 6-pounders, three 5.5-inch mortars and many 32-pounder rockets, however, were brought into action on the ridge on the first day.

The composition of Gough's force is shown in the note, page 24. The attack on the western forts was entrusted to the naval brigade under covering fire from the guns and rockets mentioned, while at the same time the 18th Royal Irish and the Royal

29

Marines under Major-General Burrell had the task of attacking the north fort nearest the wall, and Colonel Morris with the 49th Madras Native Infantry and Bengal Volunteers were to assault the north fort farther away from the wall. In the event, Colonel Morris' force, having the advantage of a shorter and better route, succeeded in carrying both of the northern forts with little loss. 'The two western forts were at the same time gallantly carried by the brigade of seamen, who were exposed to a heavy fire from gingals,[1] wallpieces and matchlocks from the city walls, by which they suffered some loss.'

Thus in the space of little more than half an hour from the time the advance was sounded, the heights overlooking the north wall of the city had been gained and ' the British flag waved in triumph upon all the forts which commanded it '.

There were, however, two other features outside the walls which needed clearing of enemy, a village occupied by Chinese troops near the north-east corner of the city, and a Chinese camp on a hill in the same vicinity. The enemy were soon dislodged from the village by the 49th, and Major-General Burrell with the 18th, a few marines and a detachment of the 49th was ordered to attack the camp. The approach to it was along a narrow causeway; and while making the attack, Burrell's men – like the naval brigade earlier – suffered casualties from Chinese manning the face of the city walls. But in spite of this the Chinese were driven out of the camp and its buildings and magazines were destroyed.

The men were oppressed by the excessive heat, and although the day was now far advanced, it still had not been possible yet to bring up all the guns. Gough decided to postpone the final assault on Canton until the next day.

In the morning the city looked very quiet except that a number of refugees could be seen making off, with as much of their property as they could carry, from the gates of the city remote from the British force. Gough was still waiting for news of his guns when all at once, about ten o'clock, a white flag appeared on the walls of the city.

Gough sent forward an envoy to find out what the Chinese wanted, and the envoy, on Gough's previous instructions, in-

---

[1] Gingals were similar to our duck guns fired from punts, and were fired from stands or over walls.

formed the mandarin with a red button who confronted him demanding peace terms to spare the city, that he should consult with Captain Elliot with the advanced squadron in the reach before the city. Gough was not ready for peace terms to be discussed. He had not yet gained the hill within the city walls from which he could dominate the town of Canton. Without this hill in his possession he did not consider the time ripe for a truce, and he hoped that Captain Elliot would not be unwise enough to arrange one prematurely.

There followed a long wait all day long during which Gough managed to bring up the remainder of his guns and make the final preparations for an assault should the arrangement of a truce come to nothing.

Soon after six o'clock next morning, just as Gough was preparing to give his final orders for an assault, a letter arrived from Captain Elliot announcing that a truce had been agreed to. All further hostile operations against the city were abandoned on the agreement of the Canton authorities to pay a ransom and remove the regular Tartar garrison sixty miles from the city. Hall explains the nature of the ransom as follows: ' Various stories were current concerning the mode in which the ransom of the city was first proposed. One of the most credited accounts was that the Hong merchants were ordered by the authorities to go as far as ten millions of dollars, if a less sum would not suffice; but on no account to return without effecting the object. They must have known that they would themselves have to pay the greater part of the amount, and naturally wished to make the best bargain they could. It is said that in the first instance they pulled alongside one of our men-of-war, and offered three millions for the ransom of the city. As they evidently appeared to be in a hurry to make a bargain of some sort or other, they were told that a much larger sum would be required. Four millions were then proposed, and then five millions; and at length, in great trepidation, and with many protestations of poverty, they raised the offer to six millions. In the first instance they were scarcely thought to be in earnest, but as the thing now looked serious, they were directed to go and confer with Captain Elliot, who granted a truce until 12 o'clock the following day, the 27th; and, in the intervening time, terms were definitely agreed upon.'

Yishan, the Commissioner-General in Canton gives his reasons for asking for the truce in his memorial to the Emperor as follows:

On the night of the 21 May, then, a great fight was fought . . . By the burning of the houses and the disabling of the guns, the artillery was rendered ineffectual; and troops of all arms, including officers of rank, also suffered loss in wounded . . . This condition of things compelled all to retire within the walls of the city. A whole people weeping and wailing, sending up loud cries to heaven, choked every pathway; and earnestly did they beg that peaceful arrangements should be entered into. Your minister as he looked upon them lost all heart, and bowing to their desires, he went to the city wall to ask the foreigners what they wanted. They all said the price of the opium they had delivered up, amounting to several millions of taels, had not yet been given to them; and they earnestly wished that a million of taels of silver might be granted to them when they would immediately call in their forces and retire without Bocca Tigris (Bogue); they had nothing else to ask for, and all the people would thus be left in the ordinary state of quiet. Inquiring of them regarding Hong Kong, if they would give it back, they answered that it had been given to them by the minister Kishen and that of its being so given they possessed documentary evidence.

Your minister, calling to mind that the city had been so frequently troubled and endangered that the whole people were as dead men, thought it right temporarily to accede to and promise their requests. In turning the matter over again and again, in his mind, it seems to your minister that for a solitary city thus to stand all the brunt of battle is utterly destructive to its property, and that in such a position the grand army can find no opportunity for displaying its strength: he deemed therefore that it was his undoubted duty to draw the enemy forth without the Bocca Tigris; and then to renew the fortifications (*example of Chinese wiles*) and seek another occasion for attacking and destroying them at Hong Kong, and thus to restore the ancient territory.

In typical Chinese fashion Yishan also asks for he and his colleagues to be punished for their offences.

The truce, however, was not quite the end of the matter. Although the authorities of Canton sought peace and the regular Tartar garrison had been sent away according to the armistice terms, a group of Chinese patriots gathered from the villages around the city, and massing at San-Yuan-li in the heights to the north, decided to continue the struggle. For some time the

(*Top*) Sir Henry Pottinger, an able British plenipotentiary who took over from Captain Elliot in 1841 during General Gough's operation in the First China War

Major-General Sir Hugh Gough, 1779–1862. After storming Canton and forcing a passage of the Yangtze, he compelled the Chinese to sign the Treaty of Nanking, 1842

(*Top*) 'The Indefatigable Mr Parkes'

Silver model of pagoda commemorating the
Treaty of Nanking, 1842

peasantry of the province, particularly in the neighbourhood of the city, had been encouraged to form themselves into societies, or 'patriotic bands' as they were called, for mutual defence against the foreigners. Although imperfectly armed with spears, swords, a few matchlocks, and shields, and totally ignorant of military matters, they yet believed that by mere force of numbers, and a little courage at a distance, they could achieve what the regular Tartar army had been unable to accomplish. They were held up to the nation at large by the government as models of patriotism and self-devotion, and so impressed were they with the high value of their proffered service, that they believed Yishan and the high officials of Canton had betrayed them in making terms with Captain Elliot for the ransom of the city, and that 'the anxiety of the inhabitants to save their own property had induced them to make unreasonable concessions, at the very moment when the patriots were advancing to exterminate their enemies by falling upon their rear.'

These forces under local Chinese gentry were a feature of China in the nineteenth century. Made up to some extent of roaming peasants who had deserted the land, they were similar in composition, though not in aims, not only to the prevalent bandit groups, and secret societies like the Triad and White Lotus, but also the rebellious Taipings, and to the best known anti-foreign society, the Boxers.

Two days after the city had been ransomed, a considerable body of these Chinese patriots began to collect on the heights to the north-east, at about three or four miles in the rear of Gough's men. It was obvious that Captain Elliot's premature armistice had left the British troops in an exposed position which they would not have been occupying had Gough been permitted to assault and take the town and to obtain the dominating hill within its walls, which had been his objective.

The number of Chinese patriots continued to increase throughout the day, and Gough, being fully prepared to expect some act of treachery or bad faith under cover of the flag of truce, ordered Major-General Burrell to take over the command on the ridge and be prepared to repel any attack from the city, while he himself organized a force to disperse the patriots.

As the 26th Regiment under Major Pratt had now joined Gough's force from the Factories, this regiment, with the 37th

B

33

Madras Native Infantry were mainly used, supported by Captain Knowles with his rockets.

The gunners fired these with great accuracy at the Chinese bands, but it was not sufficient to disperse them, and with the 26th on the left and the 37th MNI on the right the British infantry advanced to attack them at close quarters. Although both wings of the British force drove off the Chinese patriots on their own fronts, they became separated, and Captain Duff in command of the Indian troops detached a company of the MNI to form a link with the 26th. The day was sultry and the heat oppressive, and in late afternoon a thunderstorm burst upon them with inconceivable fury. The rain descended in such torrents that the firelocks got wet, and as scarcely a musket would go off, the British troops had to resort to the bayonet, which proved sometimes not a very successful weapon when matched with the long crooked spears of the Chinese, and put the British momentarily at a disadvantage.

It was on this occasion, and in the midst of the terrific storm, that the detached link company of the MNI won great fame. Hall describes the action as follows:

This company having missed the road during the storm, did not succeed in joining the 26th, who, in the meantime, had, in fact, retired. Their muskets became completely useless owing to the wet, which emboldened the Chinese to attack their rear with long spears. They were soon surrounded; and one or two of the men were pulled over with the long crooked spear, something in the shape of a small reaping-hook, fixed upon a long pole. The musket of one of the men who had fallen, was picked up by the Chinese, the powder being so damp in the pan that it had not gone off with flint and steel. The Chinese soldier, however, deliberately placed the musket to his shoulder, and, taking steady aim at one of the officers, Mr Berkeley, applied his match to the damp powder, which ignited, and the musket went off, and unfortunately wounded Mr Berkeley in the arm.

The gallant little company of Sepoys were now moved to some rising ground, where they could better defend themselves. For a moment, the rain ceased; and then with the utmost difficulty they were enabled to get a few muskets off, with unerring effect upon the dense mass of Chinese who surrounded them. But fortune was determined to prolong their trial still. The rain again descended in torrents, just as they had begun their retreat and the Chinese, taking fresh courage, resumed their attacks. Nothing now remained but to form a square, and stand true to each other, until the morning dawned, and enabled them to fight their way through the enemy.

The absence of this company, when all the rest of the force was concentrated, caused great anxiety concerning their fate. It was rightly attributed to the severity of the storm, but it was feared that they might possibly have been cut off by the Chinese. Without loss of time, Sir Hugh Gough ordered up two companies of marines, who were comparatively fresh, and armed with percussion muskets, to return with Captain Duff in search of the missing company. As they advanced they fired an occasional shot as a signal to their comrades of their approach, and to animate their spirits. At length, they came up with the missing company, drawn up in square, surrounded by thousands of Chinese. A couple of volleys sent into the midst of the confused crowd, by the unerring percussion muskets of the marines, accompanied by a loud shout, dispersed them with great loss, and they fled in confusion.

The hostility of the Chinese during a truce could not be endured, and Gough sent a message to the prefect of Canton saying that if these demonstrations continued, he would haul down the flag of truce and renew hostilities against the town. When the prefect arrived, he rode off immediately, accompanied on this hazardous duty by a British officer, to confront the irregular forces. To everyone's surprise, for all thought some treachery would be perpetrated, the irregular forces were induced by the prefect to disperse.[1]

During all the hostilities upon the heights, the greater part of the wounded were brought down and put on board *Nemesis*, which versatile little ship was employed to convey them daily to their respective vessels and transports, so that, for the time, the medical arrangements were a model of efficiency.

The days spent by the troops lying out upon the heights – days which would have been fewer had Gough been allowed by Captain Elliot to take Canton – caused eventually probably more casualties than the fighting in which only 15 British were killed and 112 wounded. The heat of the sun on the heights had been so oppressive, and the weather so sultry, that both officers and men suffered great exhaustion. Major Beecher, the deputy quartermaster-general, whose exertions had been unremitting

[1] This action at San-Yuan-li has been written up by the Communists into a great national victory (see later).

throughout the previous days, fell down, and almost immediately expired from the heat; and many officers and men went sick. Then, on their return to camp in Hong Kong, as at Chusan, many soldiers died; and it is believed that this was due more from the undermining of their health before Canton than from unhealthy conditions of the camp at Hong Kong.

Although politically the ransom of Canton was not very successful, for as Yishan's memorial suggested, the forts guarding Canton were soon rearmed, it was a well conducted and well fought operation. General Gough's General Orders of 5 June reflect his satisfaction:

The operation before Canton having now closed Major-General Hugh Gough feels the highest gratification in recording that every individual of the force, native as well as European, gallantly and zealously did their duty . . . It was the first time that Sir Hugh Gough had had the honour to command a body of seamen, and the whole conduct of Captain Bourchier's brigade was such that it will always be a matter of proud recollection to the major-general to have had it under his orders on this occasion (he also praises the commanders of the 18th, 26th and 49th Regiments of Foot, the 37th MNI, the Bengal Volunteers, the Royal Artillery and the Madras Artillery).

Having thus expressed his sense of the services of officers commonly . . . Sir Hugh Gough has no less pleasure in noticing the praiseworthy conduct of sailors and soldiers under his command; during eight days that the force was on shore, there were but two cases of drunkenness, and the soldiers of the 49th, having found a quantity of samshoo in the village they had taken, brought it to their officers and broke the vessels in their presence. It is by conduct such as this that the sailor and soldier secure the confidence of their officers, and that their gallantry in action remains untarnished.

Discipline is as indispensable to success as courage, and the major-general has the satisfaction to find that the trust which he reposed in the force under his command has been fully justified.

The chain of command in the First China War was a complicated one. Captain Elliot received his instructions from Lord Palmerston, the Foreign Secretary, and the naval commander through the Admiralty; but Sir Hugh Gough got his orders from the Governor-General of India who had appointed him and raised his force. Lord Palmerston wanted the acceptance by the Chinese of absolute equality of communication – his own words

– as well as compensation for the opium surrendered by the British merchants; but he expected Captain Elliot to achieve this by operations more in the way of ' Communications ' than hostilities. The Governor-General of India Lord Auckland's views of how operations were to be conducted coincided with Palmerston's. He had recommended Gough to carry out ' only attacks on the shipping along the coast '. Fortunately the new Governor-General, Lord Ellenborough, realized the futility of operations along the coast as a means of bringing the Chinese Government to reason, and suggested that ' the great waterway of the Yangtze-kiang, completely navigable for warships up to the immediate neighbourhood of Nanking, afforded conveniences for effecting the objects which the English Government wished to secure '.

This attack into the heart of mainland China up the Yangtze, severing the lifeline of the Grand Canal from Hangchow to Peking, and controlling Nanking, was the plan Gough had already considered the most suitable. And when for the last year of the war, Captain Elliot was replaced by the much more decisive Sir Henry Pottinger, who also advocated more vigorous action, the stage was set for the completion of the matter.

The assault on Canton has been described in some detail. The combined operations which followed on the coastal ports and towns along the Yangtze until Nanking itself was threatened, will only be given in outline. Sometimes there was more resistance than had been met at Canton, sometimes considerably less, but always the result was the same. The feeble Chinese armies were no match for the well-trained, well-led British sea and land forces.

NANKING

By 21 August Gough was ready to move. The 55th Regiment had now reached Hong Kong, making the expeditionary force up to 2,700 men, and its navy consisted of two battleships, seven smaller warships, four steamers and twenty-three transports. The first objective was the port of Amoy on the coast opposite the island of Formosa.

The resistance at Amoy was slight, as although the Chinese defenders had plenty of guns on the headlands and islands guarding the harbour, as well as behind the granite ramparts of the

harbour itself, they appeared unable to make much use of them.
A British landing in the rear took them by surprise, and by the
second day, Amoy was in British hands for the loss of two men
killed and fifteen wounded.

The next objective was Tinghai on the island of Chusan, and

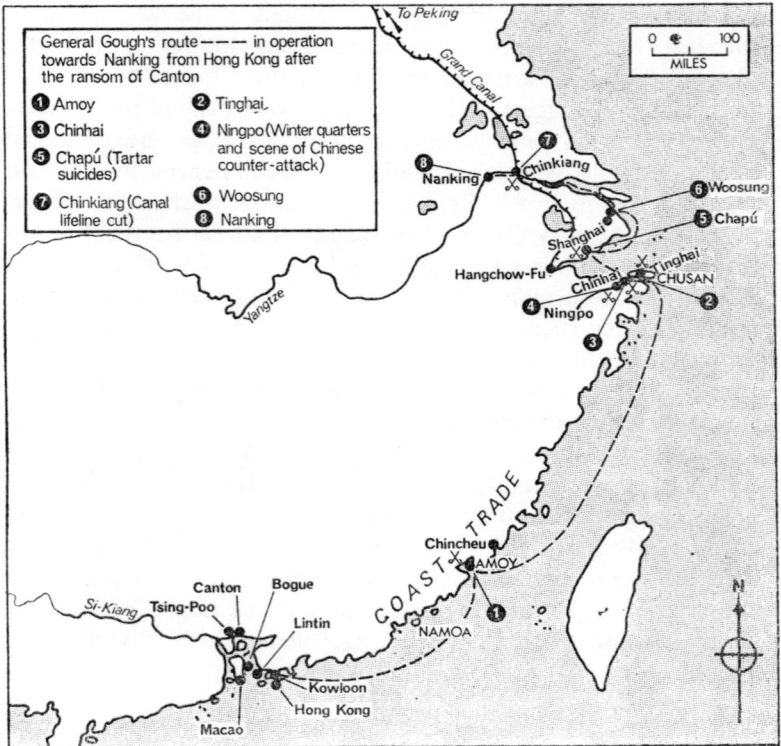

General Gough's route --- in operation
towards Nanking from Hong Kong after
the ransom of Canton

❶ Amoy ❷ Tinghai
❸ Chinhai ❹ Ningpo (Winter quarters
❺ Chapú (Tartar and scene of Chinese
suicides) counter-attack)
❼ Chinkiang (Canal ❻ Woosung
lifeline cut) ❽ Nanking

Map 3   First China War 1839-1842

this place did not last out for long either. The resistance was
slightly stronger than the first time the British had stormed it
before it was exchanged for Hong Kong, but it was captured in
three days, two British being killed and twenty-seven wounded.

The expedition was soon ready to continue its northward advance towards the Yangtze, and en route captured two ports on
the coast opposite the island of Chusan, Chinhai at the mouth

of the Ningpo river with slight resistance on 10 October, and Ningpo further up river on 13 October without a fight at all.

There was a slight difference of opinion between Sir Henry Pottinger and General Gough after the occupation of Ningpo. Pottinger wanted the place sacked because previously two British prisoners of the Chinese, Captain Anstruther and Mrs Noble, had been confined in small cages and ill-treated there. Gough, however, resisted this and even organized a corps of Chinese police to protect private property.

At Ningpo the army went into winter quarters. But after two months of quiet in which they were able to enjoy the good things of life which included fare like pheasants, woodcock and duck from the neighbourhood, they were counter-attacked in position in March 1842 by Chinese forces sent down against them from the north.

This counter-attack took Gough by surprise, and hard fighting was needed to repel it. The Chinese got into the streets beyond the western gate of Ningpo, and a howitzer had to be brought into position to force them back. The damage inflicted by the gun at point blank range was immense. Officers present who had fought in the Peninsular War said that they had not seen such carnage since the siege of Badajoz.

The Chinese attacks and similar ones on Chinhai, where a small garrison had been left, were repulsed successfully in the end. But life at Ningpo was never quite the same. The Chinese had succeeded during the attacks in planting a ' fifth column ' in the city, and its members became adept in the art of abducting British soldiers. They would lure a solitary soldier into some low haunt – sometimes with the help of a prostitute – ply him with samshoo until he became unconscious, and then take him off to Hangchow as a prisoner-of-war. Some forty men were abducted in this way before the British left Ningpo. This also occurred at Tinghai. Sergeant Campbell's abduction is described as follows:

Sergeant Campbell had been employed in the commissariat department at Chusan since 1 February last; on 24 March 1842 he went to Tinghai to purchase some fowls, but after a fruitless search in the market he was on the point of returning home, when a Chinese boy whom he had employed for several months told him if he went to the east gate he would find plenty of them. He followed him; and

39

on coming to the gate the boy pointed to a house a hundred yards further on. The boy ran into the house at the door of which Sergeant Campbell waited for his return; but after standing at the place for ten minutes, and getting tired, was retracing his steps when at the corner of the building he was attacked by 20 or 30 Chinese. Four of them he knocked down with his stick, but the odds were too great; he was felled to the ground by a stone that struck him over the left eye. They then sprung on him, tied his hands and feet, and filled his mouth with clay. Immediately afterwards he was put in a bag and two men carried him on a bamboo. Walking at a good pace for a couple of hours they brought him to a row of houses, on the southern part of the island. Here he was taken out of the bag only to lose his left ear, which one of his captors cut off with a pair of scissors, upon which they put him back in the bag; and travelled as before till 10 o'clock p.m. when the Chinese ate their suppers. This done they took him on their shoulders, and twenty minutes walk brought them to a creek, where, through the sack, he could see several small junks. Into the hold of one of these he was lowered, and left there three days and three nights, his clothes saturated with water, without a single morsel to eat, and supported entirely by some samshoo and water they gave him at intervals. On the fourth day after capture he was landed at a place which he subsequently ascertained to be Chapú. There he was taken before the chief officer, who immediately ordered his feet and hands to be untied, and treated him very kindly giving him an abundance to eat. They kept him there but two hours, after which he was sent, under the escort of a petty officer and twelve soldiers to the canal, and embarked in a flat-bottomed boat. This officer was most civil, and insisted on his eating in company with him. The canal runs through a perfectly flat country so they had no locks to get over; at times whenever the bank of the canal would allow it, the boats were tracked, but for the greatest part of the way the boatmen were obliged to scull. They stopped only to take whatever provisions the party required till the 30th when they reached Hangchow-fu. Another month was spent on their travels backwards and forwards until he and some fellow prisoners were handed over to Captain Napier of HMS *Pelican* at Chinhai. Campbell had a good view of Chinese soldiers on his travels through the streets of the towns. They often formed a long line on either side of the procession; he observed that the soldiers had weapons of all kinds: matchlocks, spears, swords, cutlasses and bows and arrows, the latter of which they seemed to be very fond and very proud of; every tenth soldier had a matchlock.

On the renewal of the advance to the Yangtze and Nanking,

Chapú, a naval base on the coast south of Shanghai, was the next town to be stormed, and resistance here was the strongest the British had so far encountered. They suffered casualties of nine dead and fifty-five wounded in taking it. Some of these casualties at Chapú were the result of inter-regimental rivalry between the 18th Royal Irish and the 49th as to which regiment should gain the honour of taking a defended joss-house. The Regimental history of the 18th Regiment records:

The joss-house was quickly and skilfully prepared for defence. The other windows were manned by picked shots, the interior passages and the central hall were loopholed; mats were hung to exclude the light, so that if the British succeeded in making their way across the threshold they would plunge into semi-darkness, and not see the loopholes from which they would be shot down by a cross fire. A party of the Royal Irish tried to force their way into this death trap, but were so warmly received that Lieutenant Murray, who was in command, drew off his men to wait for reinforcements; and after a similar attempt by some of the 49th had been repulsed, the house was surrounded by skirmishers to prevent the escape of any of the enemy. Before long more companies of the 18th and 49th came on the scene, and the officer in command of the latter corps, who was the senior officer present, decided not to press the attack until the Tartars had been shaken by artillery. The decision was a wise one, but unfortunately Lieut-Colonel Tomlinson (of the 18th) overheard some expressions which he considered a reflection either upon his regiment or himself, and instantly led a headlong charge towards the entrance of the house. At the door he fell, so desperately injured that in five minutes he had ceased to breathe, while every man who tried to enter with him was killed or wounded. After he was shot down, it became almost impossible to prevent the rest of the 18th from rushing madly at the building, for the men burned to avenge their Colonel, whom they described as ' the best officer who ever said " Come on! " to a grenadier company '. In more formal language General Gough recorded the same opinion, saying in his despatch that Tomlinson fell ' in full career of renown, honoured by the corps, and lamented by all '.

When a few artillerymen came up with a light gun and some rockets they opened on the house without result; equally fruitless were the efforts of a party of sailors to set fire to the woodwork of the upper storeys; then the explosion of a powder-bag made a small breach in a wall through which a few of the Royal Irish tried to force their way, only to be driven back with loss. A second attempt to set fire to the woodwork, however, was more successful, and the explosion of another powder-bag brought down more of the wall, and thus exposed many of the Tartars to our musketry. Soon the whole place was in a blaze, and when at last our men rushed through the doorway from which they had been so often repulsed they found themselves in a hell on earth. Three hundred Tartars had defended the building; now all but fifty-three lay dead upon the floor; and of the survivors nearly all were wounded. Many of their wadded uniforms had taken fire, and to the horrors of the reek of blood and the stench of singeing flesh were added the cries of the wounded, as they feebly strove to beat out the sparks which fell from the roof upon their clothing. In the midst of this scene of carnage sat an old Tartar colonel, who when the red-coats began to show through the smoke, laid down his pipe, snatched up his sword, and cut his throat. This stout old warrior failed to kill himself, and with the rest of the wounded was tended by our doctors and then released—a chivalrous recognition of their bravery which greatly astonished the prisoners and convinced them that the 'Foreign devils' were not as black as the mandarins had painted them. The discovery, unfortunately, came too late to prevent an epidemic of suicide among the population of Chapú.

At Chapú, as has been seen, the Tartar troops fought with great gallantry, and when they knew they were beaten, committed suicide. Some even drowned their wives and hanged their children before cutting their own throats, turning Chapú into a city of horror. The Chinese losses there were severe, estimated at between 1,200 and 1,500.

When the British main fleet were anchored outside Woosung at the mouth of the Yangtze, they were joined by reinforcements including the 98th Regiment under the command of the Major-General Lord Saltoun, and Gough's force rose to about 9,000 men.

One of the new arrivals was Captain James Hope Grant of the 9th Lancers who, as we shall see, was to return to command in China in 1860. It is said that he partly owed his appointment as Lord Saltoun's brigade-major to his skill in playing the violoncello. Saltoun himself was a keen violinist, and he insisted on having a violoncellist on his staff to play with him in the evenings to relieve the tedium of the China campaign.

Chinkiang, the next town to be assaulted, occupied an important strategic position: it was at the spot where the Grand Canal crossed over the Yangtze, just east of Nanking. The Grand

Canal was one of the main supply routes of China. To cut it was to hold much of the country to ransom; and it was natural that the Chinese should fight hard to retain Chinkiang, as indeed they did. Gough had to employ three brigades to attack it, and his troops were soon engaged in some of the heaviest fighting which had been experienced in China.

Entering Chinkiang at last, after a hard struggle, the British found all the horrors of Chapú repeated. The Tartars again massacred their wives and children before taking their own lives. Chinese looting added to the misery of Chinkiang, and Gough, who hated looting either by his own troops or by the Chinese, was greatly upset on both scores. Writing about the Tartar suicides and murders, he says: ' It would appear that the Tartar soldiers did not calculate the rapidity of our movements, and considered the city impregnable; a great number of those who escaped our fire committed suicide, after destroying their families; the loss of life was appalling, and it may be said that the Mantchoo (*sic*) race in this city is extinct . . . finding dead bodies of Tartars in every house we entered, principally women and children thrown into wells or otherwise murdered by their own people, I was glad to withdraw the troops from this frightful scene of destruction.'

Gough established a force on the hills outside Chinkiang to dominate the unhappy town, the stench of which, from unburied corpses, was appalling. He then moved on towards Nanking.

By this time the Emperor and his advisers had become really worried, and hurriedly sent off three Imperial Commissioners to negotiate with the British to save the town of Nanking. With their arrival the proposed attack was called off and hostilities were generally suspended. It was just under a year since the expeditionary force had left Hong Kong, and the intervening months had shown that the ill-armed and badly led Chinese were no match for British and Indian troops. The campaign had been a particular triumph for the British navigators who had had to take their ships along poorly charted coasts and finally up the unknown Yangtze, and had done their work with great efficiency. The Army and Navy, moreover, had worked in perfect harmony. The naval vessels had not merely carried the troops to the points chosen for action, but had ably assisted in the ensuing engagements. Gough's despatch, before Nanking, of 29 August 1842, describes the end of the war as far as he is concerned: ' I have the satisfaction to add that I have this day witnessed the signature of the Treaty by Sir Henry Pottinger on the part of Her Majesty and by the commissioners Kiying, L'lipu and Niu Kien on that of the emperor, and that the ratification of peace is no longer doubtful, the emperor's assent to the terms having previously been received.'

But the Nanking treaty was not quite the end of the matter, as it was followed by a further sequence of treaties all introducing reclarifying clauses significant to the story of the relations of the West with China in the nineteenth century.

The main clauses of the Treaty of Nanking of 29 August 1842 were that the Chinese would accept a British representative in China; that Hong Kong be ceded to Britain; that the ports of Canton, Amoy, Foochow, Ningpo and Shanghai would be opened to British trade, and that an indemnity of 21 million dollars would be paid – 12 million towards the cost of the expeditionary force and 6 million as compensation for the opium destroyed by Lin – but with no mention of the opium trade, although Sir Henry Pottinger did try at one time to persuade the Chinese to legalize the opium trade.

Then the Treaty of the Bogue of 22 July 1843 granted extra-territoriality, allowing the trial of British offenders in China in British courts or on British ships; it also introduced the ' most favoured nation ' principle to Britain allowing her to gain any further concessions which might be allowed to other nations.

In the Treaty of Wanghai achieved by Caleb Cushing for the United States on 3 July 1844 the principle of extraterritoriality was more closely defined, and under it the Americans gained all the concessions Britain had received.

The Treaty of Whampoa, signed by the Chinese with France on 24 October 1844, brought France officially into Chinese affairs. The French had less trade with China than either the British or the Americans, and although the treaty was very similar to the Treaties of Nanking and Wanghai, the most prized concession gained by the French was the granting of tolerance for their missionaries. This at first applied only to Roman Catholics, but a year later was extended to other Christian Churches, and under their ' most favoured nation ' clauses, to Britain and America.

44

France's missionary involvement in China had special significance. It was a breach of the principles of religious toleration and extraterritoriality which allied France and Britain in the next conflict between the West and China.

# 2 The Second China War, 1856-59

In 1856 there began a conflict between Britain and China which developed into what became known as the Arrow War. It came about because of China's failure to keep the terms of various treaties – the Treaty of Nanking of 1842 which allowed European access to Canton, the Treaty of the Bogue of 1843 which permitted British Courts to try British nationals, the Treaty of Wanghai of 1844 between America and China which defined more precisely extraterritoriality for all nations, and the Treaty of Whampoa of 1844 between France and China giving general toleration for religion.

The dispute began when Auguste Chapdelaine, a French missionary, whose only crime was to preach Christianity in China, was tried and executed by the Chinese; and twelve Chinese seamen from the schooner *Arrow* were taken off the (Hong Kong) British-registered ship by mandarins and soldiers and tried for piracy. These represented two flagrant examples of treaty-breaking, and to them was added the old grievance about lack of access to Canton.

There had been dissatisfaction for many years because British and other European merchants were still compelled to live in the old factories' area and were not given free access to Canton itself as the treaties allowed. In addition, Commissioner Yeh, Viceroy of Kwangsi and Kwangtung, was most unco-operative and treated Europeans as inferiors, and the central authorities in Peking ignored British representatives, and left all matters to be dealt with locally by Yeh.

The fluctuating policy of the Government in Britain came into it as well. When the old Whig Lord Palmerston was in charge, full support was given to the men on the spot to enforce legitimate British claims; but the Tories under Lord Derby and the

46

Radicals had different views. They did not believe in pressing the China Government to the point of war.

In 1856 the incident on the schooner *Arrow* set the match to the powder keg, and there followed the drawn-out complicated *Arrow* drama in Canton, and the exciting parliamentary duel at Westminster. Later still came war and, because of Chapdelaine, Britain had France as her ally.

The *Arrow* had arrived at Canton from Macao with a cargo of rice, had deposited her papers in the usual way with the acting British Consul, Harry Parkes, and on the morning of 8 October was preparing to leave again for Hong Kong. Her master, Thomas Kennedy, was having breakfast with two friends on the deck of a neighbouring vessel off Dutch Folly by the Factories' area, where some merchants were already pacing up and down taking the only exercise Canton allowed them. The three men noticed two boats pass, each with a Chinese mandarin and about thirty uniformed men on board. The morning was already hot, and the mandarins were protected by cotton umbrellas from the sun. A few minutes later the breakfasters noticed that the boats had stopped alongside the *Arrow*, and supposed they were dropping off passengers to take to Hong Kong. But the next thing they saw made them jump up from their breakfasts and row hurriedly upstream to the *Arrow* in a sampan. All three clearly saw one of the uniformed men from the boats haul down the British ensign from the stern of the *Arrow*, and immediately afterwards the Blue Peter. When Kennedy reached the *Arrow* he found that his whole crew had been arrested and were lying bound in the Chinese boats alongside. One old man had been tied with a thicker rope than the others and was being kept apart. Kennedy could make nothing of this, and did not know enough Chinese to ask questions. He managed to convey to the mandarins that he would be helpless if left without any crew, and persuaded them to leave behind two of their prisoners. The two Chinese boats then pulled away while Kennedy hoisted the ensign again, and hurried off to tell Parkes what had happened.

Parkes, when told, acted vigorously. The Chinese police raid was clearly illegal. By the Treaty of the Bogue, when Chinese authorities wished to arrest anyone serving on a British ship, they had to apply to the British consul. This procedure had been ignored in the case of the *Arrow*, and Parkes hurried to the spot to protest. The Chinese officer left in charge on the *Arrow* explained to Parkes that the old man bound with thick ropes had been recognized as the father of a notorious pirate; other members of the crew might be involved, and all were needed to give evidence. He refused to allow Parkes to fetch the prisoners and take them to his consulate, and in the argument one of the Chinese struck Parkes a blow. Parkes, however, did not bring up this matter of personal violence with the authorities. He preferred to restrict his complaint to the faults in procedure in the arrest of the men of the *Arrow*, saying in his letter of 8 October 1856 to Commissioner Yeh: 'I hasten to bring to your Excellency's notice an insult of a very grave character which calls for immediate reparation, confident that your superior judgement will lead you at once to admit that an insult so publicly committed must be equally publicly atoned. I therefore request your Excellency that the men who have been carried away from the *Arrow* be returned by the Captain, Leang-kwo-ting, to that vessel in my presence and if accused of any crime, they may be conveyed to the British Consulate, where in conjunction with proper officers deputed by your Excellency for the purpose, I shall be prepared to investigate the case.'

Yeh was prompt in answering Parkes' complaint. On 10 October he offered to send back all the men except three who were wanted on charges of piracy. He said that one had been recognized, because some of his front teeth were missing, as the leader of an attack made on a Chinese junk about a month earlier. This was not acceptable to Parkes. He now referred the case to the Governor of Hong Kong, Sir John Bowring, who was his superior. Bowring was both Governor of Hong Kong and Superintendent of Trade – as Captain Elliot had been in 1841. He had long been anxious to free the conditions of trade for the merchants of Canton, and saw in the *Arrow* incident an excuse to demand the full concessions of the treaties of the 1840s. Having been restrained by the British Government, and told not to use force to improve on, or even defend in minor matters, the rights granted, he was delighted to find in the *Arrow* incident a good opportunity to demand both freer trade and admission by the Chinese that the British were their equals. Most of those who thought about these matters on the Western side had concluded that the Chinese would never treat the Powers as equals until they were represented by ambassadors in Peking, and this became again one of the British objectives in the *Arrow* and Third China Wars. But Bowring was more interested in getting the better of Yeh. It was Yeh and the Cantonese who had, in Bowring's view, humiliated the British by refusing their acknowledged right of entry into Canton. That right must be asserted, and Yeh humbled. The *Arrow* incident should enable him to disobey his Government's orders – not to assert right of entry to Canton. By using naval force to settle the one matter, he could settle what was to him the outstanding question, that of entry into the city of Canton by Europeans.

Bowring, therefore, not only approved of the line Parkes had taken, he authorized him to demand an apology, an assurance that the British flag would be respected, and the return of the twelve. If Yeh did not accept those conditions within forty-eight hours the British naval authorities were authorized to seize an Imperial junk in reprisal. But Bowring noticed something which Parkes had missed: the *Arrow*'s register had expired eleven days before the seizure of her crew. Although this weakened the case against Yeh, and was a matter for legal dispute later, Bowring maintained his demands.

Yeh now denied that the British flag had been hauled down although reliable witnesses had seen it done, and, although he sent back the twelve and was willing to adopt Parkes' suggested procedure, he now maintained that the lorcha[1] *Arrow* was not a foreign schooner. Nor would he apologize or return the men in the public manner stipulated by the British. Both Parkes and Bowring remained adamant on these points, and a naval war was begun by them to ' bring Yeh to his senses ' and enforce entrance to Canton.

The Navy did their best for Sir John Bowring and young Mr Parkes, but manpower was limited, and it was not very effective. On 23 October 1856 the four forts below Canton were captured and dismantled, only two resisting with five Chinese killed, the first casualties of the war. Next, the Navy opened fire on the city wall of Canton and Yeh's residence within, firing a shell every few minutes. Yeh was not unduly disturbed. To give him his due

---

[1] Lorcha – a vessel of about 100 tons, having a hull of European build, and originally commanded by a European captain, but rigged with Chinese masts and sails, and manned by Chinese sailors (Giles).

he was as brave as he was cruel.[1] Only reluctantly was he led away to safety. On 29 October, the wall of Canton having been holed by gunfire, a body of marines led by the admiral passed through the breach and went on through Yeh's house before withdrawing.

The Americans in south China were even more anxious than the British to gain right of access to Canton, and Mr Keenan their Hong Kong Consul, after acting as observer to the naval bombardment, accompanied the British carrying his country's flag. Later an enquiry was ordered in Washington to investigate this strange action by a neutral consul. But Keenan explained that he had only gone into Canton out of curiosity, and the ' Stars and Stripes ' were carried by a marine, which explanation the American authorities accepted.

There followed several months of ' phony ' warfare, each side hopeful that the other would give way. Although the Navy gained control of the estuary and channels up to Canton, and sank Chinese junks, demolished forts, and opened fire on the wall from time to time to keep the breach open, there were not sufficient men to hold the city, or even protect the factories' area.

Near Canton, the Chinese, for once, offered some resistance. A British armed steamer off French Folly had to face not only the fort's 26 guns but also a fleet of 25 war junks assembled to guard it. In the fight that followed the Chinese used a weapon which the British sailors called ' stinkpots ' – earthenware vessels filled with powdered sulphur, and other materials, lit with a match and thrown aboard the British vessel and small boats. On explosion the ' stinkpots ' created such a nauseating smell that it was impossible to stay near them, so the sailors dived overboard. But in spite of ' stinkpots ' and other missiles, and the accompaniment of a continuous beating of gongs, the massed war junks were not even equal to the firepower of one British gunboat. Before the arrival of British naval reinforcements, the junks were all afire, the fort's parapets levelled, and its guns spiked.

Yeh, however, was more resolute than Bowring had imagined. He could do little to counter the British on the sea, but he made

[1] When fighting the Taipings, Yeh killed all rebels and their families as soon as captured. The execution ground outside the walls of Canton was reported as having a toll of 200 heads a day.

life uncomfortable for them in the factories. He issued a proclamation offering thirty taels for every English head, and on 15 December set fire to their houses. Mr Lane of the British Consulate perished in the flames. Yeh denied that he was responsible for this, but it is probable that the Chinese seen running from factory to factory with lighted brands were acting on his orders. The British, meanwhile, were compelled to leave their commercial and naval foothold outside Canton's walls and move to Hong Kong.

Nor was this the only disaster before the year ended. On 30 December 1856, while a postal steam-packet was on its way from Canton to Hong Kong, Chinese soldiers disguised as ordinary passengers captured the ship and killed all the foreigners on board.

When the merchants from the factories settled in Hong Kong, they found the island a troubled area, with conditions closely resembling those during Mao's cultural revolution of 1967. In 1857 the colony had been in existence for fifteen years. It had its governor, bishop, attorney-general and most of the ingredients of an established British colony. An American visiting the island at this time was reminded of one of the boom towns of the American West. He meant this as a compliment, but like the American West the colony had grown too quickly for its own good. It had attracted Chinese smugglers, fugitive Taipings as well as ordinary fishermen, shopkeepers and coolies, who as today, found life better in Hong Kong than on the mainland. The Governor, Sir John Bowring, felt some anxiety even before the arrival of the merchants from Canton. He had spoken of a few Europeans among the 80,000 Chinese on the island, and ' plenty of mischief makers, both Imperialist and rebel ', in a letter to the Foreign Office. In the next weeks his fears grew rapidly. Mysterious fires broke out on the island. As earlier at Canton, the Europeans' Chinese servants absconded and Europeans were assaulted in the streets. Yeh was known to have considerable influence over the people in the Kowloon fishing villages across the harbour, and it was firmly believed that he would attempt to seize the colony. The Europeans felt exposed, and a worried Bowring recruited extra police and borrowed detachments from the French and American naval commanders.

On 15 January 1857 there was a poison scare. Bowring, his

family, and other leading members of the British community were taken suddenly ill from what was shown to be arsenic poisoning. Fortunately no one died. It was said that the poisoner used so much arsenic that the food tasted too nasty to eat, and the few that did stomach it vomited at once. The baker concerned, from a bakery in Pottinger Street, but previously from Macao, was thought to have been hired to do the foul deed by Yeh. But when charged, he was acquitted by a Hong Kong court from lack of evidence. Nevertheless, it is certain that Yeh encouraged acts of terrorism against the British in Hong Kong in 1857 just as did the Communists in 1967.

With hostilities against the Chinese flagging from lack of numbers, and with a threat to Hong Kong by subversion, Bowring decided to ask for additional armed forces. Previously he had sought permission for his naval war from the Government at home, and this was granted. But it took three months for naval reinforcements to arrive, and the war had begun without them. Now he asked for a full scale expedition to be launched. He wrote to the Foreign Secretary, Lord Clarendon:

The gate of China is Canton, and unless we can subdue the resistance and force an entrance there, I believe the difficulties of obtaining any improved position in China will be almost invincible. But success at Canton will, I am assured, be followed by a general and satisfactory change in the state of our relations with the entire Empire. Everything that could be fairly hoped for from the prudence, enterprise and valour of HM naval forces has been accomplished, but they are not able to take the city of Canton, and I deem its capture absolutely necessary for our final triumph. I have had a conference with the naval commander-in-chief, and he deemed military aid to the extent of 5,000 men, with a small body of artillery an absolute necessary auxiliary . . . In the colony I hope we shall be carried through our perils. A large premium is offered for our heads, enormous recompenses are promised to any Chinaman who shall fire the town, a great part of our servants have left in consequence of the menaces of the mandarins and the severest punishments have been proclaimed in the neighbouring districts on all who shall supply our markets. But behind the present darkness we see the promise of brighter days, in the full conviction that HM Government will come to our aid.

By this time the *Arrow* incident was the chief topic of political talk and disagreement in England; and before Bowring's demands were met, a parliamentary battle about them had to be fought out at Westminster.

News of the outbreak of the war in China caused heated debates in both the House of Lords and the House of Commons. The Tory leader Lord Derby rejected Thomas Kennedy's claim that the *Arrow* was a British ship. He said it was ' Chinese built, Chinese captured, Chinese sold, Chinese bought and manned, and Chinese owned '; and the naval bombardment of Canton he termed ' an inglorious operation '. The Prime Minister and the Foreign Secretary, however, were convinced that Sir John Bowring was right. But when they proposed that an expedition be sent to China, all Opposition groups united to condemn the ' violent measures resorted to in Canton in the last affair of the *Arrow* '; and opponents included leading politicians of the day, such as Cobden, Bright, Disraeli and Gladstone. They found a wide variety of points for attack. Cobden thought Parkes too young, and without discretion. Disraeli believed that Palmerston's Chinese policy ' if pursued, will end in ruin '. Gladstone objected on principle. He was interested in the moral, not the legal foundations of policy. ' The lorchas,' he said, ' were mostly smugglers, and often smugglers of opium ', a trade Britain should not encourage on the grounds of Christian principle. He also condemned the way in which the fighting had begun, saying, ' War taken at the best is a frightful scourge to the human race; but because it is so, the wisdom of ages has surrounded it with strict laws and usages.' The Government, in his view, had dispensed with these and ' turned a consul into a diplomat, and that metamorphosed consul (presumably Parkes) is forsooth to be at liberty to direct the whole might of England against the lives of a defenceless people '.

Some of the points made by the Opposition were reasonable enough, but they were not successful in trying to prove that the *Arrow* was not a British ship within the meaning of the act, for the suggestion that she was legally a Chinese ship was shown by the Attorney-General to be untenable. Any lorcha or schooner receiving a sailing letter or register from Sir John Bowring, the Superintendent of Trade, automatically ranked as British, and its crew could be regarded as British subjects as they were ordinarily resident in British territory and living under British rule.

Yet although the law was on the side of Britain, and Palmerston's party managed to defeat Lord Derby's condemnatory motion in the House of Lords, Parliament was not satisfied that the case for armed intervention had been proved. On 26 February when the vote was taken on Cobden's Commons' motion condemning the violent measures already resorted to at Canton, Palmerston was defeated by 16 votes. *Punch* recorded the result as follows:

> For hauling down the British flag, apologizing to the Chinese and putting Derby, Dizzy and Gladstone in office     263
>
> For maintaining the honour of England and keeping Pam in place     247
>
> Chinese majority     16

In his discomfiture Lord Palmerston had the sympathy of Queen Victoria, who wrote to him saying, ' though prepared for an unfavourable result the Queen is not less grieved at the success of evil party motives, spite, and a total absence of patriotism.' In her journal she noted ' the wretched cant and humbug displayed in the debates '.

The triumph of Lord Palmerston's opponents, however, was short-lived. Instead of resigning, the Prime Minister decided to test opinion in a general election. In this the Government was returned to power with an increased majority, and Cobden and Bright paid for their attempt to bring Palmerston down by losing their seats.

The result was that Palmerston was given a mandate to support Sir John Bowring in Hong Kong; and to do this he chose the experienced Lord Elgin to go to China as plenipotentiary, backed, preliminarily by a force of 1,500 troops, and with more men and ships to follow. Lord Elgin was forty-five, a notable plenipotentiary with a previous diplomatic success to his credit in Canada where he had introduced responsible government on the principles outlined in his father-in-law Lord Durham's Report. He was the son of the Lord Elgin who brought the ' Elgin ' marbles from Greece, a mild-mannered ambassador with the face of a bewhiskered cherub, ' his snow-white hair contrasting strongly with his sun-scorched face '.

Elgin spent six busy weeks in England preparing for his expedition. He saw the Queen who ' was kind as usual '. He chose his personal staff and his tropical clothes, and attempted, not without difficulty, to get his instructions from the Foreign Office.

These eventually told him to go north from Hong Kong to the mouth of the Peiho river, which was the traditional gateway to the capital, and open negotiations at Peking with a representative of the Empire. He was to ask for reparations for the losses and injuries suffered by British subjects and British-protected persons in the recent disturbances, and demand the observance of treaties in future at Canton and elsewhere. These were essential requirements the refusal of which would entitle Elgin to use force. He was also to ask the assent of the Chinese Government to the residence at Peking, at least at times, of a British Minister, and permission for British officials to communicate directly with the Peking authorities. He was not empowered to use force solely to obtain these new demands; but if the essential requirements for compensation and treaty keeping were not met, he was entitled to use force. Once started, force would be continued to be used long enough to obtain the new demands as well.

These instructions appear rather complicated, and to secure what was required Elgin was offered at first only an additional force of 1,500 men from England. He was, however, promised 1,000 more from the garrisons of Mauritius and Singapore, and told more troops and gunboats would be available later.

General Ashburnham was appointed to command the land forces for him, and he was told it would be his own decision when to use force. But Admiral Seymour, the naval commander, and General Ashburnham would decide upon and actually carry out the naval and military operations.

For several years it had been the custom of the British to consult with other Western Powers and the United States over Chinese affairs, and to concede to them anything won for themselves from the Chinese. The position of the Americans was a strange one. As has already been seen, at Canton, and as will be seen later, the men on the spot looked after their own interests and co-operated with the French and British. Another example occurred on 15 November 1856 when, soon after the *Arrow* men were seized, Chinese batteries fired on the US corvette *Portsmouth* on its way up to Canton, although the Stars and Stripes were clearly displayed. Within a week the Americans bombarded and captured the forts from which the fire came. They were told later from Washington, however, to co-operate with the British and French, but to stop short of the use of force.

The main French interest was the protection of Roman Catholic missionaries, and when this interest was strikingly offended in 1856, it caused their alliance with the British in the punitive expedition against China.

On 29 February Père Auguste Chapdelaine, a French missionary, was arrested at Silin in the west of Kwangsi, put on trial by the local mandarin, ordered to confess his 'crime' of preaching the Christian gospel, and subsequently flogged and put in a small cage where he was left to die. When he unexpectedly survived this confinement, he was beheaded and his head was thrown to the dogs. The Chinese authorities excused this appalling action on the score that Taipings were rife in the neighbourhood, and it was believed the Father was supporting them. Such excuses did not satisfy the French, and they set out to punish the Chinese for the incident. They appointed Baron Gros as their plenipotentiary to work with Lord Elgin, and despatched warships to Chinese waters.

By the time Baron Gros arrived in China, it was too late in the year for the two plenipotentiaries to travel north to Peking, and it was decided to present the allied demands to Yeh. Having occupied two months in assembling their armed force in case it was required, and blockading the Canton river, formal demands were presented.

On 12 December 1857 Elgin wrote saying that all the open ports were open to commerce except Canton, and the British and French sought admission of their subjects into the city of Canton in accordance with the treaty rights already agreed by the Chinese. The British also sought compensation for recent losses by British subjects. If Yeh accepted these demands of England and France within ten days, the blockade of the river now enforced would be raised. However, they proposed to occupy the island of Honan and the forts on Canton River until a new treaty had been agreed upon with a Chinese official of equivalent rank to Lord Elgin. If Yeh refused these terms renewed operations against Canton would be ordered. When two days later Yeh in reply refused Elgin's terms an assault on Canton was begun.

The qualms Elgin felt about launching this attack are shown in a note of his written just before the battle. He said, ' On the afternoon of the 20th, I got into a gunboat with Commodore Elliot, and went a short way up towards the barrier forts, which were last winter destroyed by the Americans. When we reached this point, all was so quiet that we determined to go on, and we actually steamed past the city of Canton, along the whole front, within pistol-shot of the town. I never felt so ashamed of myself in my life, and Elliot remarked that the trip seemed to have made me sad. There we were, accumulating the means of destruction under the very eyes, and within the reach of about a million people against whom these means of destruction were to be employed. " Yes," I said to Elliot, " I am sad, because when I look at that town, I feel that I am earning for myself a place in the Litany, immediately after plague, pestilence and famine." I believe, however, that as far as I am concerned it was impossible to do otherwise than as I have done.'

Early in the morning the great guns started to boom; the bombardment of Canton had begun. The tide was low at first and landings were delayed. Then with the French and the British naval brigades on the flanks, and the British infantry in the centre, ashore they went. The French and the 59th (East Lancs) Regiment moved along the castle wall of Canton as far as the heights occupied by General Gough's troops in the First China War, taking on the way first a large Buddhist temple and then a fort. Fire was opened from the east wall of the city but most of this passed over their heads. In positions among the widespread Chinese graves which formed natural rifle pits around the north and east walls of Canton the Allied troops stayed for the night; but an hour before daylight were again under arms and with the town surrounded, the assault began. Ladders were placed against the walls, and French and English ' clustered up them like bees, holding on to one another's legs and nearly pulling each other down in the eager scramble '. The five-storeyed Pagoda and Magazine Hill offered no resistance. But when the North Gate was reached, the Chinese rallied. A heavy fire was opened, but this did not stop the Allies, and the gate was captured.

Next morning, the white flags appeared. Canton was taken. In the afternoon the Allies moved round the wall from the North Gate westward, and at the West Gate watched a rush of people leaving the city in panic. The outlying forts at the north-western corner of Canton were now blown up. An eye-witness describes this as follows: ' On Friday Lord Elgin and Baron Gros came up to camp, and sat upon the roof of the Chinese battery on Magazine Hill to see the forts blown up. Seated at only five hundred yards distance, you could just see a small glimmering slow match burning down. Then came a succession of loud, sharp, cracking shivering explosions, throwing fragments high in the air. There were at least twenty successive explosions at the larger fort. When the smoke cleared, a thousand years seemed to have passed in a few seconds. The square substantial fortifications were picturesque ruins.'

For nearly a week the victorious allies occupied the walls from Magazine Hill to the south-east corner of Canton, without going down into the streets of the city. But on 5 June 1858 three columns of Allied soldiers and sailors set off to try and find Commissioner Yeh. Parkes, always one to hear any news going around, had been told that Yeh was in the Imperial Library, but this proved untrue. Questioning an old man reading there, they were told that Yeh had left four days ago to seek refuge in the house of the Tartar general. They nearly missed him even there, but two British naval officers hearing people obviously getting out by the back way, rushed round there in time to seize a fat old man trying to escape by the narrow back passage. This proved to be Yeh himself, and was the end of the matter, for Canton was now handed over to the control of three Allied commanders, and Yeh was banished to India where he soon afterwards died.

The first task of the Anglo-French expedition had been accomplished. The city of Canton was quiet and Yeh had been removed. Now it was time for the other requirements from China to be sought.

Elgin had been told to proceed with a naval force to the mouth of the Peiho and arrange with representatives of the Chinese court for formal talks on treaty revision to be held at a suitable place. In April Elgin and Gros thus sailed for the north. They were accompanied by the ambassadors of the United States and Russia, as neutral observers, but firmly resolved to secure for their countries all concessions that Britain and France might win from China by the use of armed strength.

On their arrival off the mouth of the Peiho, they sent a note to Peking asking that plenipotentiaries should be appointed to meet them for negotiation in Tientsin or Peking. The Emperor sent two commissioners, but they were of much lower rank than had been expected and not capable of representing the Imperial Government. Elgin and Gros were not going to put up with this kind of treatment, and when no more important commissioners arrived, they decided to occupy the forts guarding the entrance to the Peiho at Taku and then to proceed up-river to Tientsin.

The Chinese had made some attempt to block the mouth of the Peiho with a boom of spars, chains and hawsers. This was strong enough to stop a junk but snapped at once when a small British steamer struck it at full speed. Other vessels followed, and although guns were fired from the forts, the heavier guns of the British ships soon silenced them, and no defence was offered when the landing parties went ashore.

The Imperial authorities were severely shaken by the fall of the Taku forts, and soon began negotiations, at one time being represented by the aged Kiying who had negotiated the Treaty of Nanking as long before as 1842. Finally, on 26 June 1858 the Treaty of Tientsin was signed. This provided for the rights of foreign diplomatic missions to live in Peking, the confirmation of extraterritorial rights, the right to travel through China, the protection of missionaries, the addition of further treaty ports (making sixteen in all), and an indemnity to cover the expenses of Britain and France for the recent expedition. Great store was set on compelling the Imperial Court itself to handle foreign relations, and it was therefore decided to send British representatives next year up to Peking to obtain the ratification of the Treaty of Tientsin. What happened on the journey there was the direct cause of the Third China War.

In 1859 both Elgin and Gros had returned to Europe, and Britain was represented by Frederick Bruce, Elgin's brother, and France by M de Bourbulon. Bowring was left with the single post of Governor of Hong Kong, and the two envoys had the task of reaching Peking to obtain the ratification.

Once again a small British fleet, this time consisting of a battleship, two frigates and thirteen gunboats, set off for the mouth of the Peiho, with the intention of sending the smaller boats up river towards Peking as had been done as far as Tientsin in the previous year. For land fighting, if any should be necessary, Bruce relied on sailors and marines, and he also took north a transport corps of Chinese coolies, an example followed on the 1860 expedition. To support the British the French sent only a frigate and a gunboat, as the rest of their Far East squadron was in action against Annam. The American envoy whose country was non-belligerent went north in a United States frigate accompanied by a small steamer. All three envoys were at the mouth of the Peiho by 18 June 1859.

Bruce had been warned by Robert Hart of the Chinese Customs that the Taku forts were rebuilt and the mouth of the Peiho blocked again, and that an army of 50,000 Chinese under General Sankolinsin was massed nearby. These were clear signs that the journey to Peking was going to be a difficult one.

When Admiral Hope, the British naval commander, approached the shore by boat to demand a passage to Tientsin there were no soldiers or officials to greet him, but a crowd of shabby men who claimed to be the local militia forbade him landing and refused to clear away the obstructions across the river as asked.

Bruce would not stand for this. In agreement with Bourbulon he ordered the admiral to deliver an ultimatum demanding the clearing of the river at once or else the Allied ships would force their way through. In answer to this a message arrived from the Emperor telling Bruce to go farther north to Peh-tang where arrangements would be made for him to be taken to Peking. Believing it would be undignified to allow himself to be diverted to the back door, when the front door was shut to him, he refused to stop Admiral Hope and his ships who were already preparing to attack the boom. It is interesting to note that the American envoy did eventually go to Peking via Peh-tang, and got his treaty ratified at the cost of some unceremonious treatment; and that the Chinese later justified their bellicose action at Taku in 1859 on the score that Bruce tried to enter China by the wrong route. An Imperial Decree of 9 August handed to the US Minister, Mr Ward, stated:

Last year (1858) the ships of the English sailed into the port of Tientsin and opened fire on our troops. We accordingly instructed Sankolinsin, Prince of the Khor-chin tribe, to adopt the most stringent measures for the defence of Taku; and the envoys of the different nations coming up to exchange treaties on this occasion (1859) were told that Taku was strictly guarded and that they must go round by Peh-tang. The Englishman Bruce, notwithstanding, when he came on the 5th moon, did not abide by his original understanding but actually tried to force his way into the port of Taku.

Admiral Hope was late in mounting the attack. Although it should have been begun in the morning, it was not until mid-afternoon that the British gunboats started to force the Peiho obstacles. There was no firing when the sailors and marines started to remove the first obstacle of iron stakes; but as the ships began to move through the barrier, and the landing parties put off to capture the forts, the Chinese batteries opened fire with devastating effect. The fire was murderous and at close quarters, as is evidenced in a letter written at the time by Midshipman John Fisher, afterwards Admiral of the Fleet and famous before and during the First World War. In a letter to his mother, he wrote: 'We had a hard fight for it, but what could we do against such a fearful number of guns, and us poor little gunboats enclosed in such a small space, not much broader across than the length of our ship. I had to fling all my weapons away coming back from the forts, and was nearly smothered once, only one of our bluejackets was kind enough to heave me out. You sank to your knees at least every step, and just fancy the slaughter from thirty pieces of artillery in front of you and on each flank.'

Admiral Hope gallantly went into action in a gunboat at the head of his men, and was severely wounded along with most of the crew. Transferred to another boat, he was wounded yet again, and when reports of the British admiral's wounds reached Commodore Tatnall, of the United States Navy, who had brought north his envoy and was watching the fight, the American was moved to help. Ignoring his country's neutrality, and declaring that 'blood is thicker than water' he ordered his ships to tow up the British reserves which had no other means of reaching the battle, then he jumped into his barge, and told his sailors to pull for the ship in which Hope was lying wounded.

Tatnall came from the south of the United States and may have seen the Taku battle as essentially a struggle between men of different colours, for in excusing his breach of neutrality he explained that he could not stand by and see white men butchered before his eyes. 'No, sir,' he is reported to have said, 'old Tat-

61

nall isn't that kind. This is the cause of humanity.' And in pursuing the cause of humanity he offered his sympathy to the British admiral while the neutral American sailors obligingly took a turn at the British guns.

Neither Tatnall's help in bringing up the reserves nor his dash to help Hope could save the British from defeat. The Taku forts remained untaken, and Hope had to withdraw his fleet, having lost four gunboats and 434 men, killed and wounded. The Allies' catastrophe was a triumph for General Sankolinsin, the organizer of China's victory, and for his Chinese soldiers who had handled the guns so well. After their success the general was China's national hero for the rest of 1859.

Bruce did not come out of it so well. Palmerston agreed that ' the British and French envoys had been right in not consenting to go round by the back door, representing as they did the two great powers of the West '; but the Cabinet were not with him in this. They felt that Bruce had not handled the affair at all well, and that Elgin would have to be sent out again to negotiate with the Chinese.

One thing, however, was clear – and in this the French fully concurred – the rebuff to the Allies could not be allowed to go unavenged: both Britain and France decided to send considerable forces to punish the Chinese for their ' insulting behaviour '. The Third Chinese War was about to begin.

# 3 The Third China War, 1860

For the Third China War Palmerston, the British Prime Minister, only gave general instructions. It was left to the Foreign Secretary, Lord John Russell, to brief Lord Elgin, and to Sidney Herbert from the War Office to instruct the commander of the British contingent, Lieut-General Sir Hope Grant.

Elgin's orders were received in a general instruction of 17 April 1860. Russell said that he hoped that when told of the misconduct of his officers in firing upon British ships without warning, the Emperor of China would be ready both to apologize and declare himself willing to abide by the Treaty of Tientsin already agreed to. In order to ensure that the Treaty was adhered to and the indemnity paid, Lord John suggested that it might be necessary to occupy some part of China or take ' a cut ' from Chinese Customs duties for the gradual payment of the indemnity. If the customs arrangement was not possible, he said, ' you will concert measure with the French Ambassador (Baron Gros) for the joint occupation of Chusan, or some other portion of the Chinese territory, in addition to the city of Canton, by the British and French forces till the indemnity is paid.' He then suggests some other requirements, saying that the British and French Ambassadors should reach Peking, and that they should be received there with honour; but ' their continued residence at the capital must be a matter left to your joint discretion '.

He continues: ' With respect to decisions which turn more upon naval and military considerations, such as the march upon Tientsin, and the further advance of the Allied forces beyond that town . . . your discretion will be guided by the opinions of the Allied Military and Naval commanders.' He then goes on to say that care must be taken not to press the Imperial authorities so hard as to destroy their control over China, which was already

63

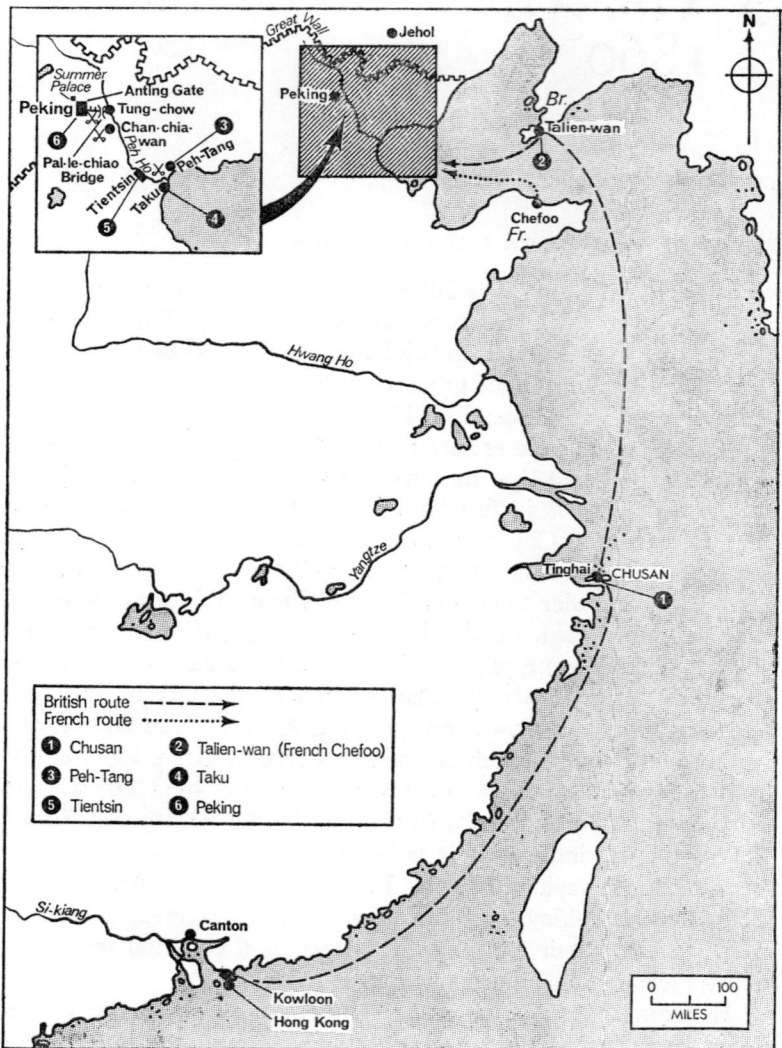

Map 4 Lord Elgin and General Sir Hope Grant's Expedition, 1860

Sir John Bowring Governor of Hong Kong, during the Second China War 1856–59

Commissioner Yeh from a sketch by Colonel Crealock

The Hon. Frederick Bruce, brother of Lord Elgin, who failed to reach Peking in 1859

Lord Elgin

menaced by the Taiping rebels. He ends by reiterating the three essentials – an apology, the ratification of the Treaty of Tientsin in Peking, and the payment of the indemnity to the Allies for military and naval expenses; and he enclosed a copy of the similar Instruction, in French, to Baron Gros from M Thouvenal.

In a further letter in April Lord John Russell hopes that Lord Elgin may acquire the Kowloon peninsula opposite the island of Hong Kong 'in any new Treaty with China . . . and not to lose any favourable opportunity which may occur for securing that cession'.

The British military commander, Sir Hope Grant, came of a well-to-do Scots family. A 9th Lancer, he had by the time of the Third China War seen a great deal of active service. He fought in the First China War, and he was later engaged in the First and Second Sikh Wars, and in the Indian Mutiny. His instructions from Sidney Herbert were on similar lines to those to Lord Elgin, but they were sent to him several months earlier, in January 1860. Besides the three 'musts' above, he was given some details of the forces he might expect. He was told: 'Her Majesty has determined to reinforce the squadron now in Chinese waters under the command of Admiral Hope, and to despatch from England two batteries of Field Artillery (via Egypt) and a battalion of the Military Train (by long sea), a battalion of Infantry, *viz* the 1st Battalion of the 2nd Foot (Queen's) from the Cape of Good Hope, and a force from India consisting probably of at least five battalions of Queen's British Infantry (they included a battalion of the 3rd Foot, the Buffs) two squadrons of British Cavalry (the KDGs), three batteries of Field Artillery, and a company of Royal Engineers, with some native irregular Cavalry (Fane's and Probyn's Horse)[1] and Infantry: the whole force exclusive of the troops now in China, amounting to 10,000 men.'

'To act in conjunction with these forces the Emperor of the French (Napoleon III) is about to despatch 5,800 Infantry, four batteries of Field Artillery, and some "Compagnies de Débarquement", in all about 8,000 men under the command of General Montauban.'

The British field artillery consisted of smooth-bore 9-pounders

[1] Fane's and Probyn's Horse: the former Sikhs, Pathans and Punjabi Mussulmen, the latter Sikhs, 'black princes' to the Chinese.

and two batteries of the newly invented Armstrong rifled breech-loading guns. These were not very successful, and it is significant that the British Army reverted to muzzle-loaders for a period after the China War.

General Hope Grant was told in his instructions to suspend operations and allow Lord Elgin and his French colleague to parley when required, but to resume hostilities if nothing was likely to emerge from talks. He was also to try to confine hostilities ' to the part of the Chinese Empire in which the outrage of which we justly complain was committed ', and preserve good relations with the inhabitants of the great seats of commerce which had remained perfectly tranquil.

He was told by Sidney Herbert to pay great attention to his medical and commissariat arrangements, and in fact all his administrative services worked very well. The Military Train was handicapped by a shortage of suitable transport animals, and by being too military in its organization. It had been used as cavalry during the Indian Mutiny, and its officers did not seem content to organize efficiently the humdrum services required from a transport corps. There were, however, other possibilities. In the Second China War a Chinese coolie corps had been organized for supply. This Canton Coolie Corps was now worth its weight in gold to the British and French alike. Even during action they brought up supplies and, being from the south, watched the defeat of their northern countrymen with satisfaction. Their only failing was bad behaviour in billets and their fondness for looting and wrecking the towns of their fellow Chinese. ' Patient, lusty, enduring, but the scourge of the inhabitants of occupied cities ', is how they have been described.

The campaign was opened by a landing from the sea, and proceeded along a navigable river towards Peking, so that help as regards transport or supplies could also be given by the Royal Navy. The most fortunate feature of the campaign, however, was the plentiful supply of food and provisions which could be bought locally. Unlike the terrain met with in many of Britain's colonial conflicts, North China was both fertile and healthy.

In the Crimea the medical arrangements had been deplorable; in China they were almost beyond reproach. Yet the medical side was not without its problems. Hong Kong, for example, was unhealthy. In 1852, the 59th Regiment, after only twenty months

buried 180 men there. It also had few areas of flat land suitable
to provide large-scale camping grounds. Because of this the
healthier and flatter peninsula of Kowloon on the mainland side
of the harbour was acquired. It was leased from a most willing
Chinese governor for the payment of a yearly rent of a hundred
and sixty pounds a year. Another example of the topsy-turvy
nature of the war! Surgeon D. F. Rennie, whose brother was
also serving in the same capacity, has much to say about the
health of the troops during the expedition:

> Before leaving Talien-wan, I reported to the principal medical
> officer upon the health of the troops during the encampment on shore.
> A large amount of sickness prevailed. The symptoms closely re-
> sembled those which prevail at Hong Kong – fever, dysentery, *etc.*
> Yet the position is remarkably healthy; there was no intemperance as
> intoxicating liquors could not be obtained beyond the ration, the army
> had been weeded of its weakly and sick at Hong Kong, the troops
> having at the first been selected in India as men of known robust
> health. The lowest amount of sickness occurred in the 99th Regiment
> and I observed that that regiment alone is furnished with the Indian
> tent, the rest of the infantry use the bell tent.

He came to the conclusion that the bell tent with fourteen men
in it was unhealthily stuffy. At Peh-tang he discovers a sanitary
paradox:

> It would be difficult to indicate a more filthy and foul smelling
> locality than Peh-tang . . . it was expected that the troops would
> suffer severely from malaria disease; such, however, was not the case,
> their health having been much superior to what it was in the beauti-
> ful climate and pure atmosphere of Talien-wan.

Allied casualties throughout the campaign were relatively slight
and the close contact with the navy enabled medical services to
be excellent.

> Soon after the forts were occupied . . . our own wounded had been
> carefully conveyed on board the hospital ships where every comfort
> that skill and invention could supply was prepared for them.

Even during the advance towards Peking, the wounded could
be evacuated by boat down the Peiho river.

The British were suspicious of the French and did not welcome them as allies. They would have preferred to mount the
expedition on their own. ' It is a great bore (between ourselves)

being tied down by the French,' General Hope Grant writes, ' their force is so small that by the time it gets to China, having in all probability a five months' voyage, it will scarcely be of much use.' Sidney Herbert asked his general to be friendly. ' I need scarcely impress upon you the necessity of a most open, cordial, and conciliatory bearing towards the French forces,' he writes. Grant likes what he hears about the French admiral, ' a nice person – as long as we have gentlemen to deal with we shall get on well '; but he is not so sure about the general. ' I hear that Montauban is a great Turk,' he says. Grant was annoyed by General de Montauban's delay in preparing his force. The French had no convenient base like India. They held the British back, and it seemed they would never be ready to start.

However, at last both forces assembled in the north, the British at Talien-wan and the French at Chefoo. On leaving these two forward camps, the Allies sailed across the Gulf of Pechili towards the Taku forts at the mouth of the River Peiho where on the last occasion in 1859 the British had been repulsed in spite of American help. Before reaching the forts this time, however, they veered off northwards towards Peh-tang eight miles from Taku and the so-called proper way of entrance into north China. Loch and Rennie write:

It was an interesting sight seeing the ships getting under weigh, every available steamer being employed in towing large sailing transports clear of the harbour, while others, impatient to be off, relied on their own efforts. The steamers were dashing backwards and forwards, while the despatch vessels and gunboats were enforcing orders and bringing up the lazy and slow, and by noon upwards of two hundred ships and steamers were bowling along before a strong breeze. At noon I counted ninety vessels under full canvas bearing down on the anchorage, a fine strong and fair wind having set in. The sight was a magnificent one, not likely soon to be witnessed again. At this time a number of junks that had been cruising in the neighbourhood, though at a respectable distance, made sail in the direction of the Peiho, in all probability to report our approach . . . looking out for land I saw in the distant haze three dark masses, apparently equidistant from each other and of symmetrical shape, looming obscurely above the horizon. I looked at them through my glass and concluded they were the Taku forts.

As the weather became unsettled and Peh-tang was still ten miles off, it was decided to defer the landing till the next day,

1 August. By then, although the day opened with heavy rain, the sea had gone down.

The landing party consisted of General Sutton's brigade of foot, with a nine-pounder and a rocket battery carried in large troop boats, each holding fifty soldiers. All were towed ashore by two small gunboats. The boats anchored under the mud bank on the southern side of the river about a mile from the forts. Wolseley describes it thus:

No enemy showed himself beyond what we should have called a couple of squadrons of mounted Tartars who kept near the gate through which the road (a raised causeway) leads to Sinho and the Taku forts. There was about a mile of deep muddy flat to be waded through immediately on landing, so there was little of the pomp and circumstance of war about that operation. The first man to jump ashore and lead up the mudbank was the brigadier. He was an old campaigner well known for his swearing propensities, and famous as a game shot in South Africa. I shall never forget his appearance as he struggled through that mud, knee deep in many places. He had taken off trousers, boots and socks, and hung them over his brass scabbarded sword which he carried over one shoulder. Picture a somewhat fierce and ugly bandy-legged little man thus accoutred in a big white helmet, clothed in a dirty jacket of red serge, below which a very short slate-coloured flannel shirt extended a few inches, cursing and swearing loudly 'all round' at everybody and everything as he led his brigade through the hateful mire. I remember many funny scenes in my soldiering days, but I never laughed more than I did at this amusing disembarkation of the first brigade that landed in northern China.

As the landing proceeded, the Tartars rode off, and the Allies moved across the mud to the causeway and bedded down for the night, spending it, not very pleasantly on the mudflats and causeway, without water, or anything to eat, wet through and lying on very moist ground.

During the night the indefatigable Mr Parkes, accompanied by a staff officer, entered the town and learned that the forts, though mined, were deserted. Next morning the town, noisome, smelly and surrounded on all sides by mud, surrendered. When the inhabitants had evacuated it and hobbled off to Taku – many of the women with their tiny bound feet having to be carried! – it was divided equally between the French and British for quarters. Not a very happy arrangement as the British commander noted,

' I regret very much that our troops are thrown so closely in contact with the French. We have been obliged to occupy the town, the French taking one side and we the other. The plunder and robbing that has been committed by them is a very bad example to our men. The officers appear not to try to stop it.' Among other things the French soldiers, in search of food, chased pigs and dogs through the muddy streets, and when they caught them bayoneted them. On their behalf it must be said that, unlike the British, they did not get full rations and had to live off the country.

The main advance on Taku, via Sinho and Tang-ku, was not started until eleven days after the landing at Peh-tang. There were several minor enemy defence works on the causeway and road leading to Sinho, and bodies of skirmishers had been sent to test their strength. A larger scale reconnaissance had also been completed. Colonel Wolseley with a party of cavalry had followed a cart track to the north-west of the causeway and found quite a good route, muddy at first, but passable for cavalry and artillery, by which Sinho could be approached from the north.

General Grant and General de Montauban had come to an agreement that their forces should take precedence of march by turns, and that the British should have the first right to the privilege. The British commander, therefore, planned to lead the advance on 12 August with a drive down the causeway by Sir John Michel's 1st Division, and a right flanking attack at the same time by Sir Robert Napier's 2nd Division down Wolseley's cart track. The French, after complaining of the state of the muddy ground, agreed to help, but only with a thousand men. There followed a series of minor engagements against the entrenched camps protecting Sinho, attacking what were described as ' merely strong cavalry outposts;' and then the occupation of Sinho itself.

Sinho offered a most pleasing contrast to Peh-tang. It was surrounded by well kept kitchen gardens, full of vegetables, and beautiful to eyes accustomed for the last few days to look upon nothing but mud. Although the opposition had been slight, a very large force (some said twenty thousand) of Tartar cavalry had been stationed in the area, and a plentiful supply of grain for the troops and enough hay to last six weeks were taken over.

It seems that the Chinese General Sankolinsin himself may have been there, for behind one of the crenellated walls blocking the road stood a very large blue awning set up on poles suitable for the use of a very high ranking mandarin.

General Sankolinsin had won renown by once defeating the Taiping rebels and by rebuffing Admiral Hope in 1859. The British soldiers turned his name into ' Sam Collinson ', and there was a most unlikely story among them that he was a renegade Irishman from the Royal Marines. On the approach to Sinho, Napier's Second Division, which had advanced along Wolseley's cart track, were assailed by a mass of Sankolinsin's Tartar cavalry. Here the Chinese horsemen showed their skill at shooting from the saddle. After being fired at by the British infantry and artillery, and charged by cavalry, the Tartars galloped off followed by the KDGs on horses still not fit enough to catch the sturdy Chinese ponies.

The British moved on, but after their departure, bands of Tartar horsemen came out again over the same area; this time they scored a small success; they managed to capture sixteen coolies and two British soldiers following a cart containing rum and supplies in the rear of the 1st Division. This was not all. The captured stragglers were brought before the Chinese commander, resulting in a well known story of British military history. Written up by the enthusiastic Mr Bowlby of *The Times* – present with the expedition – and further dramatized in Doyle's poem, there emerged the famous legend of the ' Private of the Buffs '. This is how it is described in the Buffs' regimental history:

It was at the end of the operations on this day that there came to light an incident that had occurred in the morning which, though of no military significance, led to the name of a man of the Buffs being handed down to posterity as an example of the dauntless spirit of the British soldier. It appears that on the 12th August whilst the Second Division was toiling along the track to Sinho, a body of Tartar cavalry, having worked round to the rear of the column, came upon a body of coolies carrying the rum of the Division who, due very probably to the state of the ground, had lagged some distance behind. In charge of the party was a sergeant of the 44th Regiment who had with him No. 2051 Private John Moyse of the Buffs and a number of Indian followers (Chinese coolies). The whole party was captured by the Tartar Cavalry, and taken off to the Chinese camp. On the morning of the 13th, Moyse and his companions were brought before the Tartar mandarin, Sankolinsin, who declared to them that if they would but *kow-tow*,[1] or touch their foreheads on the ground before him, no harm would befall them. Moyse refused to do this and he was then warned by an interpreter that if he did not obey he would be beheaded by one of the escort on a given signal by the mandarin, but he still stoutly declared that he would sooner die than disgrace his country, whereupon, he was instantly cut down and killed, and his body was dragged away. His companions who had complied with the demands of the mandarin and thus saved their lives were brought back under the flag of truce on the evening of 14 August to Colonel Sargent's advanced post in front of Tang-ku and here the circumstances of Moyse's death were made known by them. Very soon after this event the action of Private Moyse was immortalized by Sir Francis Hastings Doyle in the poem, the first verse of which is quoted below:

### The Private of the Buffs

Last night among his fellow roughs
He jested quaffed and swore;
A drunken private of the Buffs,
Who never look'd before.
Today beneath the foeman's frown,
He stands in Elgin's place,
Ambassador from Britain's crown,
And type of all her race.

There is some doubt whether this story is quite true. Wolseley and others who heard about it considered that Moyse had died of drink; or at any rate not so dramatically as they had been led to believe.

After Sinho came Tang-ku. This was a more formidable proposition. A causeway with deep ditches on each side joined the two towns and there were swamps on the east of the causeway and firmer ground on the river side. Tang-ku's fortifications consisted of a crenellated wall three miles long encircling it from a point on the river to the west round to the river again in its rear. General Grant commanded again – the French had made an

---

[1] The *kow-tow* was the conventional form of obeisance in China and consisted in a series of triple kneelings, bowing the head to the ground. In the earlier period refusal to make this servile gesture was one reason why the Emperor would not receive our ambassadors.

abortive rush alone on Tang-ku immediately after the capture of Sinho, and had thus lost their turn. The attack was made on the firmer ground on the right of the causeway, with the English near the river and the French along the causeway. Sir John Michel's First Division led for the British. By throwing bridges across the ditches flanking the causeway towards the river, and then over several little intervening streams, the Allies found that they could approach to the very walls of Tang-ku on an extended front. While they were doing so the enemy opened on them from the other side of the river with some guns in two junks hauled up on the mud near the village of Taleang-tze, and from a battery on rising ground in the same vicinity. The Allied guns soon silenced this fire, and a naval officer crossed the river with a few men and spiked the guns.

On the night before the assault on Tang-ku, trenches were dug within seven hundred yards of the wall to give cover to the riflemen, and the protective ditch dammed near the river to check its flow. Thirty-six guns, French and British, including two batteries of Armstrongs, supported the attack, and in addition a rocket troop was used. The heavy fire from these guns soon silenced the Chinese weapons and knocked the wall to pieces, for the commander Royal Artillery advanced his guns cleverly by alternate batteries so that ' the enemy pieces were dismantled and the parapets ruined '. The flags with which the walls had at first been bedecked were fast vanishing. One brave fellow mounted on the battlements, and proudly waved a banner in the air, until a shot from one of the guns struck him and he disappeared. Meanwhile some companies of the Royal Scots and 60th Rifles crept through the orchards and sedge along the bank of the river, crossed the dam, reached the foot of the fort, and succeeded in forcing their way through the broken wall. The French on the left had scaled the wall in their sector. Now caught in the flank as well, the Chinese abandoned the wall and fled. Inside, the Chinese scampered back from the wall across to the village, with rockets whizzing through the air to accelerate the speed of their flight. From Tang-ku some of the fugitives made off down the causeway in the rear of the village, over a floating bridge of boats, and then to the safety of southern Taku. Forty-five cannon were captured from behind the wall. There were not a great many casualties on either side, though a few dozens of bodies of Chinese lay about the guns. There were no Allied killed – unless General Michel's horse be included – and only about fifteen wounded.

After Sinho, Tang-ku; and after Tang-ku, Taku; and each Chinese defence work was becoming progressively more difficult to assail. The attack on the northern Taku forts saw also the first major difference of opinion between the British and French commanders.

On 20 August Mr Parkes and Captain Graham, with a flag of truce were sent by Sir Hope Grant to demand a surrender. But the Chinese showed no sign of yielding, and the two envoys were compelled to return. The northern Taku forts were very formidable, having the usual crenellated walls, but with two broad ditches round them, and on the space between the walls and the ditches, the ground was thickly studded with upright bamboo spikes. They had also, like the Peh-tang forts, a ramp inside leading to a cavalier, or raised platform, from which guns could be fired in all directions. The country between Tang-ku and the first northern fort was much as before, saltmarsh and swamp; but without a causeway leading across it. The British built a road north of the main swamp, bridging ditches, and carrying it forward until firmer ground near the forts was reached. The Allies also built a bridge of boats across the Peiho.

The French general now proposed that the two armies should cross the river and attack both the entrenched town of Taku and its triple southern fort. This plan had the advantage of bottling up the enemy in the fortifications and not allowing him to escape to fight another day. It appeared, however, too hazardous for Sir Hope, as the Allies would lose the right flank protection for the river, which they had in operations on the north bank. Sir Hope Grant had also made a careful survey of the positions of the forts, and had come to the conclusion – confirmed in the event – that if they captured the first small fort on the north side, now immediately in front of them, they would command by fire from it all the others, and would have them at their mercy. General de Montauban disagreed. ' L'attaque des forts qui reste sur la rive gauche (north forts) me semble complètement inutile,' he said. Sir Hope was still determined to go ahead with his plan. It looked like stalemate; but in the end De Montauban did co-operate with the British. He was satisfied with writing a memorandum to free himself from military responsibility with reference to his own government in the event of its judging the question in the same way as he did.

The attacking force on Taku consisted of 2,500 British and 1,000 French. Heavy guns were used as well as six batteries of field guns and a rocket battery. The Allies had a stroke of luck when an eight-inch shell falling on the powder magazine of the nearest fort blew it up with a terrific explosion. For some time the fort was so shrouded in dense clouds of vapour and smoke that it appeared to be completely destroyed. But when, by degrees, it cleared away, the enemy recommenced firing and seemed determined not to give up without a desperate struggle. Heavy guns from the cavalier were still firing, but not for long after being struck time and time again by the shells of the massed Allied guns. The British marines brought up pontoons to try and bridge the broad ditches near the fort, but met with too much matchlock fire from the walls to do so. The French were more successful and constructed a way across the ditch by means of scaling ladders carried by Chinese coolies. The Chinamen jumped into the water up to their necks and supported the ladders on their hands and shoulders to enable the French soldiers to get across. The Allied force now pushed forward. Some of the British swam across the ditch, and others got across with the French. Sir Hope's aide-de-camp, Major Anson, getting across by a raised drawbridge, cut the ropes keeping it up, and let the bridge fall down into position. This made a good way across. The difficulty now was to get over the high walls by scaling ladders. There was, however, a small breach made by the guns, and both the British and French, at the same time, forced their way in through it. Ensign Chaplin of the 67th Regiment (Royal Hampshire Regiment) was one of the first of the British to get inside, and managed to plant the Queen's Colour of his regiment on the cavalier, being severely wounded in doing so. For this, along with five other officers and men, he won the VC. The *London Gazette* announcing the awards, speaks of them swimming the ditches, entering the North Taku Fort by an embrasure during the assault, and being among the first of the English established on the walls of the fort. Lieutenant Rogers, 44th Regiment (The Essex Regiment), who also won the VC, is given as the first.

The combined navies had brought up their gunboats near the forts at the mouth of the Peiho, and one of their shells exploded a magazine in the other northern fort. After the capture of the first northern fort, white banners were seen on all the other forts, but this did not appear to mean very much at the time, for when the willing Mr Parkes was sent to summon the other northern fort to surrender, he got 'a very insulting answer'. Another joint attack was therefore staged on the bigger fort, but the French would not wait for the British, and this time their enthusiasm paid off. Dashing ahead alone as they had done after Sinho, they entered the fort through a large embrasure without a shot being fired, and captured it, two hours after the fall of the first fort, without resistance.

Next, flags of truce were sent across the river to Hang-Fu, the Governor-General of the province. By this time General San-kolinsin and his Tartars had fled back up river towards Tientsin and Peking, and according to Mr H. B. Loch, Lord Elgin's private secretary, who accompanied the peace mission across the Peiho, Hang-Fu, although friendly, was not prepared to treat for some considerable time, not seeming willing to take the responsibility, and at least pretending to search for the missing Chinese general. By the next day, however, all the forts on both sides of the river were taken over by the Allies, and the formidable obstacles – chains, stakes, spikes, and booms – were removed by the navies from across the mouth of the river, obstacles which had for so long blocked the route to Peking. The first task of the expedition had now been carried out. The guns which had sunk the ships of Admiral Hope in 1859 had been captured. The obstacles which had stopped him going up the river with the plenipotentiaries had been removed. The British defeat of the year before had been revenged. 'My dearest Mother, the Third China War is over,' Wolseley wrote, after the surrender of the Taku forts.

But he was quite wrong. There was a great deal left still to be done.

Up to the surrender, the main operations had been military. Although Hang-Fu, the Chinese Governor-General of the province of Chihli, had tried to ward off the blow threatening China by writing a series of letters to Lord Elgin asking him to appoint some time and place so that an amicable settlement might be arranged, Lord Elgin studiously avoided negotiating with the provincial official. He was aware that Hang-Fu's only purpose was to gain time until the onset of winter would halt operations. Lord Elgin, however, in consultation with Baron Gros, did write to Hang-Fu telling him the terms on which he was willing to call off naval and military operations, namely: an apology for the attack at Taku in 1859, the ratification of the Treaty of Tientsin of 1858, the payment of an indemnity to the Allies for the expenses of the war, and – before their capture – the surrender of the Taku forts. To further correspondence from Hang-Fu, he made the same invariable answer.

With the Taku forts in Allied hands, diplomatic as opposed to military action began in earnest, and it was agreed that a meeting and discussion should be arranged in Tientsin. Thus an advance was made on that city, with gunboats moving forward in the van, taking with them Lord Elgin's diplomatic assistants, Wade, Loch and Parkes. Parkes, a former consul at Canton, and a firm believer in Palmerston's ' gunboat ' methods, had done important work already. Always to the fore, he had arranged the purchase of Kowloon, he had found Peh-tang unmanned and discovered the nature of the mines left in its forts, and he had persuaded Hang-Fu to sign the document of surrender of the Taku forts, including nominally the whole of the province and the town of Tientsin. From now on he was to play an even greater part.

There were two roads from Taku to Tientsin, one on either side of the Peiho, the high embankments of which could occasionally be seen from the river. The countryside on leaving Taku was cultivated, and there were a few trees near the villages. The villagers were friendly, and anxious, as in 1858, to sell fowls, vegetables and eggs to the invaders at ' twenty times the proper value '. Ice and grapes were particularly popular with the troops and sailors. The Chinese saved the ice from the winter, and not only drank it melted, but laid it under rugs on which they took cool siestas.

Admiral Hope led the Allied advance, and finding the Tientsin forts empty, took over the town. The river was crowded with junks and boats, and the people flocked in thousands to the banks showing no alarm. Lord Elgin and Sir Hope Grant were not far behind, and Baron Gros arrived in one of the French gunboats which had been sent out from France in pieces and bolted together on arrival. These were poor things with thin plates, and too small to be of much service.

Mr Parkes and Mr Wade put the terms to the three Chinese envoys, now Kweilang, who had drawn up the Treaty of Tientsin, Hang-Fu, and Hang-ki, the last a member of the group of Chinese who wanted peace.

There were a series of meetings and discussions and all seemed to be going well. But when it came to signing it was discovered that the envoys from the Emperor had neither the official seal nor yet the power to agree to anything. The Chinese were, of course, trying to delay the Allies until the winter, when, with the help of the cold weather, they thought they could drive the ' barbarians ' away.

So that no time should be given the Chinese to prepare new defences, the order was at once given for a further advance on Peking. During the march from Tientsin, Lord Elgin received almost daily letters from the Chinese authorities imploring him to stop his army. But he replied that because they had tried to mislead him at Tientsin, he would not think of signing any convention until he reached Tung-chow, a city about twelve miles from Peking.

Approaching Tung-chow, but with only part of the main force on the move owing to the time needed to bring supplies up the river, Parkes and Wade again went forward to negotiate. This time Tsai, Prince of I, was the principal Chinese commissioner.

When Parkes and Wade returned after the first visit to the Chinese commissioners the preliminary arrangements appeared almost settled. The Allied armies were to advance to an area ten miles from Tung-chow and then encamp while Elgin and Gros proceeded with a large escort to Peking. Unfortunately Parkes had to go back to Tung-chow to make a few final arrangements. He took with him under a flag of truce, De Normann, a diplomat, Loch, Bowlby, *The Times* correspondent, Colonel Walker of the quartermaster's department, Thompson of the commissariat, and an escort of about two dozen troopers of the KDGs and Fane's Horse under Lieutenant Anderson. (In the event all of these men except Walker and Thompson and a few troopers were captured or killed, in spite of the flag of truce in the form of a white flag on a lance under which they moved.)

Parkes' party first inspected briefly the camping area short of Chanchiawan. This lay on a plain between the road and the river, just short of a stream with a bank along it. On the left of the road, as they approached, was a small village near which they noticed trees had been felled – the first sign of treachery. They passed through the walled town of Chanchiawan safely and reaching Tung-chow were taken to their quarters in a temple.

At the meeting with the commissioners, Lord Elgin's letter accepting the conditions of a convention was read. In it he said he hoped there would be no delay in being received at Peking, and in the delivery of the letter of credence to the Emperor. On this request the Prince of I became almost offensive and refused to continue with negotiations until Parkes agreed to defer the question of the letter and also cut down the size of Lord Elgin's escort. After this it was arranged that the Chinese would set up and provision the camp for the Allies, and issue a proclamation to tell the people that peace had been established between the Emperor of China and the Allies.

On the next day Parkes, Loch, Walker and Thompson, with an escort went back to the camping ground with the intention of leading the Allied forces to it. The remainder of the party went sightseeing in Tung-chow. When Parkes' group reached the camping ground they found it in the process of being occupied by the enemy. Obviously a trap was being prepared to catch the Allied forces when they came forward to use the area. Enemy troops were manning the bank by the stream, and masked batteries were being set up along it. On the flanks and to the front cavalry were manoeuvring. The position of Parkes' party was a most critical one. It was now only too apparent that treachery was intended.

After a hasty council, it was decided that, to prevent an immediate attack on the party, it was better not to show any distrust of the Chinese. Walker, Thompson, and five of the KDGs, were therefore to remain moving backwards and forwards along the bank, ready on the first appearance of hostility to turn their horses' heads and gallop for their lives over the plain, across which the Allied forces would soon be advancing. While they were doing so, Parkes was to ride back to Tung-chow to find out from the Prince of I what was happening, and to warn those left behind of their danger, and Loch was to try and push through the Tartar cavalry screen and warn Hope Grant of the trap awaiting him. The first Chinese line of cavalry through which Loch had to pass was about a quarter of a mile in advance of the village

79

with the felled trees. The cavalry made no movement to stop Loch and his Indian escort, so he pushed on at a canter through their open ranks, and came up with the Allied advance guard half a mile further on. Hope Grant was both indignant and perturbed to learn that Chinese troops and guns were occupying the very site which had been promised to the Allied force.

Loch, very gallantly, went back to help Parkes and the others escape, and Captain Brabazon persuaded Grant to let him accompany him. By the time that Loch found Parkes, seven of the original party had made their way to safety. This is how one of the main body described it:

We looked through our telescopes along the line of Chinese troops, and made out Colonel Walker and some men of the Dragoon Guards on their horses, but to our surprise they did not come out to meet us . . . Suddenly we heard a heavy fire of matchlocks and gingals, and a number of horsemen were seen galloping furiously towards us. They turned out to be Colonel Walker and his party. They soon reached us, and told us their story. They had been detained by the enemy, but were civilly treated, when a French officer rode up and began a dispute with some Tartars about a mule he was riding. At last he drew a pistol and fired it, when his mule was immediately shot and himself murdered. Colonel Walker rode to his assistance, but his sword was struck out of his hand, and though it was restored to him by a Chinese officer fresh efforts were made to wrest it from him and in his endeavours to retain it, his fingers were so badly cut that his hand was disabled. Then finding that their only hope of safety was to force their way out, he shouted to his party to ride for their lives. All charged through the enemy and made their escape – *viz*, Colonel Walker, Mr Thompson of the commissariat, one sowar, and four Dragoon Guards, one of whom was shot through the leg. Mr Thompson received several spear-wounds in the back, and one horse was shot through the body, but managed to convey its rider back in safety.

Meanwhile Parkes had not been able to find the Prince of I, who having laid his plot, had gone to Peking to report to the Emperor. Parkes then sought out General Sankolinsin and asked for a free pass for himself and the remaining members of the mission, but Sankolinsin laughed in his face and accused him of having caused all the trouble that had arisen in China. This time Parkes accepted his fate. ' I fear we are prisoners,' he said to Loch.

After Loch and Brabazon had been absent for two hours, and

Lieut-General Sir Hope Grant in command of the British Contingent in 1860

General C. de Montauban, the French Commander, 1860

Cantonese coolies serving with the British Military Train: 'patient, lusty, enduring' – and the scourge of the inhabitants of occupied cities

(Top) Sikh Sowar, Punjaub Irregular Cavalry, China 1860

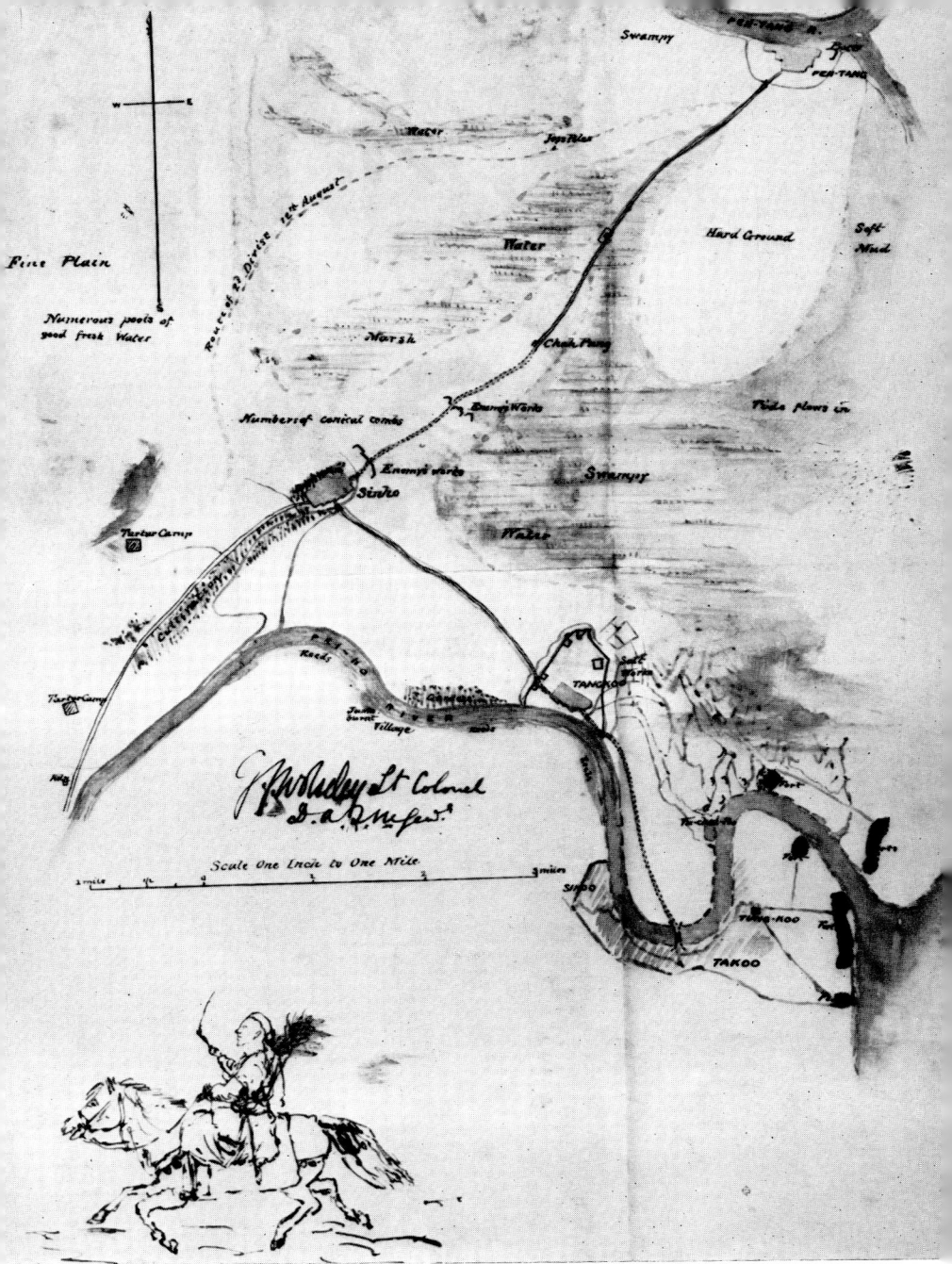

Lieut-Colonel Wolseley's original map of the approach march
on Taku Forts, 1860

French troops capturing the bridge of Palichao (from which General Montauban took his later title of Count Palikao), September 1860

(*Top*) The 44th Regt (later Essex Regt) and 67th Regt (later Royal Hampshire Regt) attacking the first Taku fort. A breach was made by the guns and then Ensign Chaplain of the 67th and Lieutenant Rogers of the 44th led the way in. These two and four other officers and men won the V.C. The assaulting troops with scaling ladders can be seen and the second line manning a bank in the foreground

it was evident they had been detained, Hope Grant gave the order for the attack. The French advanced on the right and got into difficulties. But to assist them the British had lent a squadron of Fane's Horse, and this gallant little force of cavalry, with half a dozen Spahis (mounted orderlies) and all the cavalry the French had – the whole led by Colonel Foley, the Commissioner with the French – now charged the Tartars, and, though a handful compared with them, used their sharp swords with such effect that the enemy were compelled to retreat.

On the left among the British it was much the same, with the Tartar cavalry overrunning the position. Here relief was given through a charge by Probyn and a hundred of his Sikhs. Then, when reserves were brought up – the 99th Regiment, a nine-pounder battery, an Armstrong battery, and the KDGs – the enemy crumbled and their whole position was captured. Wolseley describes thus the battle of Chanchiawan:

Our force then advanced, when the action became general along the whole front, the hordes of Tartar cavalry trying to surround us and intimidate us by their vast numbers, but John Bull is not easily frightened so in we went at them over and over again. Through and through them until all had retired behind the river (stream) leaving all their guns in our possession amounting to over seventy in numbers. We pursued them through the town of Chanchiawan, and took a number of their camps which we consigned to the flames.

After the battle of Chanchiawan the Allies moved forward west of Tung-chow towards Peking, with the French on the right, the British infantry and artillery in the centre, and the cavalry on the left. A canal joining Tung-chow to Peking lay across the Allied front. The French were approaching the Palichao bridge over the canal, and the British a wooden bridge on their left, when the French left was attacked by Tartar cavalry, the enemy coming between the Allies. Hope Grant immediately turned a battery on them at two hundred yards range, and then sent in the KDGs and Indian Cavalry – it was here that the KDGs distinguished themselves – and chased off the enemy cavalry over a ditch. But the battle was not finished. When Montauban's French troops advanced on the Palichao stone bridge they found the élite of the Chinese Imperial Guard drawn up to resist them. After some gallant fighting, however, spurred

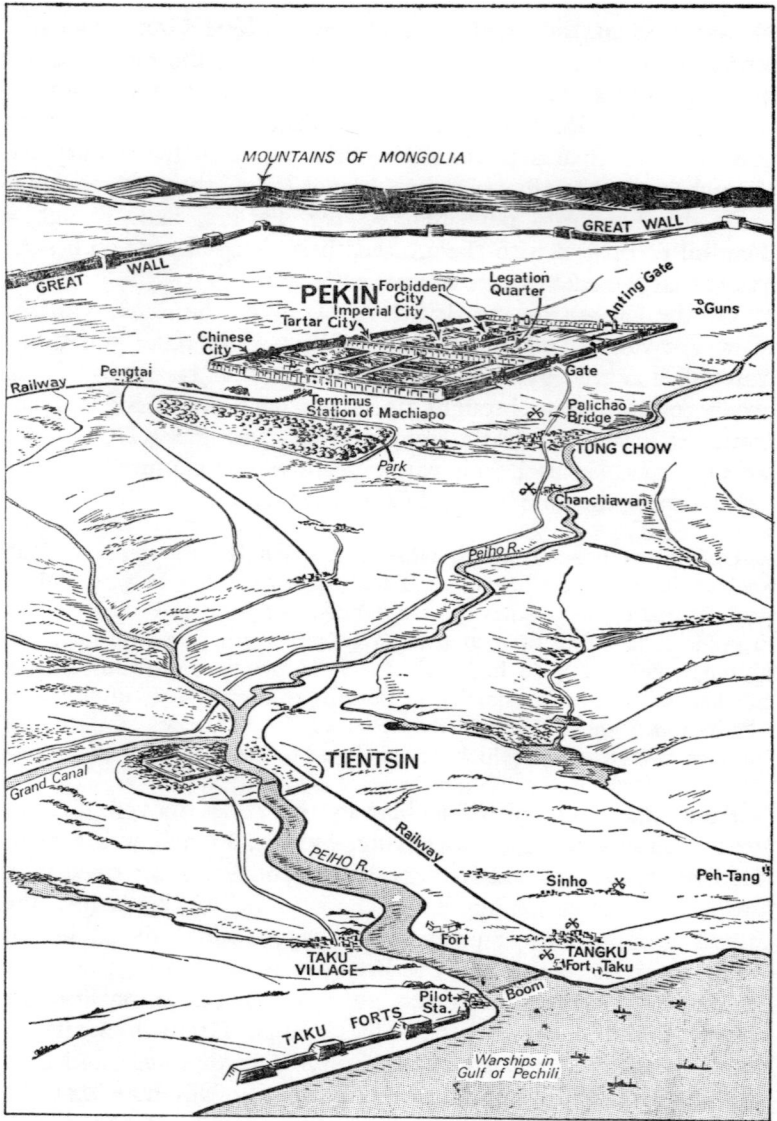

MOUNTAINS OF MONGOLIA

GREAT WALL

GREAT WALL

**PEKIN** Forbidden City
Imperial City
Tartar City
Chinese City
Legation Quarter
Anting Gate
Guns

Railway
Pengtai
Terminus Station of Machiapo
Park
Gate
Palichao Bridge
TUNG CHOW
Chanchiawan
Peiho R.

Grand Canal
TIENTSIN
Railway
PEIHO R.
Sinho
Peh-Tang
Fort
TAKU VILLAGE
TANGKU Fort, Taku
Pilot Sta.
Boom
TAKU FORTS
Warships in Gulf of Pechili

Map 5  The Way to Peking. 1860, major battles. The route from
Tung-chow to Peking crossed by Palichao is a waterway and there is
no railway. 1900, the railway shown played an important part. The
Grand canal from Hangchow ends at Tientsin

on by their general, they secured the bridge. The battle of Palichao was over.

The enemy had apparently disappeared. But there was one
final incident before the day ended. The British camp was being
pitched by the bridge when the enemy opened fire from across
the canal. The Musbee Sikhs,[1] however, soon dealt with this.
They crossed the canal, took the guns, and killed seventy of the
enemy.

The next morning, 22 September, a flag of truce was sent in
from the highest mandarin of the empire, Prince Kung, who
from now on, played the main part in the negotiations. He and
Hang-ki seemed genuinely to be seeking for peace, but there was
still pressure in the opposite direction from a war party with the
Emperor at Jehol, a town away to the north beyond the Great
Wall, where the Imperial Court had now moved.

Prince Kung announced that the Emperor was willing to call
off hostilities if the Allies agreed to restore the Taku forts and
leave the country. Lord Elgin replied that he would not even
discuss terms until all the prisoners were returned and, unless
they were sent back, the Allies would move up and storm Peking.
It must have been a difficult decision to make. Particularly as
the Chinese said the prisoners would be massacred if they did so.
There was, however, a delay. As at Taku Sir Hope Grant was
not prepared to attack without his siege train – the 8-inch guns
and howitzers, the two 32-pounders and three 8-inch mortars,
without which he believed it would be futile to try to break down
the rampart walls of the city. These were thirty-five to forty feet
high and sixty feet wide at the top, and presented a formidable
obstacle even against heavy guns. Nevertheless the deliberate
nature of the campaign as fought by Grant met with disapproval
from the diplomatists, and even from some of the officers. ' I
wish we had either of our Major-Generals at the head of the
army,' one wrote home.

The poor prisoners – and there were French as well as British
– certainly suffered from this delay. Captain Brabazon and Abbé
Voss had been executed. The remainder were divided between
' the worst prison in China ', Parkes' description of the headquarters of the Board of Punishments, where he and Loch were

[1] Musbee Sikhs – low caste Sikhs enlisted as pioneers who fought and did
pioneer work as well.

first in custody, and the cells of the Summer Palace, where Bowlby of *The Times* and De Normann died. The casualty rate among the prisoners was high. The Chinese prisons were infested by small maggots. If these got into wounds caused by the rubbing of fetters, inflammation, fever, delirium and death followed in succession. Parkes and Loch were luckier than the rest, although the Peking prison itself was very bad. Loch says of his arrival:

I found myself in the presence of, and surrounded by, as savage a lot of half-naked demons as I had ever beheld; they were nearly all the lowest class of criminals, imprisoned for murder and the most serious offences (they were kindly disposed to the Englishmen all the same). On one side of the room, running the whole length, was a wooden bench extending about eight feet from the wall, sloping a little towards it; this was the sleeping place; chains hung down from several of the beams, reaching nearly to the bench, with the use of which I was soon to be made practically acquainted . . . My hands were handcuffed, the short chain which connected them being passed through the link in the one which descended from my neck to my feet . . . I was then laid on the bench which I have described, with my feet towards the wall, directly under one of the chains hanging from the beam above; to this the chain round my neck was attached and I was thus only able to lie flat on my back, and even that was painful with my elbows pinioned.

Parkes and Loch, however, were later used as a means of communication with the Allies, and were moved to comfortable quarters near the Anting gate – even having their meals sent in from a nearby restaurant. While there, they composed several letters at the dictation of the Chinese. They were also allowed to receive fresh clothing from outside. On the letters and the clothing secret messages were sent in both directions. Hindustani was used, a language unknown to the Chinese. Finally, to placate the Allies, Hang-ki persuaded Prince Kung to release them. The two Englishmen were returned secretly in a closed cart to the Allied lines outside the city. Apparently, only just in time, for soon after they left Peking a message arrived from the war party in Jehol enclosing the Emperor's orders for their execution.

Parkes and Loch, and some of the others, were returned on 8 October, and the remaining survivors on the following day. But two had been killed, and eighteen had died.

While arranging for the final attack on Peking, Elgin lost touch with the French. They had moved northwards, and, coming on the Summer Palace a few miles outside Peking, had turned aside to plunder it. Montauban assured Elgin and Grant, when they rode over, that the soldiers were strictly forbidden to loot, although even while he was speaking, French soldiers could be seen helping themselves to jade, jewels, silks and furs. In the end it was agreed that the British should have a share. Their allotment was sold by auction and the money distributed among the officers and men of the force. Generals Grant, Michel and Napier declined to accept anything, but every British private got about four pounds.

Before the final move on Peking, the later famous Charles George Gordon joined the Engineers of Sir Hope Grant's force. While negotiations were going on Gordon utilized the period of inactivity by going on 8 October 1860 to see the Summer Palace. The grounds covered a large area and in addition to the main building contained more than two hundred summer houses and kiosks. Gordon describes the inside of the main house as follows:

You would scarcely conceive the magnificence of this residence or the tremendous devastation the French have committed. The Throne room was lined with ebony carved in a marvellous way. There were huge mirrors of all kinds, clocks, watches, musical boxes with puppets on them, magnificent china of every description, heaps and heaps of silk of all colours, embroidery and as much splendour and civilization as you would see at Windsor. Carved ivory screens, coral ditto, large amount of treasure, *etc.*; and the French have smashed everything in the most wanton way . . .

The main objective was now the occupation of Peking, and as all demands for its surrender were refused, the heavy guns were placed in position opposite the Anting gate with the intention of breaking it in with gunfire unless the Chinese capitulated. Gordon, who helped with his engineers to mount the heavy guns in a protected position, indicated how the Chinese left their surrender to the last moment. He writes. ' The Chinese were given until twelve on the thirteenth to give up the gate. We made a lot of batteries and everything was ready for the assault on the wall which is battlemented and forty feet high but of very inferior masonry. At 11.30 p.m. however, the gate was opened and we took possession.'

With the Emperor still at Jehol, it was left to Prince Kung to conclude the matter. On 24 October 1860, Elgin, with a large and imposing escort, marched to the Hall of Ceremonies. All he demanded was now granted, and in addition, Kowloon was ceded to Britain, and Tientsin added to the list of open ports. At last the Treaty of Tientsin, under the name of the Treaty of Peking, was ratified. Two days later a similar treaty was signed with the French.

Meanwhile, the Summer Palace, having been plundered by the French, had been burned to the ground by the British. Both Loch and Wolseley thought that the burning of the Summer Palace 'hastened the final settlement of affairs and strengthened our ambassador's position ', and ' was felt acutely by the Chinese authorities as a punishment directed specially against the Emperor and themselves '. But Gordon who helped do the job of burning believed it ' a wicked shame '.

In a letter to the Foreign Secretary from Peking on 25 October 1860, Elgin justifies his action – which caused horror throughout the world – in these terms:

It was necessary, therefore, to discover some act of retribution and punishment, without attacking Peking, and in such a manner as to make the blow fall on the Emperor who was clearly responsible for the crime committed (murder of the envoys) without, however, so terrifying his brother (Prince Kung) whom he had left behind to represent him, as to drive him from the field . . . The destruction of the Yuen-ming-yuen Palace . . . seemed to me to be the only combination which fulfilled . . . these conditions.

The Third China War had achieved what it set out to do. Except for the murder of the envoys, it was carried through, albeit slowly, without any real hitch. The administrative arrangements were sound, and the soldiers fought well. With remarkable skill the plenipotentiaries got the China Treaty ratified in Peking itself. It was, moreover, a lasting settlement. The friendly relations established between England and China by this Treaty remained unbroken for forty years.

After the settlement it only remained for congratulations to be given and awards made. Elgin was offered, and gratefully accepted, the post of Viceroy of India, General de Montauban was raised to the French nobility as Count Palikao – after the bridge captured so gallantly by the French – and Grant received the GCB. He also received a letter from Sidney Herbert, sum-marizing the Government's view of the war: ' The public here are, I think, very pleased with the way everything has been done in China – firmness, temper, skill, success . . . a first-rate general, a capital staff, an excellent commissariat, and a good medical de-partment are four things the English public are especially pleased to see, and the more so when all are got together.'

# 4 The Taiping Wars

In the three China Wars already described Britain was attempting to make China receive her ambassadors and to accept from her commodities – which included opium – in exchange for silk, tea, rhubarb and silver. By contrast, in the battles with the Taipings and other rebels, Britain was a respected ally, lending China generals like Gordon, and providing, on request, officials like Robert Hart to control the Chinese Customs. The cause of this topsy-turvy state of affairs – with British armies fighting against China in the north and as her ally in the south – stems from the nature of the Taiping kingdom and the uncontrolled behaviour of the Taipings and other rebels in the vicinity of Shanghai where many British merchants were based. The form of Christianity adopted by the rebels was, as will be shown, such that European Christendom was unable to accept the Taipings as allies, while fear of the looting propensities and destructive behaviour of rebel troops in the Shanghai area caused Britain to support – after frantic pleas by the merchants – the Imperial cause in that neighbourhood.

The setting of the Taiping rebellion seems to have been similar to other rebellions throughout the long history of China, but it differs radically in one way from the uprisings which preceded it. There had been attempts to overthrow the dynasty; the Taipings not only tried to overthrow the dynasty, but also the ruling class of scholar-gentry who, with their Confucian principles, had always formed the basis of the government for whatever dynasty was in control, including the alien Mongols and the Manchus.

The setting contained the elements characteristic of periods of dynastic change: rapid population growth had produced by the middle of the nineteenth century severe pressure on the land; farmers were overtaxed; and high rents led to the desertion of the land by the peasants so that there arose a roaming population willing to enlist under bandit leaders or rebellious organizations based on secret societies. Although the Triad provided in theory an overall organization for secret societies, such societies in the South were more independent and became prototypes for any rebellious organization which could attract discontented dispossessed people. There were other examples of group strife. The original Miao tribes of the South staged uprisings against local Chinese officials; and the Punti, descendants of the first Chinese settlers there, were at enmity with the Hakka peoples who had spread into the South at a later date. Thus there was armed strife between Punti and Hakka villages as well as Miao rebellions and banditry.

The local gentry tried to keep order in their regions even if they were not employed as mandarins by the Peking Government; and the officials legally responsible were often content to permit defence forces to be created by local gentry to deal with bandits, secret societies, rebellious tribes or village strife, instead of calling in the regular military forces of the central power. Thus there were many groups at war with each other in the South, and plenty of scope for new ones like the Taipings.

These were not the only difficulties facing the Manchu dynasty. It had severe economic troubles of an external nature, and possessed a particularly weak military organization to meet either external aggression or internal disorder.

As we have seen, the vast illegitimate import of foreign opium turned a favourable balance of trade between China and the West into an adverse one. Formerly the value of exports had been higher than that of the imports, and the balance had been covered by an import of silver into China. Through the import of opium the imbalance was not only reversed, but the outflow of Chinese silver became great enough to disturb the Chinese fiscal system.

The Chinese currency system was based on silver and copper. The farming population had its taxes and rent calculated in silver but received its income in copper. The outflow of silver debased the value of copper in terms of silver from $1:2$ to $1:3$ and upset the farmers by lowering their profits.

The Opium Wars demonstrated the total inadequacy of the Manchu military forces to defend China against Powers such as Britain and France. But these military forces were hardly ade-

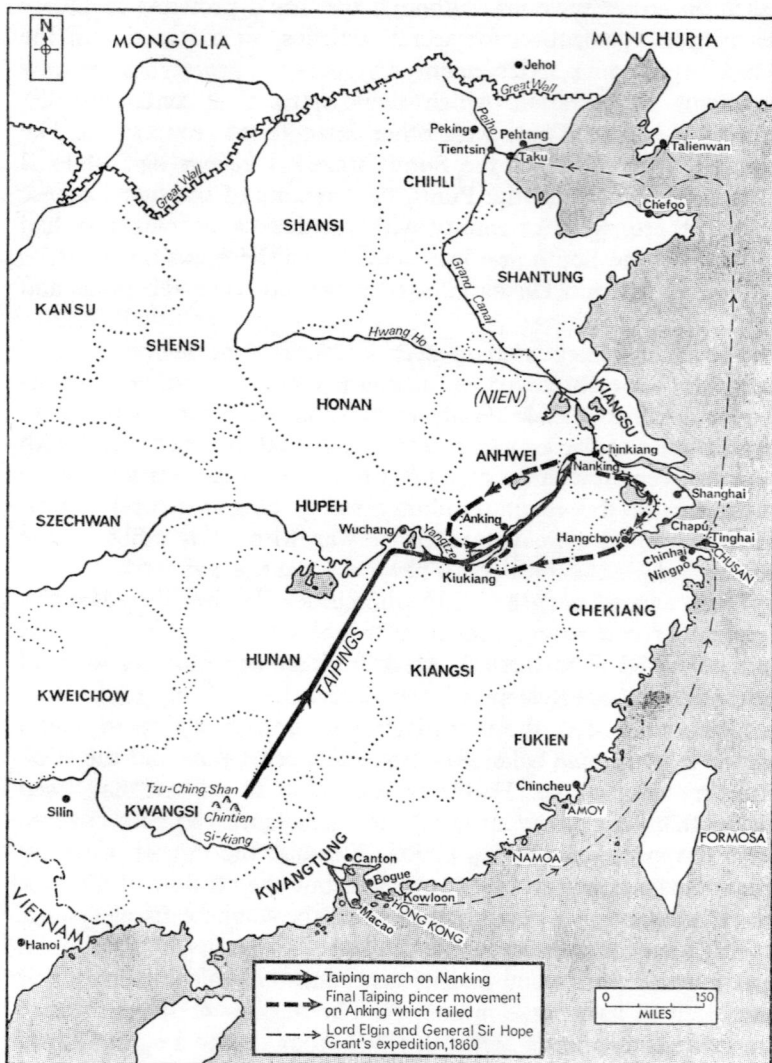

Map 6   The Provinces – and Taipings

quate to deal even with the Taipings.

The army of China under the Manchus consisted of three parts. The first part was made up of the Tartar Army of the Twenty-four Banners,[1] originally composed of Eight Banners of Manchus, Eight of Mongols and Eight of Chinese. This part of the army traditionally had the role of guarding the palace, the city of Peking and the frontiers of Mongolia and Turkestan. At the time of the Taiping Rebellion there was one division in Shensi province, six were in Kansu, three in Shansi, and the remainder, about half of the total of 293,274 involved, in a cordon round Chihli and along the Yangtze River, including 3,491 at Nanking, and in Chekiang, Fukien and Kwangtung, with small garrisons in Honan, Shantung and Szechwan. Kwangsi, Hunan, Kiangsi and Anhwei were without Banner troops.

Most of the Bannermen in the provinces were commanded by Tartar (Manchu) generals. Service as Manchu Bannermen was a hereditary privilege and almost every adult male Manchu was in some way enrolled under the Banners. The larger garrisons in the North and West retained their fighting qualities to some degree, but the small garrisons in the South degenerated. For example over 5,000 Manchu Bannermen at Nanking surrendered to the Taipings without a fight. On the other hand, as has been seen, 300 Tartars fought to the last at Chapú in 1842 against the British under General Gough, and killed themselves and their families rather than surrender.

The second part of the army of China was made up of volunteers from all parts of the country. Officers might be Manchu or Chinese, but the rank and file were Chinese. This army, known as Tents of the Green Standard, and dating back to pre-Manchu days, was evenly distributed through the eighteen provinces of China. It numbered 618,319 in 1850. The troops of the Tents of the Green Standard under the Viceroy were in some provinces checked by the Tartar general stationed in or near the capital city of the province with his Bannermen. The Tartar general ranked above the Viceroy and was directly responsible to Peking.

Hung, the man who started the Taiping Rebellion, came from near Canton in the province of Kwangtung, and was of Hakka

---

[1] The Eight Banners of each group were coloured: yellow; white; white with yellow; yellow with white border; red, white with red border; blue, white with blue border.

stock. His father was a small farmer who worked his own fields, and he had two brothers who helped their father on the farm. An intelligent child, Hung was sent to school to prepare for the examinations held in Canton for admission to the administrative class, the so-called scholar gentry, but in 1827 after eight years' schooling, he failed in his examination. Those who failed tried again whenever the examinations were held, and Hung tried several times more, the last in 1843, but he never succeeded. He thus became one of a body of disappointed, frustrated, unsuccessful scholars from whom in periods of crisis leaders of rebellions sometimes come.

During the latter part of his studentship he taught in the village school to support himself, and in 1837, in the middle of this period, he became critically ill, probably from nervous strain due to his failures. He was so ill that his family feared for his life, and this severe illness and the delirium which accompanied it played an important part in his career.

Before his breakdown a religious tract, admonishing the reader to believe in God and Jesus Christ and obey the Ten Commandments, had been given him in a street in Canton by a Chinese convert. He paid little attention to it at the time, but after he recovered from his illness, his cousin, having mastered its contents, brought it to his notice. Then the fantasies of his delirium appeared to Hung to be explained. During them it seemed he had left the world and moved up to Heaven, and had met God and Jesus Christ. He had certainly battled with devils and demons. This was his wild behaviour during the delirium viewed and reported by his family. The mission which he now believed he had to perform was to bring the Chinese to worship the Christian God described in the tract. To begin with he and his cousin baptized each other in the way prescribed in the pamphlet. Then, having enlarged on the ideas received from the tract by a few months' instruction from a Baptist missionary, he put down on paper the beliefs which were to form the basis of his movement.

It was only natural that Hung's views of God and Heaven should be coloured not only by his delirious visions but also by his Chinese ideas of the family. God was an imposing figure with a golden beard who sat in Heaven like an emperor in a dignified posture in a black dragon robe surrounded by his heavenly family. God had a Heavenly wife and Jesus also had a Heavenly wife.

When Hung was in his dream Heaven, Jesus' wife, a kind-hearted woman, was like a mother to Hung, and exerted her modifying influence on Jesus when angry with Hung for not learning his biblical lessons well. Christianity to Hung was now a battle between God and evil ones or devils, some of which he had struggled with in Heaven during the ravings of his illness. When Hung was in his dream Heaven he had learnt that he was God's son too, a younger brother of Jesus Christ and therefore charged to take his role in the battle against the evil ones represented on earth by all people who refused to accept God's will as now interpreted by Hung – especially Manchus. Such was the ideology of Hung's movement.

Another early convert besides Hung's cousin was a fellow teacher Feng. These three removed the traditional idols from their schoolrooms and refused to praise the local gods at the Lantern Festival early in 1844. This attack on tradition seems to have cost them their jobs. At any rate about this time they set forth as travelling Christian preachers and made their way westwards out of Kwangtung province into Kwangsi. Hung now returned home leaving Feng behind, and it was Feng who formed the nucleus of the society which developed into the Taiping following of millions. In the scattered villages of the mountain area of Tzu-ching-shan he founded the God Worshippers Society[1] in 1844, forming an organization of the followers of the new faith.

Feng's God Worshippers Society resembled in some ways traditional Chinese secret societies, but the acceptance of a new religious faith was contrary to all Chinese ideas. Once formed there can be little doubt of the sincerity of the members of the Society. In the records preserved of their prayers to be offered on ordinary and special occasions can be found genuine religious feeling and great trust in God whose blessing is sought at the beginning and end of each day, at birth, marriage, and death, and in the ordinary affairs of life.

But the God Worshippers Society had from the first a militant character. Conversions were often of whole occupational groups or of villages, and, what was most important, of Hakkas. These

---

[1] The God Worshippers became officially known as the Taipings on 11 January 1851 when Hung at Chintien declared the formation of a new dynasty, the Taiping Tien-kuo. But he had been using the term Taiping for the movement since 1847.

Hakka religious groups next armed themselves to protect themselves against the rival Puntis, and following on from this against the local gentry's forces and the forces of the state directed against them from Peking. Hung's religious experiences and the formulated beliefs based on them caused him to turn his followers against all who would not be converted to his distorted Christian ways. The evil spirits of the supernatural world, disbelievers among his fellow Chinese, and above all the Manchu ruling class, became objects of God Worshipper aggression; and the movement took on a rebellious character.

In August 1847 Hung joined Feng at Chintien, a small town at the foot of the mountain area whose villages were providing the nucleus of the movement, now consisting of over two thousand converts mostly peasants and miners. Together Hung and Feng brought about a rapid expansion of the group. Hung believed it was God's will for him to organize the faithful to establish on earth a Christian kingdom of peace, the Taiping Tienkuo; and it was about this time he began to use the term Taiping and call himself the Chun Wang[1] or noble king.

Hung's Christianity was of a simple nature. The rules of the Ten Commandments, which were set by Hung into poems, were used as a system of discipline for the God Worshippers and enforced as a code. The group was also made into one great family with common property and a common treasure, and until the kingdom of peace was established, and while fighting and expeditions were necessary to create it, all, including husbands and wives, were supposed to live in chastity. This last must have been an impossible condition to enforce even with beheading as a penalty, and that it was imposed indicates symptoms of insanity in Hung's condition as early as 1837. Nevertheless in the chaos and crisis of the early part of his rule during the establishment of the Taiping kingdom, his claim to divine guidance carried conviction with his followers – indeed, the similar claims of Hung's leading lieutenants were accepted. For example, Yang, the chief of staff of the movement, added to his importance as the Tung Wang[2] by claiming to be the Holy Ghost on earth, while the Hsi Wang claimed to represent Jesus Christ whose spirit spoke through him to the God Worshippers. In the event, the new

[1] Later the T'ien Wang or Heavenly King.
[2] Wang means King or leader.

family system of the kingdom of God that Hung proclaimed seemed to his followers to promise a better world, and instilled in them a religious fervour that lifted their organization above the level of a troop banded together for local fighting to that of a disciplined army, ready for rebellion. But the military character of the Taiping movement cannot be overstressed, and it was Yang not Hung who turned the Taipings into an efficient military machine, just as it was Feng, not Hung, who created the movement. Historians perhaps have credited too much to the part played by Hung and too little to the parts of the others involved in the Taiping rebellion.

At first Feng's God Worshippers had to deal with opposition from gentry-led local corps, and Feng was captured by them and brought before the magistrates. The magistrates, however, in the first instance, refused to take action between the local corps and the God Worshippers, just as they seldom intervened in clashes between the Hakka and Punti. The officials obviously regarded the God Worshippers as just another force for local defence. But Feng was captured several times by local corps troops and eventually, when they claimed he was planning a rebellion, he was put in prison, being released only on the payment of a fine collected by the God Worshippers, and a promise to return to his home province, Kwangtung.

In April 1848, during the period when Feng was in prison and Hung also absent from Chintien, Yang took over control of the God Worshippers. Yang was a shrewd and ruthless man. He had lost his parents at an early age and had become a charcoal burner, and seems to have established himself as leader of the charcoal burners and miners who joined the God Worshippers. He managed to make himself commander of the Taipings' central corps, and the chief of staff and thus the most powerful leader of the movement. He was helped to attain this position by his organizing skill and ability as a trainer. He gained importance as leader of the charcoal burners and miners whose special skill with explosives and in sapping were essential for military success, and he strengthened his position by copying Hung and claiming divine inspiration. Much of the initial success of the Taiping movement must be credited to the military ability of this strange man. Certainly after his assassination the fire went out of the Taiping rebellion.

As regards his claim to divinity, according to Yang's own account, he had been taken ill and had been deaf and mute for two months. Then suddenly he spoke up in the meetings. He had trances – simulated or perhaps genuine seizures – in which he claimed to be possessed by the Holy Ghost. Since neither Hung nor the group had a clear understanding of the concept of the Holy Ghost, they accepted Yang's view that he received direct orders as Holy Ghost from Heaven as to what the God Worshippers ought to do. Divine sanction indeed appeared to them to have been given to Yang's orders, and he controlled them to such good effect by these means that they became an efficient fanatic military machine. But while Hung may have been genuinely convinced of his own ascent to Heaven and of his divine mission, Yang's actions seem to indicate that he was playing a part.[1]

Modelled militarily on the classical Chou-li[2] system, disciplined and organized by the masterful Yang, when Hung and Feng returned to the movement it had become an effective force of some 20,000. This was large enough to deal with any local corps sent against it, or even small governmental forces. In 1851 it fought a number of successful battles against forces under the prefect of Hsün-chou and others. At this stage although Yang was the most important figure, Hung was still in actual control. Hung personally issued the orders and edicts on the Taiping system and made decisions on moving the camp. Under his name had appeared also orders nominating the five commanders of the army, with Yang in command of the all important central division and guard. This delegation of authority and creation of minor kings or wangs proved the final undoing of the movement. The rivalry between the wangs which Hung either could not or would not control led to their quarrelling and murdering each other. The final murder of Yang undermined the structure and fighting power of the Taipings, which he had done so much to create.

From Chintien the Taipings marched north-east on Nanking,

[1] This chapter is based on the works of F. Michael and his team of American and Chinese scholars who claim to have made comments and notes on all known Taiping documents.

[2] In this system, the civilian and military organizations were combined. The people were farmer-soldiers who took up arms when the need arose. Their officers were also their magistrates and military and civilian aspects of government were not separated.

(*Right*) Prince Kung, the most
reasonable of the Chinese
negotiators

The Paper Dragon at war

Li Hung-chang when Governor of Kiangsi, at the time General Gordon was fighting the Taipings in co-operation with him

Sir Robert Hart, Chief of Chinese Customs, and friend of Imperial China

the main town of central China. They were animated by the religious thunderings of their heavenly inspired wangs, and encouraged by their traditional Chinese hatred of the Manchus. ' The Manchus are non-believers or demons;[1] they have usurped the throne and enslaved the Chinese; they are no better than swine and dogs, and a great reward is promised to anyone who cuts off the head of the Manchu emperor, the Tartar dog Hsien-Feng,' the wangs proclaimed, adding, ' the Heavenly Father and his agents will establish a new type of Chinese empire to take the place of the prolonged misrule of the Manchu barbarians, a kingdom in which all the children of God are members of one family.'

For this end an extraordinarily strict discipline was established. Men who threatened to desert or retreat in battle, or who hesitated to attack, were at once killed by their officers, and capital punishment was the penalty for violation of a number of other disciplinary rules. But the appeal of being supported from a common treasury did more to confirm the faithful in their allegiance, and this also brought in new followers from a population suffering economic misery. Such was the nature of the call to rebellion, and its appeal – a call offering a new religion and a better way of life, but possessing a racist undertone.

While the Taipings were organizing their rebellion and moving north-east on Nanking, the Imperial government was building up its resistance, and in Hunan, halfway to Nanking, the Taipings suffered their first major defeat. In Hunan they had not only to fight regular soldiers of the Tents of the Green Standards whom they defeated, but also a local defence army led by gentry at Soh-yi Ferry, and the local corps repelled the attack of a much larger Taiping force, inflicted heavy losses on them, and killed Feng the founder of the God Worshippers. This victory had a greater significance than the immediate military results. For the first time a local corps had successfully opposed the Taiping army although the Green Standard troops had been beaten. The contrast between the militia's victory and the regulars' defeat taught a lesson which was instrumental in persuading the Manchu court to permit and encourage the establishment of local defence forces by the gentry. This was because the gentry leaders were obviously

---

[1] Demons were all those who refused to accept God's will as interpreted and represented by Hung.

D

trying to defend Chinese tradition. When the Emperor appointed Tsêng Kuo-fan to suppress the Taipings he was allowed to use this type of militia organized into armies similar to the one which had been so successful in the engagement at Soh-yi Ferry. With a large number of such forces encircling the Taipings and pressing them back to Nanking, Tsêng Kuo-fan eventually put down the rebellion. According to Hail, it was the Imperialist hero Tsêng Kuo-fan and not, as is so often claimed, General Gordon, to whom this honour is due. Certainly General Li Hung-chang who co-operated with or employed Ward's, then Burgevine's, and finally Gordon's mercenaries operated mainly between Shanghai and Nanking, and it was Tsêng Kuo-fan's armies forming the ring round the rest of Taiping territory which played the major role and delivered the *coup de grâce* by capturing Nanking and mercilessly exterminating the rebels; lest a residue be left to carry on the Taiping ideas and renew the attack against the traditional order, which Tsêng Kuo-fan wanted to protect.

This was much later, however. After Soh-yi the Taiping march continued. The Taipings did not tarry long when they could not overcome determined resistance; and it was the speed of their movement that gained them success and awed their government enemies as well as the population. They failed to take Ch'ang-sha, which they invested from September to November 1852, but succeeded on Tung-t'ing Lake in capturing a large fleet of several thousand boats which enabled them to use water transportation on the lake and the Yangtze River for a rapid movement of their whole army.

At this stage many more joined the Taipings, not all voluntarily. When the Taipings captured Wu-chang in January 1853, practically all its population was incorporated; and many did come of their own free will, especially from local bandits and secret societies. Numbers soon began to approach the half million mark.

From Wu-chang, the Taipings moved down the Yangtze towards Nanking. They took Kiukiang after a week's siege and required less than another week to occupy Anking, the capital of Anhwei province and the main stronghold guarding the approach to Nanking. On 19 March 1853 they captured the city of Nanking.

With the seizure of Nanking, the Taiping movement changed

its character. Up to that time the Taipings had been a mobile force whose success had in part depended on its mobility and the rapidity of its movement. Now the core of its million people – for many more had joined – was anchored, and could become the object of a planned, concentrated attack by the Imperial forces. But it took the Imperialists eleven years to accomplish the destruction of the Taiping Kingdom and during that time several aggressive expeditions were made against them in their turn, one in the autumn of 1853 approaching within sixty miles of Peking.

It seems that besides the increased vulnerability of the Taipings when they were no longer on the move, there were three other factors which played a part in their disruption and overthrow. These were the murder of Yang, a great military commander and irreplaceable; the mistake of the Taipings in attacking Shanghai and thereby causing the Europeans to resist them;[1] and the persistence of the Imperial Generalissimo Tsêng Kuo-fan who was determined to maintain the Chinese traditional way of life. He never admitted failure and finally prevailed.

Hung, the Taiping leader, believed that his people should obey strictly the Ten Commandments but not the wangs, or himself. In the margin of Chapter 1 of The Epistle of Paul to Titus, he writes, ' God has sent an edict to the effect that high officials may marry more than one wife.' He interpreted the rules on sex matters particularly liberally as regards himself, and this was one of the reasons for the missionaries' lack of sympathy towards Taiping Christianity. Hung seems to have selected women for his harem at the very beginning of the uprising. At the time of his death he had ten wives and countless concubines and was waited on mainly by women at his palace in Nanking.

The religious side of the movement was fully developed on the lines worked out personally by Hung, the self-styled Heavenly King. Nevertheless, from 1848 until his murder in 1856, Yang, the Tung Wang or East King, and self-styled reincarnation of the Holy Spirit, managed to establish himself as the real leader of the Taipings; and under his strict command they were a highly disciplined and effective group. Li Hsiu-cheng, later the Chung Wang, writes: ' The law was so strict. Thus, in 1853, operations were carried on with great success and people's minds were submissive. The Tung Wang's orders were strict, and the soldiers

---

[1] General Gordon played the most important part in doing this.

and people looked upon him with awe.' To help him maintain his position as leader, Yang set up an elaborate and effective spy system; and what his spies told him about the domestic affairs of the Heavenly King and his fellow wangs, Yang represented as coming to him from Heaven. In this way the Heavenly King received orders from Heaven, via Yang to the effect that he must not kick his concubines as they might be pregnant and it could do them a mischief. The system of administration depended on a merits and demerits system, and this again put power into Yang's hands. Each officer reported on the merits and demerits of the people under his command, and their reports passed up the chain of command to Yang and to the Heavenly King himself who in turn would issue edicts for promotion and demotion. But Yang seems to have taken the decisions, the Heavenly King merely giving his approval as a formality.

Yang was particularly successful in the military field. Michael writes:

Yang, the Tung Wang, was also the obvious author of a series of regulations for the Taiping's military forces which was the basis of the effective operations of the Taiping army. These regulations, issued in 1855, under the title *The Elements of Military Tactics on Troop Operations,* go in great detail into the form of military operations, into training, inspection, security measures, discipline, and the drilling of troops. They prescribe that plans for military moves should be outlined on paper for distribution to the corps commanders prior to action and that plans should be made to prepare for any eventuality on the march and during battle. The regulations describe the organization of land and water forces. They deal with signs and signals to be used for communication between the different military units, including the signals to be given in battle by means of such instruments as horns, drums, rattles, and flags. The regulations contain an elaborate disciplinary system enforced by military police. They deal with medical care for the wounded and sick, with military drill of the troops, and elaborate on specific techniques of warfare, going even into such details as a description of how to construct and use various types of booby-traps. The extraordinary versatility of Yang's mind, his organizational talent, and his understanding of military problems are demonstrated in these regulations, which were the foundation for the organization and success of the Taiping armies and their strategies.

By 1856 Imperialist forces and gentry-led militia under the

general command of Tsêng Kuo-fan were blockading Nanking, and it looked as if the Taipings were likely to be overcome. Then a battle to the south-east of Nanking went in favour of Yang's forces and the blockade was broken. The common danger had kept the rival wangs co-operating with each other. When it was removed the way was open for a power struggle among them. There had been dissatisfaction because of the dominating position of Hung and Yang with their divine sanctions to support them, and the other leaders did not like according such pre-eminence to Yang even while willing to acknowledge Hung as the Heavenly Father and prophet of their movement. The concept of the Taiping system in which all men were brothers and sisters and formed the family of God made distinctions between the brotherhood of all followers and the special brotherhood of the leaders, the original kings of the movement at the beginning who shared the dangers and adventures of the rebellion and expected to share the rewards. But they were jealous of the advantage among the special brotherhood claimed by Yang as spokesman on earth for the Holy Spirit. In his reach for personal power and for the leadership of the Taipings Yang disregarded the principle of collective leadership implicit in the brotherhood idea by assuming the role of a leader with divine sanction. Opposition seems to have come from both Hung, the Heavenly Father, who gradually became frightened by the challenge by Yang to his own position as the true prophet of the movement, and from the two most important wangs, Wei Chang-hui, the Pei Wang or North King, and Shih Ta-kai, the I Wang or Assistant King. Wei, in particular was upset at Yang's ruthlessness in command and his off-hand treatment of Wei's staff and the staff of the other wangs. The size of Yang's harem, which according to government accounts was the largest of the Taiping leaders, also caused jealousy. It is by no means clear exactly how or why it happened, but on 2 September 1856 Wei, the North King, assassinated Yang and killed all Yang's family and followers in Nanking. Over 20,000 men and women are believed to have perished in the slaughter.

That Yang and all his followers could be caught by surprise and slain is proof of the decline of his authority over the movement, outside his own following. But the background of the conspiracy for the assassination of Yang has remained unclear, and the stories on it are conflicting. According to one version, it was

Hung himself who gave the order of assassination and chose Wei to carry it out, and the plan was known and agreed to by Shih Ta-kai, the I Wang. But whoever was involved in the conspiracy the blame was placed on Wei alone.

At the time of the assassination Shih was fighting in Hupeh. When he heard the news he returned immediately to Nanking and is said to have reproached Wei for his wanton slaughter. Wei, determined to make a clean sweep of it, and being stronger than Shih – whose main troops were still in the field – attempted to assassinate Shih as well. The latter, learning of the threat and unable to fight it out, escaped from Nanking by being lowered over the city wall in a basket, and joined the troops under his command; but Wei murdered all Shih's family in the capital. Shih next marched with his troops against Nanking to take revenge; but Hung decided to take action at this stage, and before Shih's men arrived, the Heavenly King's own men assassinated Wei with his whole family and following.

After this holocaust, the fortunes of the Taipings turned dramatically. The period of swift campaigns and sweeping victories ended, and the Heavenly King was hard put to it to find new leaders to defend the rump of his Kingdom around Nanking. The battle was still to go on for several years – till 1864 – but after Yang's death no other leader was capable of organizing the movement and giving it that central direction and plan that alone – if that were at all possible – could have carried it to victory.

After the assassination of Yang, Hung sent the head of the slain leader Wei to Shih Ta-kai as a sign that his family had been revenged, and asked him to become his chief of staff. But Shih had not the qualities for such a post and only held it from November 1856 to the end of May 1857. Hung's brothers thought that Shih's popularity with the troops might make him a new rival of the Heavenly King, and believing his life to be threatened by the brothers, Shih left Nanking and proclaimed his determination to lead an independent campaign. He took with him a substantial part of the Taiping forces. These followed him when, in his proclamation, he asked the troops to decide for themselves whether to go with him or remain with the main movement. With him went some of the best military commanders, and his departure was thus another grave setback to the Taiping movement.

Shih led his army in combat south-west through Kiangsi into Hunan, and eventually into the south-western provinces. There he became a military adventurer rather than a revolutionary – comparable to the Nien rebel leaders in the north of Anhwei. The Peking authorities asked Tsêng Kuo-fan, the Imperialist generalissimo, to go and deal with Shih, but Tsêng wisely decided to treat Shih as just another 'roaming bandit' and concentrate on the Taiping forces in and around Nanking.

Since Yang's assassination Hung had put his confidence in his own family and relations, and at this stage Hung's brothers tried their hand at running the Heavenly Kingdom. To help improve the administration they brought about a proliferation of new minor wangs; but both the brothers were deficient in talent and military tactics, and among their nominees there was no one really capable of carrying on the government; so 'the morale of the soldiers and people was broken and troubled.'

Then two new military commanders rose to importance in the Taiping camp. These were Li Hsiu-cheng, later the Chung Wang, and Ch'en Yü-cheng. They gained some success against the Imperialists by co-operating with the local Nien[1] rebels in the north of Anwhei. These operations and the alignment with the Nien provided a respite for the Taipings at Nanking; but by this time the control of the Yangtze and the lake communication system had been lost to the Taipings, and having used up the vast stores[2] acquired on the original capture of Nanking, supply became difficult and the Taiping economic position tenuous.

In the spring of 1859, however, an efficient new leader did emerge in Hung's cousin, Hung Jen-kan. Hung Jen-kan had no great political expectations when he arrived at Nanking. His welcome and immediate success surprised him. In his own words:

I arrived at Nanking on the thirteenth day of the third month and was blessed by my Sovereign, who conferred on me the noble rank of Fu. On the twenty-ninth day I was made a noble of the rank of I and a chief general. On the first day of the fourth month, I was pro-

[1] The Nien rebels were anti-government but had no ambition to establish a new dynasty, let alone the kind of revolution at which the Taipings aimed.
[2] The amount of silver in the Taiping treasury at Nanking was reported to have been 18 million *taels* compared with 3 million *taels* in the Imperial treasury at Peking. There was also enough rice to feed the Taipings for many months.

moted a founder of the dynasty, loyal chief of staff, upholder of Heaven, adjudicator of court discipline, and the Kan Wang. I tried to decline these honours on the ground that I had only just arrived and that such rapid promotion would tend to create resentment among the generals. However, the Sovereign insisted. My original desire was merely to go to the capital, represent to the Tien Wang the distressed state of my home, and rely on his gracious protection in order to enable me to live out my normal span of life. To my great surprise the Tien Wang showered great favours on me, and out of consideration for my industry and aspiration to seek fame he did not shrink from the odium of creating a spirit of jealousy among his ministers but elevated me to this extraordinary appointment. Since my appointment I have felt it my duty to exert myself strenuously to carry out the work before me as a return for favours received.[1]

After his appointment to the position of Kan Wang and chief of staff, Hung Jen-kan tried his best to serve the cause of the Taiping movement, in which, from all evidence, he strongly and sincerely believed. What has survived of his writings as leading administrator of the Taipings, and, at the end, as a prisoner of Tsêng Kuo-fan awaiting execution, shows him to be a man of strong religious faith, of character, and of great political and strategic vision.

Hung Jen-kan tried to accomplish two things: to turn the Taipings over to a form of Protestant Christianity similar to the one he had been studying himself when working for Western missionaries; and to bring about a better relationship with foreigners. But the new position as political leader conferred on him by his cousin, the Heavenly King, forced him to begin with a programme of reorganization with which he became so involved that he never had much success with his first two aims.

In the successful period of the rule of Yang, control of the Taiping movement had been centralized under the chief of staff. But since his death, the generals in the field had created their own staffs and had adopted the habit of going their own way without much concern for the Tien Wang or their colleagues. Hung Jen-kan was well aware of the decline of the central control and of the disorganization that had resulted; but he found it

---

[1] This is from Hung Jen-kan's confession. After capture and before execution, the Taiping leaders were asked to make their confession and describe their part in the rebellion. Most of them complied.

difficult to establish an administration under his direction acceptable to the Tien Wang and to the generals. The Tien Wang's mind had become even more unstable and his main concern now was his own harem. He was personally of little account as a day-to-day administrator, and, in fact, had never been. Although the prophet of the movement and the annotator of its doctrine, it had been Feng who had established the God Worshippers in the first instance, and Yang who had led the Taipings so successfully in battle. Yang possessed the advantage of being accepted as the Holy Ghost and receiving direct commands from God. This combined with his great gifts as a disciplinarian, administrator, strategist and tactician had been the basis of his success. Hung Jen-kan made no attempt to base his authority on the supernatural, and received the minimum of support from the crazed Tien Wang and his jealous relatives of the court. He found also the generals loath to allow any reduction of their independence.

Shortly after Hung Jen-kan was made the Kan Wang, the two major commanders, Ch'en Yü-cheng and Li Hsiu-cheng, were also given the titles of Wang. Ch'en became the Ying Wang and Li the Chung Wang. These appointments were obviously meant to placate the feelings of the two generals, who until Hung Jen-kan's arrival had been on their own and who would not easily subordinate themselves to the newcomer who had been immediately given the title of king, until now reserved for the original leadership. It was in the relationship of these three men, now all appointed to the highest rank, that Taiping politics and military strategy were fought out in these decisive years. Ch'en co-operated with Hung Jen-kan, accepted a position on his staff, and helped formulate some of his regulations on government reorganization; but Li Hsiu-cheng continued to go his own way, wrecked Hung Jen-kan's carefully drawn up strategic plan and ruined the hope of a lasting Taiping kingdom.

Hung Jen-kan's approach to government organization and to the creation of a staff was realistic. To start with, he chose the best people he could find at Nanking, and to create a more permanent staff he revived the examination system for the selection of officials. An earlier Taiping examination started by Yang had been no real test of knowledge, and practically every candidate seems to have passed. Hung Jen-kan tried to make his examination a proper basis for a career in the Taiping government, as it was in the Imperial service. This traditional attitude enabled him to appeal to the educated upper group, the gentry, to serve the Taiping government.

This appeal has sometimes been interpreted as a compromise with the traditional system and the abandonment of revolution. This was not so. Hung Jen-kan seems to have wanted to create an educated bureaucracy, but with its beliefs Christian not Confucian. The examination papers, of which a whole series survive, indicate this.

Although the Confucian classics were part of the educational material for the candidates, they were used together with the Bible and the religious tracts of the Taipings themselves. Hung Jen-kan wanted to create a Christian gentry whose common outlook would be based on the Christian teachings of the Taipings; and his examination system was a selection of qualified candidates for official service. The Taiping principle of uniting religious, administrative and military affairs in the hands of the same officials remained.

Hung Jen-kan saw it as his responsibility to make the Taiping system appeal to both the Chinese and foreigners, and so tried to rectify some of the errors and fantasies of the Taiping movement. After his arrival at Nanking he cultivated his previous contacts with foreign missionaries and tried to represent the Tien Wang as a reasonable figure. In the early days, the Taiping Christian revolutionary movement had some appeal both to the leaders of countries like Britain who thought it might offer an alternative to the Imperialist régime, and to the missionaries who hoped it might develop into a genuine Christian Chinese kingdom. Neither, however, were eventually willing to support the Taipings. The wanton destruction and lack of order in the Taiping kingdom appalled the officials, military men, and merchants in Treaty ports like Shanghai, who came in contact with the rebels, and the many missionary visitors to the Taiping capital, and the other cities under rebel control came away revolted at the idolatry of Tien Wang's court, for Hung Jen-kan was quite unable to impose his rational religious ideas on his mentally unbalanced master.

1859-62 were the key years for all this. By the end of this period many missionaries had visited Nanking, including Josiah

Cox of the English Wesleyans, and a number of American Baptists, T. P. Crawford, J. L. Holmes, and Issacher J. Roberts, from whom Hung received some instructions in Christianity in 1847. When Roberts left Nanking in January 1862 he disowned the Taipings, thus ending the last phase of missionary sympathy towards the Taipings. By this time Taiping relations with all Westerners except for some adventurers like Burgevine, had deteriorated. Besides, 1860 was the date of the signature of the Treaty of Peking, the delayed ratification of the Treaty of Tientsin. This gave Britain and France all they required in the way of freedom of trade, treaty ports and extraterritorial rights. Foreign governments were therefore happy from then on to deal with the Manchu dynasty.

Hung Jen-kan's main failure came with the collapse of his strategy to free the Heavenly Kingdom from economic strangulation by the encircling Imperial forces. He tried to carry out a complicated military operation to drive away the Imperial forces under Tsêng Kuo-fan from the upper Yangtze so that supply by water might be resumed from the west, and also remove Imperial control of the lower Yangtze to open up supply from the seaboard.

The first stage of the operation met with success. Li Hsiu-cheng moved south from Nanking to attack Hangchow, and then, having enticed the Government generals to divert troops for Hangchow's defence, rushed back to attack the Government camp south of Nanking from the south, while Chen Yü-cheng attacked it from the north. The second stage, however, failed completely. In it one army was to move north of the Yangtze beyond Anking into Hupeh province, and then cut back to the north side of the river below Wuchang. This was to be Chen Yü-cheng's army. The second arm of the pincer was to be formed by the army of Li Hsiu-cheng. After occupying Soochow and Hangchow and freeing the lower Yangtze, he was to move along the south side of the Yangtze into Kiangsi and Hupeh provinces to reach the river from the south at the same point that Chen's army was to reach it from the north. After the two armies had met, they were to fight their way into Hupeh province and clear the area on both sides of the upper Yangtze. To help all the operations on the Yangtze, both above and below Nanking, it was hoped that some twenty steamships from Shanghai could be got hold of to open up communications and supply for the Taipings.

This strategic plan was to serve several purposes. One was to secure Anking, the strongpoint and centre on the Yangtze controlling the upper river west of Nanking. Another was to regain the lower Yangtze area of Kiangsu and Chekiang, which was important to the Taipings as a source of tax income and as an access to Western supplies. It also offered an opportunity of obtaining Western ships for the campaign. But these parts of the campaign were preparatory and of secondary importance. The main assumption of the strategic plan was that the fate of Nanking depended on the control by the Taipings of the upper Yangtze area; and the main part of the plan was the two-pronged attack on both shores of the Yangtze that was to encircle this area and clear it of the enemy.

After initial success the plan failed. The reason was that halfway through the campaign Li Hsiu-cheng decided not to carry through his part. Chen reached the Yangtze on the north side as planned, but as Li had not arrived he left a subordinate in command there and moved downstream to secure Anking. Li marched and took Soochow and Hangchow. He turned north and arrived at his place on the south side of the Yangtze after Chen had done. But instead of trying to co-operate with the Taiping forces on the other side of the river, he disregarded his part of the overall plan and, collecting some remnants of the army of Shih Ta-kai, moved back to Chekiang and built up the strength of his base there. He claimed to have found the Yangtze in flood and too difficult to cross, but this seems to have been merely an excuse. He was probably jealous of Hung Jen-kan and unwilling to co-operate in his plan. He thought he should have been the first man in the Tien Wang's service, and in spite of a stern order from the Tien Wang telling him ' to sweep the north ' upstream, he returned to his southern base.

By himself, Chen was unable to secure Anking, and it fell to Tsêng Kuo-fan. Chen was defeated and killed, and Li on his own in his southern retreat was not strong enough to protect the Taiping capital from final destruction. As will be shown in the next chapter, General Gordon's Chinese force played a part in the final rout of the Taipings by supplying pressure in the south, along with Li Hung-chang's forces, while Tsêng Kuo-fan's Government troops and gentry-led militia surrounded Nanking. Li Hsiu-cheng's decision to turn back from the Yangtze when Hung Jen-kan was near to success, was thus the decisive mistake that probably led to the loss of Nanking and the military defeat of the Taiping movement.

GENERAL GORDON'S BATTLES IN CHINA

The Taipings from time to time threatened the Treaty Ports including Shanghai, and in August 1860 Li Hsiu-cheng, the Chung Wang, after dispersing an Imperial force that was laying siege to Nanking, led his troops to the very walls of Shanghai before he was recalled. To enforce the terms of the Treaty of Tientsin or Peking which, signed by Lord Elgin and Prince Kung on 24 October 1860, granted all the British and French demands, including the one for new treaty ports, a contingent of 3,000 troops under General Staveley had been left at Tientsin, and at Shanghai there was a naval squadron under Admiral Hope, 1,000 Indian troops, an equal number of French, half a battery of artillery, and a small corps of volunteers including a mercenary force of Manila men and Westerners under an American named Ward.

In February 1861 Admiral Hope began systematic visits to the ports of the Yangtze which had been thrown open by the recent treaty, some now controlled by the Taipings. The first request that the admiral made to the Taipings was for permission for a British gunboat to be stationed off Nanking to watch over British commercial interests. The Tien Wang replied that he had had a vision, forbidding him to grant the request. When this message was brought to Parkes, whom we have already met at Canton in the *Arrow* incident and on the march to Peking with Hope Grant, and who was again acting as interpreter and intermediary, he exclaimed, ' Tut, tut, tut! That won't do at all. He must have another vision.' Parkes' words were reported to the Heavenly Father, who accommodatingly experienced a further revelation, with the result that the stationing of a warship was sanctioned.

The next point to be secured was the safety of Shanghai, which had been so seriously threatened by the rebels in the previous autumn. On this matter Admiral Hope succeeded in obtaining from the rebel leader an undertaking that he would leave Shanghai alone for a year, and that, in any case, he would not approach within a distance of a hundred *li*, or thirty miles, of the town. It took Parkes five days to obtain this last concession.

The Tien Wang kept his agreement not to attack Shanghai for a year, during which time the Taipings occupied themselves in operations to the west and south-west of Nanking, in unsuccessful attempts to capture Hankow and to save Anking from being taken by the Imperial forces under Tsêng Kuo-fan.

Admiral Hope considered that he was fully able, with the regular troops at his disposal, to guarantee the security of Shanghai. He had never been very happy about Ward's odd force, especially as the high pay which Ward offered tempted the British seamen under his command to desert and join it. After consultation, therefore, with the Shanghai officials, Ward's force was broken up.

A few months later the residents suffered a scare of another Taiping advance, and the leading merchants, not satisfied with Admiral Hope's offers of protection, turned to Ward again, and entrusted him with drilling and commanding a new irregular force to protect them. This was to consist of Chinese who would be paid by the merchants. Ward readily agreed, and in September 1861, taking as his second-in-command another American, Burgevine, he established a force of disciplined Chinese dressed in distinctive uniform of European type with a turban headdress. Before long, to encourage the Chinese to enlist in it, it was given the high-sounding title of ' The Ever Victorious Army ', but it was more usually known as ' Ward Force '.

The first brunt of the attack, however, was directed, not against Shanghai, but against Hangchow south-west of it at the end of the Grand Canal, and against Ningpo, the treaty port opposite the island of Chusan, which had been a winter headquarters during General Gough's expedition in 1841.

This move on the part of the rebels, and the fact that the year's grace allowed to Shanghai was drawing to a close, led Admiral Hope to pay another visit to Nanking to ask the Tien Wang to grant Shanghai a further period of immunity from attack. This time, however, the Heavenly King refused, and when by the end of December both Ningpo and Hangchow had fallen to the rebels,

Li Hsiu-cheng, the Chung Wang, advanced on Shanghai. By the second week in January 1852, he was within gunshot of the town, and as the townspeople looked out upon the surrounding country they could see clouds of smoke by day and flames by night testifying to the ruin that the Taipings were spreading far and wide.

This attack on Shanghai was more serious than the one eighteen months before. It was a definite challenge by the rebels to Admiral Hope's requirement laid down after the earlier attack that the Taipings should not approach within thirty miles of the town. That requirement had been made both on military and economic grounds: if the rebels were allowed to occupy positions near Shanghai, the town would never be safe from attack, and unless the fertile districts around the town were kept free from rebel devastation, Shanghai would run the risk of food shortage.

Therefore, it was decided to open hostilities against the rebels within the thirty-mile limit, and drive them outside it. Reinforcements were sent for from Hong Kong and Tientsin, and Ward's mercenaries despatched against the enemy from their base at Sunkiang.

The Ever Victorious Army justified its title by two quick victories, the first under Ward against a town a few miles from Sunkiang, and the second under Burgevine, in co-operation with naval vessels, against Kachio, near the Yangtze north-east of Shanghai. This was the first naval attack on the Taipings. The ships' guns opened up a heavy fire and the European-led mercenaries, together with marines under Captain Holland, stormed the stronghold. The part that Ward's troops played in these successes won the admiration of the British as well as of the Chinese authorities, and Admiral Hope forwarded a despatch to Peking recommending that the force, which by this time numbered 1,500 should be considerably increased.

A change now occurred in the command of the British forces in the Shanghai area. Admiral Hope left to command the naval squadron, and although he returned he was soon to leave Shanghai for good; and General Staveley succeeded General Michel in command of the land force in China. Michel had felt uncertain whether British troops should be used against the Taipings, and had done little to help the more vigorous Admiral Hope. General Staveley, however, was more active. He not only got authority for Bruce, the British Minister in Peking, to use British garrisons from the other Treaty Ports to protect Shanghai, but also to clear the rebels from territory within thirty miles of it; and he received permission to lend British officers to the Imperial Army as drill instructors. As will be seen, there was still some doubt whether towns within the thirty-mile limit, when captured, should be garrisoned by British troops, or whether British officers should be permitted to command Chinese mercenaries in the field as Ward and some French officers[1] had done. But the clearing of the thirty miles around Shanghai now became the main British objective, and remained so throughout this period, as can be seen from letters from Bruce to Gordon. As late as 25 January 1864 Bruce writes, ' These events make no change in our policy which is to keep the city of Shanghai, and as large a part of the neighbourhood free from Rebel incursions as possible.' This policy began to be formulated in 1862, as a letter to his sister Augusta from Gordon indicates:

The Bu Wang, *viz.* head Rebel magistrate, sent very pressing invitations to Mr Roberts – who you will remember was sent from Nanking after a long residence there by the ill-treatment of the Wangs – he is an American missionary of great character. Well, he left Nanking in December last year, and he came to see our general to-day and told him he had been to Soutchow (Soochow) to see the Bu Wang, who had received him very well and had asked him to tell the General and Admiral that he had heard that it was our intention to defend 100 *li* or thirty miles around Shanghai. Mr Roberts told him that was true, and he then produced a sketch thus, saying:

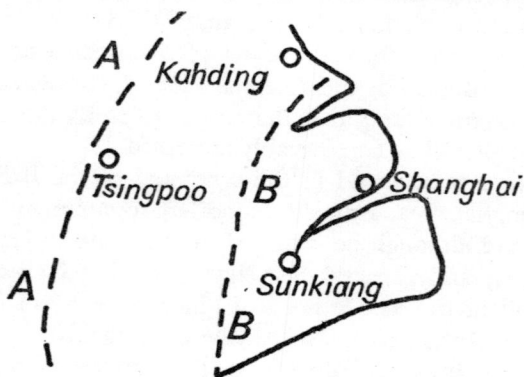

[1] Bonnefoy and D'Arguebelle.

the line A was the thirty miles; that he did not want to have any more fighting with us, and that if we would let him retake Kahding and Tsingpoo, he would not let his men come within line B which he marked himself. He said he had heard of the employment of Thomas Osborne,[1] and also of the trained Chinese attacking Nanking. Of course we will not allow him to retake those places, but we may treat on the terms. I think it is a bad thing as they are such miscreants.

In the more active operations under General Staveley, Captain Charles George Gordon of the Royal Engineers played a part. When he arrived at Shanghai from a survey project around Tientsin, Staveley, having captured Kahding, north of Shanghai and near the limit of the thirty-mile area, had chosen as his next objective Tsingpoo or Tsingpu a similar distance to the west of Shanghai. He employed Gordon to reconnoitre the approach to it. Tsingpu was a typical rebel stronghold: it was surrounded on all sides by a creek fifty or sixty yards from its walls. It could be approached by infantry along a path following another creek up which small gunboats could proceed. This was blocked in places by stakes. The only way of capturing such a place was to bombard its walls until a breach was made, and then rush men forward into the breach under cover of protecting fire. Gordon carried out a thorough reconnaissance of Tsingpu. Not paying much attention to General Staveley's warnings to be careful, he went up towards the town. Although under fire, he reached a small pagoda in whose shelter, with the aid of his telescope, he made a good sketch of the creek. He estimated its width with some accuracy, at ninety feet, and the walls as twenty feet high. He placed the creek at fifty yards from the town. When Gordon rejoined his commander, he knew just how many boats would be required to form a bridge over the creek, and how many yards the troops would have to charge over the open when they were across, in order to storm the breach. Two days later the attack was made and was entirely successful. The naval guns opened a deadly fire on the walls till a breach was made. Then the troops advanced, put a bridge of boats across the creek, and under covering fire stormed the walls and captured the town, which was then left to Ward's force to garrison.

[1] H. N. Lay and Captain Osborne had formed a Chinese naval detachment on the lines of Ward Force; but they had grandiose ideas for it, and the Chinese authorities would not let it continue.

General Staveley wrote of Gordon's part in this success as follows:

Captain Gordon was of the greatest use to me when the task of clearing the rebels from out of the country, within a radius of thirty miles from Shanghai had to be undertaken. He reconnoitred the enemy's defences, and arranged for the ladder parties to cross the moats, and for the escalading of the works; for we had to attack and carry by storm several towns fortified with high walls and deep wet ditches. He was, however, at the same time, a source of much anxiety to me, from the daring manner he approached the enemy's works to acquire information. Previous to our attack on Singpo (*sic*), and when with me in a boat, reconnoitring the place, he begged to be allowed to land, in order better to see the nature of the defences. Presently to my dismay, I saw him gradually going nearer and nearer, by rushes, from cover to cover, until he got behind a small outlying pagoda, within a hundred yards of the wall, and here he was quietly making a sketch and taking notes. I, in the meantime, was shouting myself hoarse in trying to get him back; for not only were the rebels firing at him from the walls, but I saw a party stealing round to cut him off.

Before coming to command in the south, Staveley had been Gordon's brigadier while he was doing his survey around Tientsin. Gordon's sister, Augusta, also seems to have known him. In a letter to her, Gordon wrote of his commanding officer from Tientsin in March 1861, not in very complimentary terms: ' Staveley is well; he is going to Peking in a few days. For such an essentially selfish man, I like him well enough.' Staveley, however, was more than satisfied with Gordon.

Staveley followed up the capture of Tsingpu by taking two other rebel-held towns within the thirty-mile limit. Then, just as it seemed that he had driven away the rebels, news arrived that Kahding had been retaken by the Taipings by subterfuge from the Imperial troops put in charge of it. The Government forces had attempted an advance outside Kahding on the enemy. But the Taipings arranged for 2,000 of their number to shave their heads as a sign that they submitted to the Manchu Government, and by this means gain admission to the Government ranks. Then the Chung Wang delivered his attack and, helped by the 2,000 traitors inside the camp, wrought such havoc on the Imperial troops that scarcely a quarter of them escaped with their lives.

This disaster put Staveley in a difficult position. The policy was that the British forces and Ward Force should be used to clear the rebels from an area thirty miles from Shanghai, but that any town captured should be garrisoned by Imperial troops. The new governor of the province of Kiangsu was Li Hung-chang, and he now enters the story in which he was to play such an important part. Li said that he could not provide troops, either to retake Kahding or to garrison it afterwards. General Staveley also felt too weak to deal with Kahding and decided, much to the chagrin of the Shanghai merchants, to abandon it to the rebels. Instead, Staveley called upon Gordon to erect defence works around Shanghai, which as a skilful engineer he quickly did. At one time it looked as if Gordon's defences would be tested, for by 26 August 1862 the rebels were only six miles from Shanghai. Then, to their surprise, the inhabitants saw the Taiping troops, in their white uniform with orange border, abandon their advance posts and withdraw from the neighbourhood. Something had happened to change the Taipings' plans. Before long it transpired what it was. Increasing pressure from the large Imperial force under Tsêng Kuo-fan that was besieging Nanking had caused the recall of the Chung Wang to help defend the capital.

In September 1862 Ward's Force, now 5,000 men, took the initiative, in co-operation with Li, in trying to retake Tsingpu which it had had to evacuate at the time of the Taiping advance on Shanghai. To help him in the attack, Ward took with him the steamer *Hyson* which was used later by Gordon. The first attack was driven back, but the next day Ward renewed the assault, and after a fierce bombardment from the *Hyson*'s heavy gun, he led out a strong party and forced his way over the walls. This was a great victory, much appreciated by the Chinese authorities. But six weeks later, while leading another attack on a rebel-held town near Ningpo, Ward was mortally wounded.

As soon as the news of Ward's death reached Shanghai, the British Consul saw General Staveley and suggested that a British officer should be appointed as his successor, and consent for this was sought from the British Government. Meanwhile Ward's second-in-command, Burgevine, took control of the force. Under him, with Gordon providing a small body of engineers, Kahding was recaptured. Although successful, this operation showed lack of discipline and a tendency to loot by the men of Ward Force, and it was decided to attach Captain Holland of the Royal

Marines as a chief of staff, and other officers as drill instructors, to try to remedy these faults.

Next, Burgevine was asked by Li to co-operate by moving against Nanking in support of a similar attack on Nanking from the west by Tsêng Kuo-fan. Burgevine refused. The policy of the thirty-mile limit precluded his British officers from taking part, and he was still suffering from old wounds and did not want to take the field. To put pressure on him, Li took strong action. He persuaded the Shanghai merchants who paid Ward Force to withhold supplies until Burgevine agreed to take the field.

The men without pay became mutinous, and Burgevine, a tough gangster type, who was in China primarily for money, cheap drink and women, was not willing to be treated like this. He set off with his bodyguard by steamer from Sunkiang to Shanghai, went to the house of the mandarin banker who was responsible for payment and demanded that his men's wages be handed over to him. The mandarin refused, whereupon Burgevine struck him a blow in the face, and ordered his men to seize the 40,000 *taels* which he needed.

When he returned to Sunkiang with the pay, his troops received him with enthusiasm, and the mutiny was over. But, in the eyes of the Chinese, he was guilty of a serious offence in striking a mandarin, and Li, as soon as he heard of it, decided with General Staveley's acquiescence to get Burgevine dismissed.

As a temporary measure Captain Holland of the Royal Marines was put in charge of Ward Force, and Gordon's name forwarded to the War Office with a view to his permanent appointment, although Bruce, the British Ambassador at Peking was by no means convinced that any regular officer, naval or military, should be put in charge. Gordon was eventually appointed after an unsuccessful spell in command by Holland, although Burgevine tried hard to get himself reinstated. Burgevine had the support of many important people including the American Ambassador. But receiving no appointment from the Imperial leaders, and getting an offer from their enemies, he decided to change sides.

It was not until 28 July 1863 that Bruce expressed himself happy about Gordon's appointment. Then he wrote giving his approval (although Gordon had assumed command and been winning victories for four months already), and setting out what he considered the scope of the force. This was more limited than Li liked, or even Brown and Gordon, although he did foresee expeditions as far as Soochow which was well outside the thirty-mile limit originally envisaged:

Since I wrote to Major-General Brown[1] on the subject of the command of 'Ward Force', I have received further despatches from Her Majesty's Government, from which I infer that no objection is felt to a British officer commanding that Force in the field, provided he be on halfpay and in the service of the Chinese Government.

I shall be glad if you are able to continue your operations so as to force the insurgents to abandon Soochow and the line of the great canal without which Shanghai cannot be looked upon as secure from attack.

I would rather see you in command of the Chinese than anyone else, as I think the corps in your hands will become dangerous to the insurgents, without being dangerous to the Government and oppressive to the population.

(*sgnd*) Frederick W. A. Bruce

When Gordon took over command of Ward Force in March 1863, he found need to improve the discipline of both officers and men. It was also necessary to define the position of the force in relation to the Imperial authorities, and the extent of its future operations against the Taipings. Li, the Governor of Kiangsu, had recently been serving in the army of Tsêng Kuo-fan, Viceroy of the three provinces of Kiangsu, Anhwei and Kiangsi, and Generalissimo in charge of the regular and militia forces blockading Nanking. But Li still had an Imperial force under him in Kiangsu commanded by General Ching, an ex-rebel. As soon as the area around Shanghai was free from rebels, Li wanted Ward Force to be used with Ching's force on more distant expeditions and it was because of Burgevine's unwillingness to comply with Li's demands that Li withheld the pay. It was no means clear who was directing policy, and the position which led to the quarrel between Li and Burgevine was so obviously unsatisfactory that General Staveley with Li's co-operation drew up some rules for the future conduct of the force. Arrangements were made for Li to be responsible for paying it and the Shanghai merchants to be relieved of this burden. But Li was not permitted to give it orders for expeditions outside the thirty-mile radius

---

[1] General Staveley's successor.

without previous discussion with his allies.

When Gordon arrived at Sunkiang, he found the troops discouraged by a recent reverse under Captain Holland, and the officers resentful of the removal of Burgevine. Burgevine's method of satisfying the wants of his men had been to allow them to loot opium and valuables which were in turn sold to the receivers following the army. The privates mostly smoked opium, and drank brandy when they could get it, and indulgence in this combination gave them a temporary self-confidence leading to fantastic deeds of valour – but also, at times, made them grossly insubordinate. The officers, except for British regulars like Holland and Gordon, were a cosmopolitan collection, largely American, but with some Germans, Scandinavians, Frenchmen and Spaniards. A letter of 31 March 1864, from General Brown, Staveley's successor, to the Secretary of State for War, when Gordon had dismissed sixteen of his officers, indicates the nature of these soldiers of fortune. He wrote:

Tho' Major Gordon had weeded his force to some extent by dismissing sixteen of his most insubordinate officers, there still remained in it a considerable American element, and many of the officers look with regret to the time when the Force was commanded by adventurers like themselves . . .

General Brown thought Ward Force provided valuable employment for the best of these adventurers, and stopped the worst from joining the rebels – it did not stop Burgevine, however, though Gordon managed to persuade him to come back. Brown continues:

The rowdy population of Shanghai composed chiefly of Americans, the dregs of San Francisco where the Vigilance Committee interfered with their special industrial arts of robbery and murder, and who found in Shanghai and the Taiping rebellion a wide field for their energies, had been restrained from joining the rebel party by the wholesome dread of Major Gordon's force . . .

The foreign adventurers were brave but quarrelsome, and most of them drank and whored to excess. On storming a town, the first concern was to round up the young concubines of the defeated rebel leaders. Although the concubines, it must be allowed, did not generally seem to have been greatly perturbed by their abrupt change of masters, Gordon, a devout Christian, could not approve.

He could not wholly suppress either opium or drink among his men, but he made it clear that a man who was drugged or drunk might be shot if it led to him deserting his duty. The threat was taken seriously and had a wholesome effect. His officers still had a number of young women whom they changed constantly. Gordon could do little about this as long as it did not interfere with duty. The commander himself never had a woman in his quarters, though by Chinese tradition the youngest and most beautiful should first have passed through his hands. He was secretly revolted by the sexual greed of his officers, his own instinct being for the companionship of men, and that as a receiver of affection rather than one who bestowed it. In the extraordinary circumstance in which he found himself Gordon's disinterest in women worked out as a positive advantage. He had a quick perception of men. He sympathized with their angers, their follies, and their foibles, but he was not himself subject to the same temptations as they were. Knowing that in some respects he was different from the men he commanded became a cult with him, a cult that revealed itself in a number of small ways – in his nightly praying in his tent and in his refusal to carry any arms except his cane, which became as much a symbol of authority as a field-marshal's baton.

Gordon modelled the routine arrangements for his force on the British army, and took personal control of its feeding, pay and discipline. At dawn a bugle woke his disreputable rabble, and by sunrise they were – much to their surprise – sweating at drill or setting out on marches. As an engineer, he had mantlets made to protect the gunners in his boats, pontoon equipment to cross the many waterways north and west of Shanghai, bamboo ladders to scale fortress walls, and other devices. With a reorganized army, well equipped, and a flotilla of gunboats, he was soon ready to take the field against the Taipings, and when he did so inflicted on them a series of defeats, starting with the storming of Fushan and the relief of Chanzu north-west of Shanghai, then recapturing Taitsan and finally taking Quinsan.

Most of the engagements follow the same pattern as the one described earlier at Tsingpu, and entailed a careful reconnaissance, a bombardment from gunboats, or emplaced artillery under cover ashore, to break down the fortress walls, and then the storming of the stronghold, wherever it might be. The capture of Quinsan, however, had special features.

## QUINSAN

Gordon left with an advance guard to move on Quinsan on 4 May 1863, and approached the city from the east. At the East Gate he was joined by General Ching who was in command of the Imperial troops and co-operating with him. Ching favoured an immediate frontal attack on Quinsan. But Gordon considered the eastern wall too strong, particularly as the rebels had an eighteen-pounder gun there commanded by a European. Gordon also had a mutiny on his hands in the main part of his force, and leaving the American, Captain Davidson, with the *Hyson* to support Ching, he returned to his base at Sunkiang to deal with it. The men wanted time after the victory at Taitsan to dispose of loot to established receivers at Sunkiang, and had not expected another operation so soon. By strong measures such as arresting the suspect NCOs and putting them in chains, and threatening insubordinate officers with dismissal, he restored order. Then he moved his base from Sunkiang and away from this temptation.

By 27 May Gordon was back with his whole force outside the East Gate of Quinsan. Before attacking he carried out a reconnaissance in the *Hyson* with General Ching along the creeks leading to the main waterway connecting Quinsan to Soochow to the west. Then, satisfied that the best side to attack was the west, he ordered round his gunboats,[1] led by the *Hyson*, carrying 380 of his own men, 500 of Ching's, and the field artillery. Meanwhile, Ching returned to the East Gate to draw the attention of the rebels away from Gordon's operations in the west.

Gordon disembarked his men in the neighbourhood of Chunye, nine miles west of Quinsan, pulling up the stakes which blocked

---

[1] The ordinary gunboats had a nine-pounder or twelve-pounder in their bows and could carry fifty men. The *Hyson* commanded by Captain Davidson was bigger and measured 60 feet by 24 feet and carried a thirty-two pounder in her bow and a twelve-pounder in her stern. She was a paddle-boat fitted with caterpillar wheels which enabled her to proceed along the creeks when there was not enough water for her 3 feet 6 inches draught. She was also provided with ropes for dragging up the wooden stakes with which the rebels obstructed the waterways.

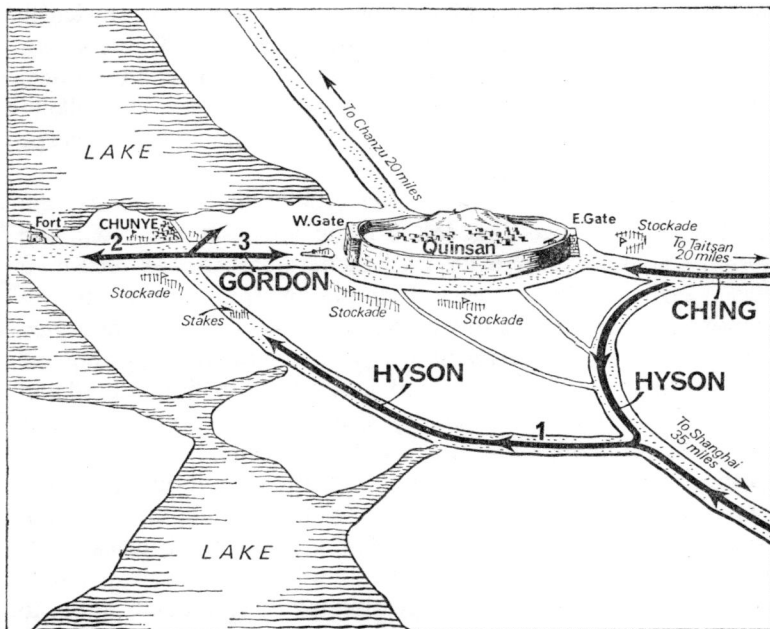

Map 7   General Gordon and General Ching – Pincer attack on Quinsan

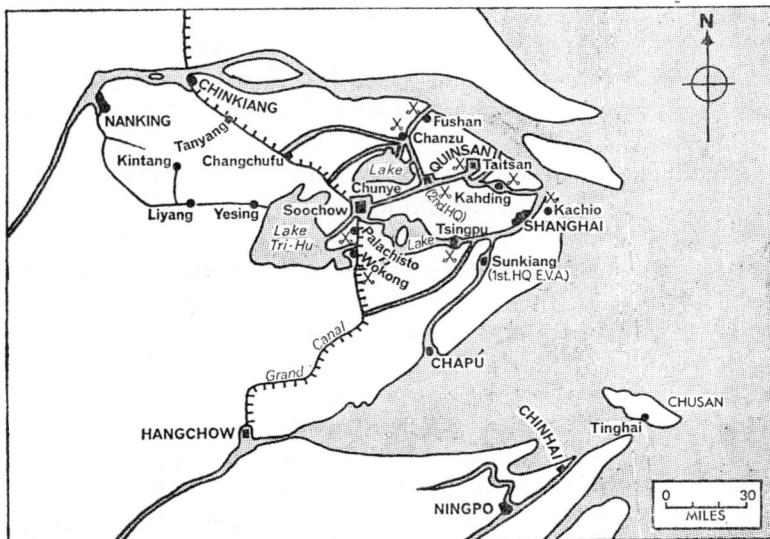

Map 8   The area of General Gordon's operations against the Taipings

the waterway, and clearing by action the rebel-manned stockades on the banks. There was little resistance, and while Ching's men were left to hold the captured stockades, Gordon split his force, sending one part after the rebels retreating to Quinsan, and following up himself in the *Hyson* the rebels who were trying to escape in the direction of Soochow.

Threading her way through the crowds of boats which the frightened inhabitants had left drifting about in the canal, the *Hyson,* under its American commander, chased the retreating rebels, giving them a dose of grapeshot from her thirty-two pounder at intervals. On this voyage westwards, Gordon occupied a fort, took 150 of the rebels prisoner and drove away the rest into Soochow. He then returned to Chunye to find a battle in progress between his remaining gunboats and some Taipings ashore on the north bank of the waterway. The *Hyson* blew her whistle and steamed up to help, and then, continuing up the main channel, steamed on towards Quinsan. Soon after leaving Chunye, Gordon saw in the darkness a confused black mass crowding along the northern bank. It was the garrison of Quinsan – some 8,000 men who were attempting to break through to Soochow. The *Hyson* again sounded her whistle, and opened fire from her gun. In Gordon's own words: 'The mass wavered, yelled and turned back . . . matters were in too critical a state to hesitate, as the mass of the rebels, goaded into desperation, would have swept our small force away. We were therefore forced to fire into them and pursue them towards Quinsan, firing, however, only rarely, and only when the rebels looked as if they would make a stand.'

The *Hyson* used grape, which produced consternation in the Taiping ranks. They turned and fled through the darkness in the direction of Quinsan eight miles away. By early morning of the following day, General Ching outside the East Gate realized what had happened, and in the absence of the rebel garrison, entered the town without opposition. So without any real assault on the walls, this important stronghold fell into Gordon's hands. The loss to the Taipings was heavy: in addition to the slaughter from the *Hyson*'s guns during the pursuit westwards towards Soochow, and the night pursuit towards Quinsan, a lot of rebels were drowned in the lake to the north of the main waterway by outraged local inhabitants who were glad of a chance to take revenge on their erstwhile oppressors. Casualties amounted to over 1,500 with the same number taken prisoner, while Gordon only lost two men killed and five wounded.

### BURGEVINE

During the first two months of Gordon's command of Ward Force all had gone well, and victories had been won within the thirty-mile limit, at Taitsan, and outside it, at Quinsan. For although Bruce tried to insist that British officers should only conduct operations inside the limit, Lord John Russell, the Secretary of State for War, finally decided that officers on half pay, like Gordon, ' should be at liberty to serve in any part of China they pleased ', and only ' the officers who retain their regimental rank should keep within the thirty-mile limit '. The next period, however, was by contrast, a troubled one for Gordon, in which his men were mutinous, his former colleague Burgevine deserted to the rebels, and he himself quarrelled with Li and Ching.

The mutiny was the result of the earlier decision to remove the headquarters of the Force from Sunkiang where the relationship between his men and the inhabitants to whom they sold their loot had been so close as to interfere with discipline. Hake describes the mutiny, and Gordon's handling of it, as follows :

The artillery refused to fall in, and threatened to blow the officers to pieces, both European and Chinese. The intimation of this serious mutiny was conveyed to Gordon in a written proclamation, and he at once took measures that showed it was no easy task to shake him in his absolute command. Convinced that the non-commissioned officers were at the bottom of the affair, he called them up and asked who wrote the proclamation and why the men would not fall in. They had not the courage to tell the truth, and professed ignorance on both points. With quiet determination he then told them that one in every five would be shot, an announcement they received with groans. During this manifestation, the Commander, with great shrewdness, determined in his own mind that the man whose groans were the most emphatic and prolonged was the ringleader. This man was a corporal; Gordon approached him, dragged him out of the rank with his own hand, and ordered two of the infantry standing by to shoot him on the spot. The order was instantly obeyed. Gordon then sent the remaining non-commissioned officers into confinement for one hour, with the assurance that within that time, if the men did not fall in, and if the name of the writer of the proclamation was not given up, every fifth man among them would be shot. This brought them to their senses. The files fell in; the writer's name was disclosed. Gordon had done justice to him some hours before: it was the loud-voiced corporal.

Hardly were these difficulties over when another arose – this time between Gordon and Ching, and then Li. Ching had been annoyed because Gordon would not agree with his plan to attack the East Gate at Quinsan. Gordon's decision to move his headquarters to Quinsan was another grievance, for Ching had intended to occupy it with his own troops. These discords were brought to a head shortly afterwards when Gordon sent some of his men after some raiders north of the Quinsan-Soochow waterway, and Ching's men shot at them when they were returning. They appeared to do this deliberately, but Ching afterwards pretended that his men mistook them for Taipings.

As soon as news of this incident reached Gordon, he wrote an indignant letter to Li and, taking the *Hyson* and a strong detachment of men with him, started down the canal in the direction of Soochow, with the intention of demanding an explanation from Ching. Li, however, alarmed at the outbreak of this quarrel, sent his European liaison officer post-haste to overtake Gordon and arrange the matter peaceably. This envoy was an Englishman named Halliday Macartney who had been an army surgeon with the 99th Regiment but had become Li's personal assistant, being engaged partly in drilling troops and partly in liaising between Li and foreigners. Macartney was placed in command of some Chinese soldiers at Sunkiang when Gordon moved his force to Quinsan, and not only organized a small force similar to Gordon's but also set up an arsenal for supplying Li with arms and ammunition.

Macartney overtook Gordon as he was steaming in the *Hyson* down the main waterway to Soochow. He urged Gordon to come to a friendly arrangement with Ching, and to some effect, for after visiting and upbraiding Ching for his conduct, Gordon finished by accepting a humble apology for the unfortunate incident.

These difficulties with Ching had only just been composed when trouble arose with Li himself. Li began to delay payments to Ward Force, and failed to settle accounts with the firms supplying boats, guns and ammunition ordered by General Brown. Gordon repeatedly complained to Li about it, but without effect, and finally he took the drastic step of threatening to resign, writing to Li as follows:

Your Excellency, in consequence of monthly difficulties I experience in getting the payment of the force made, the non-payment of legitimate bills for boat hire, and the necessities of war from Her Britannic Majesty's Government, who have done so much for the Imperial Chinese authorities, I have determined on throwing up the command of this force, as my retention of office in these circumstances is derogatory to my position as a British officer, who cannot be a suppliant for what Your Excellency knows to be necessities, and should be happy to give. As my resignation of this command will necessitate the knowledge of the British Minister and General, I have forwarded to them copies of the letters and have to add I will remain in command of the force till such time as I have received their replies.

Fortunately Gordon soon withdrew his resignation, and one of his reasons for doing so was the receipt of the serious news that Burgevine was secretly planning to join the rebels. The first intimation came in a letter from the tactful Macartney, who had done so much to end Gordon's quarrel with Ching. Halliday Macartney wrote: ' My dear Gordon, I have made further enquiries about Burgevine, and find for certain that he *is* enlisting men for some service or other, 300 are said to have been enlisted and were to leave Shanghai yesterday. The sum paid to them on joining is 75 *taels*, and they are told that they need not fear about payment, that money will be no object to him. He gives out as a blind, I am told, that he is raising a force for the North. I hear that the twelve-pounder howitzer that used to stand before his door is no longer there.'

At about the same time as he received this letter, Gordon received a letter from Burgevine in which he wrote: ' My dear Gordon, you may hear a great many rumours concerning me, but do not believe any of them. I shall come up (via Shanghai) and have a long talk with you. Until then, adieu.'

Ward Force, and a similar body under the Frenchman Bonnefoy, and Li's Imperial forces, were now in the process of investing Soochow, a very important rebel stronghold. Burgevine's defection with 300 men, an armed steamer and a twelve-pounder howitzer provided a valuable addition to the rebel strength there.

Operations about Soochow began with engagements to clear outlying rebel-held strongpoints and to reinforce similar Imperial ones: Patachiao to the south of Soochow was first taken, and then Wokong, further south down the Grand Canal, was relieved, both after hard fighting. After a battle at Wokong, Gordon returned to Patachiao, and there he carried through by peaceful means, with the help of the valuable American commander of the *Hyson*, Captain Davidson, a most delicate project.

Burgevine and his mercenaries were by now in the Taiping camp: the red shirts of the Europeans had indeed been noted among the rebels when they were counter-attacking to try to recapture Patachiao, and on the rebel-supporting *Kajow*, the vessel taken from Sunkiang. Then, through the good offices of Captain Davidson, an old friend of another American, Captain Jones, Burgevine's chief assistant and the *Kajow*'s captain, negotiations were conducted between the two American sailors, at Gordon's instigation, which led to Burgevine and his followers leaving the rebels and coming over to Gordon. This was carried through by agreement with the Moh Wang and rebel wangs in command at Soochow – Gordon having stressed the unreliability of Burgevine's men – on the promise from the Shanghai authorities of immunity for Burgevine and his followers. The strange meeting between them after Burgevine left the rebel camp has been described something as follows:

Gordon at his stiffest and most uncompromising, lectured Burgevine on loyalty and the ethics of the soldier. Burgevine laughed at him.

'That's all right for you, Kernel,' he said, 'but not for me. I'm here for the pickings. Have I showed you Yok Lin? The best legs in China. But seriously, Kernel, you and I should get together.'

'What are you suggesting?'

'You and I, Kernel, and your lot and my men, join up. Set up in Nanking, if you like. Lords of the Yangtze. You can be Emperor. I'll be the Na Wang, your chief man. Soon we'll have them all licking our boots. An Anglo-American entente. Peace and the rule of law – under you, Kernel. And all the gold and girls in China. Now I could not do this without you. But you could never do it without me. We're made for each other, Kernel. What about it?'

When Gordon heard this startling proposal, he was horrified – at the way it attracted him. This life would give him fame, riches and power. But he pulled himself together. With an effort, he heard him-

self turn on Burgevine and say, 'You had better go. This is un-
pardonable.'

Burgevine only laughed.

'Well, think it over, Kernel,' he said, and was gone.

Gordon felt lost without the intensely living figure of Burgevine.
He might smell of liquor and women, but he smelt too of life, lived
to the full and recklessly. Then, Gordon sank to his knees, the tears
streaming down his face, for one of those talks with his Maker that
were a feature of his life.

In spite of his nonchalance, this meeting seems to have affected
Burgevine. He wrote Gordon several letters afterwards, the last
from Japan. In them he shows his deep affection for the British
general regardless of what had happened between them and tries
to show that some of the hard things said of him were not true.
One of these letters reads:

My dear Gordon, I have been very anxious to see you on many
accounts, but have been unable to do so, and another wound has reopened, and still keeps me confined to my bed – as soon as I am able
to walk I shall make it a point to come up as there are many things
to explain and many falsehoods circulated to disprove. In all the foul
assertions made by the deserters, there are none I care about save the
charges of deliberately proposing to desert my wounded, and that of
treachery towards yourself. I do not intend to enter into any controversy with such a man as Jones whose vindictive and extraordinary assertions have surprised me, but I give you my word as a gentleman that they are false, and that I never for a moment entertained
such an idea.

Do not credit any idle reports you may hear concerning me – what
I told you on board the *Hyson* as to my future intentions I still ad-
here to . . . There are many things to say which I will defer to a
personal interview. Trusting this may occur in a few days, I remain,

Yours sincerely,

H. R. Burgevine.

SOOCHOW

As the negotiations with Moh Wang about Burgevine and his
followers' release led to such satisfactory results, Gordon had
high hopes of repeating this success and of gaining control of
Soochow by negotiation rather than of capturing it by fighting.
He mentioned this in writing to his mother: 'I feel convinced
that the rebel chiefs would come to terms if they had fair ones

offered them. I mean to do my best to bring this about, and I am sure that if I do so, I shall gain a greater victory than any capture of cities would be.'

After a period of attacks on outposts, followed by resistance to rebel counter-attacks to regain them, Soochow was eventually encircled. In all these preliminary assaults Gordon's force of 4,000 only represented a small part of the 14,000 men investing Soochow and the 25,000 Imperial forces nearby. But they played a major part, and Gordon himself was usually in the forefront of the battle. Nevertheless, when it came to the final attack, Gordon still felt more could be gained by attempts at negotiation than by an extensive military offensive. For he had learnt from the reports of deserters that one section of the rebels, led by Lar Wang, the second in command, was in favour of capitulation, but they were opposed by the man in command, Moh Wang, whose family was held hostage in Nanking.

In order to hasten the rebels to make up their mind, a series of attacks were planned which in the end had the required effect. Individually, however, they cost the lives of many of Gordon's men, and were not very successful. The first was a night attack on the north-east walls where it was believed that the pliable Lar Wang was in command. But rebels not in favour of capitulation heard of it beforehand, and Gordon's men were defeated. There followed an equally unfortunate choice of time and place for another assault by the investors. They attacked when the Generalissimo, the Chung Wang, was visiting Soochow from Nanking, and had to fight a bloody battle with the Chung Wang and his picked bodyguard of 300 men in yellow robes. The only achievement on this occasion was the occupation of a few of the outer stockades which Lar Wang had been told to defend, but from which he had purposely held back his troops.

The importance the Chung Wang placed on holding Soochow is shown in a rebel letter intercepted by the Imperial forces. It was dated 10 November 1862 and addressed to Hu Wang commanding at Changchow and translated by W. S. F. Mayers, an interpreter. It also shows the sound strategic sense of the Chung Wang and his understanding of the principle of concentration. It reads:

I write again because on the 28 October I despatched two letters

The Empress Dowager

General Gordon

Imperial Chinese Banner given to General
Gordon during the Taiping Rebellion, *c.* 1862

(*Left*) Li Hung-chang, General and Statesman, on a visit to England at the end of his long career

(*Right*) General Gaselee, the staunch commander of the British Contingent of the Relief Force which marched on Peking in 1900

Dr G. E. Morrison, *Times* Correspondent at Peking, who went to the rescue of the Chinese converts near Nan-tang Church in Peking in 1900

by express message with orders to deliver them within a certain time, in which I requested that with the exception of the garrison of Chang-chow all the forces might with all speed be brought together for a combined attack in order that we might derive the benefit of conjoint action; but a length of time has elapsed to my great anxiety, without the receipt of an answer. The news yesterday received from Nanking to the effect that the works around the Kao-chiao Gate have been evacuated has probably already reached you, as you are nearer the spot. I was disturbed and grieved beyond measure by this intelligence and at the same time I had no troops of whom I can dispose. If you together with the Wu-seih troops can come and make a combined effort, there will be reason to hope that the siege both of Nanking and of Soochow may be broken up. The beleaguement of Nanking is, as you are doubtless fully aware, far different now from what it has been heretofore, and I am most anxious that you should consent to join with your forces and also combine with the troops of Shih Wang. If all unite in sweeping away one division of the Imps, security will accrue on all sides, and the sooner we clear away this brood the sooner we shall be able to make a combined effort to relieve Nanking. If, however, Soochow and Hangchow are endangered, not only is it useless to talk of relieving the siege of Nanking, but Changchow and Wu-seih will also be as good as lost and it will be too late for repentance then. To yourself who know this so well it is not necessary that I should say more.

However, a few days later, when the Chung Wang had left for Nanking, the rebels started negotiating, first by means of three young wangs, later by the secret appearance of Lar Wang himself. On Wednesday 2 December 1863, General Ching came to Gordon and told him that he had heard Lar Wang himself intended to pay him a secret visit and asked Gordon to join them at the agreed rendezvous, an isolated spot by a creek about a mile to the north of the town. The two leaders went to the appointed place and waited. Soon after they arrived, a distinguished-looking man came up to the boat and asked for Ching. It was Lar Wang. In the discussion which followed, Lar Wang wanted the Imperial troops to attack his area of the wall. He said he would then facilitate their entry if he was given a promise that his own men would be spared. Gordon did not approve of this, owing to the difficulty of distinguishing who were friendly rebels and who were unfriendly. After a while, Gordon left Lar Wang and Ching to talk over between themselves some new arrangement.

The difficulty was in getting Moh Wang out of the way, and the two Chinese evolved a strange method of doing this which in the event did not have to be put into effect. The idea was for the wangs favouring surrender to bring Moh Wang to the top of the wall, ostensibly to see some sapping activity on which Gordon was engaged, and then to throw him down to Ching who would have a boat ready to take him away. While Ching and Lar Wang were evolving this complicated plot – in which the sign of surrender would later be that the rebels would cease firing, shave their heads and withdraw from the East Gate walls – Gordon went off to see Ching's superior, Li, to negotiate for the safety of Moh Wang and the rebels should they surrender. Li gave his undertaking to spare the rebels, and this is an important matter, as much of what followed hinges on Li's promise, and the promises of Gordon.

Hake describes the events which caused the plot to be unnecessary as follows:

Moh Wang, obstinate, and resolved to hold out to the last, had learned something of these parleys, and had his suspicions thoroughly aroused. He sent for his six brother kings that he might speak with them on the subject. After certain ceremonies, they adjourned to the reception hall, where Moh Wang seated himself at the head of the table, which was on a dais. Unfortunately for the rebel cause, the chiefs thus collected together in council had each a separate command, and were therefore able to enforce their differences of opinion. Moh Wang was captain of the city. He was not wise, but he was brave as a lion, and would have shed the last drop of his blood rather than surrender. Gordon knew this, and had a great respect for his character. He had in person extorted a pledge from Governor Li that Moh Wang's life should be spared, but this pledge he was never to call upon Li to keep. The council was the last at which Moh Wang was ever to preside. The question of capitulation was raised and discussed: Moh Wang and another voted against surrender. All the rest were loud in its favour. Hot words ensued, when Kong Wang jumped up, threw aside his robes, drew out a dagger, and stabbed Moh Wang nine times in the back. Assisted by the others, he then bore his victim into the outer court, and severed his head from his body.

The head was later sent to Ching, and Ching interpreted it as one of the signs of surrender, and said that he would enter the East Gate in the morning.

Next morning at daybreak there were sounds of firing under

the walls, and it was learnt that this was due to some fighting between the followers of Moh Wang and Lar Wang. Lar Wang's men had shaved their heads during the night as a sign of submission, and they were now chasing out of the Western Gates those – chiefly Cantonese and Kwangsi men – who refused to surrender. Presently the firing ceased and the Taiping troops were withdrawn from the Eastern Gate. This was the form of surrender agreed upon by Lar Wang, and so General Ching marched in and occupied the gate. At the same time Gordon advanced outside the walls to the North Gate, where he kept his men in strict military formation, refusing to let them enter the town, because he dreaded the demoralization that would follow if they were once let loose in it.

The news of the capitulation of Soochow on 5 December 1863 was received in Shanghai the following day, and six weeks later in England.

The story of what happened after the occupation of the East Gate and the virtual surrender of the city is most involved. The full account which Gordon gave may be found in printed form in *Secessional Papers: 1852–1899*, China No. 30 *c*: (correspondence relating to Lieut-Col Gordon's position in the Chinese Service after the fall of Soochow; 1864, LXIII 423). Gordon is usually most sincere, but in this account seems to dissemble. He is only really clear about his indignation with Li for breaking his promise to spare the wangs of Soochow after their surrender. Gordon and Ching had given word on this to Lar Wang, yet in the event the wangs were murdered. The following is the outline of what Gordon says about it in the papers quoted above: Ching's troops occupied the East Gate area, but Gordon's were kept outside the town to preclude looting. Gordon himself went through the town and found it quiet. He notes that the Taiping soldiers had shaved their heads as a token of submission. He went to the house of Lar Wang where he found the wangs assembled. He asked them if they were satisfied with the way things had gone, and they said they were. He then went to Moh Wang's house where he found the body of the assassinated chief still unburied, and ordered a grave to be dug for it. Under the chair on which Moh Wang was sitting when murdered, and according to the accounts of bystanders they were previously on his person, were two letters which Gordon had written to him about Burgevine's surrender. The following extract from one of them shows on what good terms they were at the time:

Your Excellency, I have given orders that the arms taken by the Europeans the other day when they came over together with a boat they took with them shall be placed above the small Bridge at 2 p.m. this day and request Your Excellency to send for the same.

The Europeans took no horses away with them, but I send Your Excellency a pony herewith, which I hope you will accept.

I send Your Excellency the rough copy of my letter in Chinese to you in order that no mistake may be made in this matter.

I cannot express to Your Excellency the appreciation I have for your sentiments expressed in your letter, and assure you that by acting in the way you write will gain your cause more friends among Foreign nations than you can imagine. As for myself, I am a British Officer, and the present position I am in quite prohibits my entertaining the idea of accepting your hospitality.

If Your Excellency would take my honest advice, you will ask all foreigners who do not wish to stay, to leave the city, and in doing so you will never have cause to regret it.

I can answer for them fulfilling to the best of their power all engagement they may be under Your Excellency and if perchance any men choose to remain you will by the above liberality secure good and faithful service from them.

I quite agree with Your Excellency in your statement that if you have paid money out, you are bound to have the same refunded and I am certain that there are men with you on whose word you can rely even if they should leave your service.

Gordon had tried to get Li's permission to round up the rebels who were fleeing to the west. But owing to another disagreement concerning the Force's pay, he never undertook this operation, and instead marched his force back to Quinsan. Next, he considered the alternative of seizing the armoured rebel gunboat, *Firefly*, on Lake Taihu. While waiting for his own boats, *Hyson* and *Tsarlee*, to steam up, Gordon returned to Soochow and paid another visit to Moh Wang's house. This time he found the body had been buried, and while going through the streets of the town, he saw Lar Wang and the other wangs riding off towards the East Gate to go to Li's camp for the conference at which, most unwisely as it turned out, Gordon had declined to be present. He said he considered it better to leave the surrender negotiations to the Chinese General; but as Moh Wang had been murdered by his fellows and Ching himself was an ex-rebel, and as Gordon had pledged his word to spare the rebels who surrendered and was indeed suspicious of treachery being afoot, it appears a most stupid arrangement to have made. So it came about that he was riding the streets of Soochow, hesitant and undecided while the really important things were happening at Li's camp in his absence.

Gordon met Macartney in the streets, and they rode along together for a time. As they did so, they heard in the distance a considerable commotion, with rifles being fired in the air from the direction of Li's camp. The next encounter was with General Ching riding back from the conference. When asked how it had gone, he gave the unexpected news that the Soochow wangs had demanded such impossible surrender terms that the conference had broken up with nothing decided, the wangs taking alarm and fleeing. Macartney now left to try and find Lar Wang and ask him what happened at the conference; and Gordon and Ching also parted when the South Gate was reached.

Gordon was by this time very suspicious. Deciding to give up his idea of an operation against *Firefly* – the enemy gunboat on Lake Taihu previously captured and taken off by the rebels from Shanghai – he went off again into the town accompanied only by his interpreter. In the streets now the rebels were standing to their arms, and the Imperial troops were busy looting. Reaching Lar Wang's palace he found it sacked and gutted. But Lar Wang's family were still there standing about disconsolately among the ruins. At their request he escorted them to their uncle's home, which they found packed with rebels and a minor stronghold. They obviously felt some comfort from Gordon's presence even with only an interpreter, and it was with great difficulty that he managed to get away. On returning to the South Gate he was delayed again. It was the Imperial troops this time. They were suspicious of him and would not at first let him pass.

Next he went up to the East Gate and found his bodyguard, yet even with this staunch band at his back he could still get little sense out of anybody. Gordon was furious with Li and Ching for allowing the town to be plundered. He met Ching again and charged him with this. Ching assured Gordon that the permission to loot was on Li's orders, and he was trying his best to prevent it. He was in a very hysterical state, and to prove his assertions, caught hold of twenty looters and had them shot.

Finally an American, Major Bailey, whom Gordon had lent to Ching as an artillery expert, led him to discover the truth about how the conference broke up. In Bailey's tent was a young son of Lar Wang. He told Gordon his father had been murdered, and pointed to the spot on the other side of the creek where his father had been beheaded, and where his body still lay.

Gordon felt he must see for himself before he could fully credit such a criminal deed. He crossed the creek and there before him lay nine headless bodies with their severed heads beside them. Among these he recognized the head of Lar Wang, which the boy had begged him to bring away. Snatching up the hideous object he returned.

Gordon was now so angry with Li and Ching that he seems to have gone berserk. He had been hesitant and undecided before. Now it was the same again only to a greater degree. First he planned to take his gunboats, now awaiting him, and search out Li at his headquarters and arrest him. He would then call on him to resign, and would have him charged before the Peking authorities as guilty of criminal treachery. If he refused Gordon would himself cease supporting the Governor and hand back to the rebels all the towns Ward Force had helped to capture. But Gordon was thwarted in this wild intention by finding that Li had already left his headquarters and was by this time entering Soochow at the head of his large army. It is not known exactly what Gordon did next. He certainly wrote Li a letter in which he gave full vent to his indignation, and set out the terms of an ultimatum. One book, which professes to base itself on contemporary evidence, even suggests that Gordon systematically hunted down Li – going out through the city, revolver in hand, to try and avenge the murder.

There followed a period much like that which followed Gordon's earlier major quarrel with Li over the pay of Ward Force. He withdrew the services of himself and his Force and threatened to resign unless the Peking authorities removed Li from his governorship of Kiangsu and the command of the Imperial forces there. He sought support for his demands from General Brown – which he got – from Bruce the Ambassador in Peking, and other British diplomats and from Sir Robert Hart, all of whom, being realists, tried to persuade him to come to terms. Then just when he had persuaded some people to back his resignation, he did a *volte face* and said he would take the field again. All this emerges from a series of letters from which the author now proposes to quote. Some it is believed have never been published before.

Brown wrote to Bruce on 17 December 1863:

The subsequent treachery of the Imperialist Authorities had, however, destroyed the confidence of all ranks, and their cruelties had turned the sympathies of the Europeans in favour of the rebels and I have found it necessary, in order to restore discipline and to avoid a perhaps total defection of the force to take Major Gordon and his force finally under my command . . . Though the Futai (Governor Li) was prepared to take on himself the whole responsibility of the murder of the Wangs, and the sacking of the city, and to fully exonerate Major Gordon from all blame, he was unwilling or unable to offer any exculpation or explanation of his conduct . . .

Brown who had met Li before writing to Bruce, went on to say that he told Li that Britain would no doubt withdraw Gordon's support to the Imperialists because of what he had done at Soochow even if he paid all his monetary dues – another of Gordon's complaints against him.

On 26 January 1864, Bruce, the realist, replied to Brown:

The perfidy of the Governor to the rebel Wangs does not differ much from other perfidy they exhibit towards each other, of which, the assassination of the Moh Wang as a means of buying their own safety, is only one among many instances. Neither party will scruple to commit such acts of treachery when their immediate interests seem to be thereby promoted, and though as a general rule the terms of capitulation granted by the Imperialists to those who surrender seem to have been kept I do not delude myself with the belief that they are guided in observing them, by any higher motive, than that of expediency . . .

Li gave his explanation as one of justifiable revenge, and Bruce passed this on to Lord John Russell in a letter dated 12 February 1864:

I am inclined to think that Governor Li, in putting these chiefs to death, may have acted in a spirit of revenge for the perfidious massacre of his own men at Taitsan . . . the orders to continue the negotiations for the surrender of Taitsan, and thereby to inveigle Imperialist soldiers into the town and put them to death were sent by the Chiefs at Soochow and were carried into execution. This may have palliated, in the eyes of Governor Li, his breach of faith towards these men. The *lex talionis* is quite in accordance with Chinese maxims. (Bruce then went on to quote what Prince Kung said to justify the massacre): By the death of a few (dangerous originators of the Taiping rebellion) the death of many will be avoided.

Meanwhile, John Gibson a consul at Tientsin, and outspoken friend, wrote on 2 February 1864, to try to persuade Gordon to carry on:

I have heard that your work is finished, that you have retreated to Quinsan and that you will have nothing to say to the Futai. I am sorry for this. The Futai was extremely wrong in murdering the Wangs whom you hoped to spare, but the Futai is the Civil Governor of the Province, it might not have been in his power to spare the Wangs, and if we consider the sort of Government there is in Nanking most probably he did right in executing them . . . Sir F. Bruce will do nothing. The Futai will be Futai still. Sir F. Bruce is going home shortly and he will not do anything to set you right with the Futai. Even if Sir F. Bruce was inclined, the Prince of Kung and the Foreign Board must be got over, and rather than see the Futai degraded or punished the Board will sooner see *you* leave the army. I speak *plain* but I think reasonably . . .

There follows a bit about how he thinks Brown was foolish to write a despatch to Bruce supporting Gordon's demands for the removal of Li, and then continues:

I don't think the Futai will murder Wangs another time. In fact don't permit him. Your troops dislike the Futai; and you can use your troops in protecting the Wangs. You can, at least, *not* promise them their *lives*. Be sure to keep out of diplomacy with the Chinese Mandarins. Englishmen are bad diplomats, and once a Chinese Mandarin discusses with you any policy be sure that he *has you* – your object is to fight, which a Chinese Mandarin is unable to do . . .

Eventually it was Sir Robert Hart who brought about a reconciliation between Gordon and Li. Hart was the sagacious Englishman who had been appointed Inspector of Customs in the Chinese service, a post he held with great success for many years. He became also the chief adviser for the Chinese in their relations with European countries, and was highly respected by them. The Peking authorities approached Hart and asked him to act as an intermediary. Hart first went to see Li at Soochow, and found him most anxious to effect a reconciliation. From Soochow, Hart went on to Quinsan to see Gordon. He found that he was inspecting the country around, and it was a few days before he was able to see him. It was the first time the two had met, and Gordon received him cordially, ordering a special parade of the troops in his honour. Gordon had now had time to think over things, and he gave a more favourable hearing to Hart's arguments than he had done to similar ones presented by Macartney just after the execution. It was now about two months since the event, and he had heard nothing in reply to his ultimatum. He had had some trouble with the discipline of his force owing to his prolonged inaction, and felt it necessary to dismiss no less than sixteen insubordinate officers. Meanwhile, Li had been scrupulous in paying the Force, as well as providing bonuses and compensation grants. Gordon had also heard some of the arguments put forward in excuse by Li, on the lines of the points in the letters above. He was therefore inclined to look upon Li with a more favourable eye than he had considered possible two months before and, when Hart laid fully before him the reasons which Li gave for his action, he expressed his willingness to go with Hart to Soochow and have an interview with Li.

On 1 February 1864 Gordon went with Hart to Li's palace at Soochow. When conversations began, recrimination was studiously avoided, but Li undertook to make a public announcement of his sole responsibility for the execution of the Wangs. With this undertaking Gordon was satisfied, and the rest of the interview was devoted to discussing plans for further attacks upon the rebels with a view to bringing the fighting to a speedy end.

Hearing that Gordon had weakened in his resolve some diplomats now wrote to try and stop him joining Li again. These included Markham, the British Consul at Shanghai; and Dent, the latter writing, ' I can't believe that you really intend to assist the Futai after his late behaviour and the disgust you expressed at it . . .' In spite of these supplications, however, Gordon stuck to his decision to take the field again, and he was encouraged in doing so by a letter from Sir Frederick Bruce, who wrote: ' In any future operations in which a foreign officer is concerned, the rules of warfare as practised among foreign nations are to be observed. I have received the strictest assurances that this will be strictly adhered to, and that the Governor Li is to be instructed to that effect. I need not impress upon you how essential it is that there should be no repetition of the occurrence at Soochow.'

## GORDON'S LAST CAMPAIGN – MARCH TO MAY 1864

The plan which Gordon and Li worked out at their meeting was that Li should invest Changchufu while Gordon crossed Lake Tai-hu, moved westwards, and captured Kintang, and Tanyang, in order to get between Changchufu and Nanking, and cut off the rebels. This would also block the routes north from Hangchow. Finally, after capturing Kintang, he was to join the investment of Changchufu.

While crossing Lake Tai-hu, they discovered the *Firefly* derelict and with its 32-pounder removed, and Gordon had a clear passage. A waterway led to the stronghold of Yesing which Gordon captured by his customary method: reconnoitre, bombard, assault. The next post, Liyang, surrendered voluntarily in the same manner as Chanzu after the capture of Fushan in his first campaign.

To complete his tasks Gordon now prepared the attacks on Kintang and Tanyang, the vital posts blocking the escape routes. Here he encountered a series of setbacks.

Kintang was a small town with few stockades outside its walls, and no customary groups of many-coloured flags could be seen on its ramparts. It was therefore assumed that resistance would be slight – an assumption which proved erroneous. After the usual breach was made, and the men were landing from the gunboats under it, such a horde of rebels suddenly appeared, and so much fire was met, that retreat was the only course. A second attempt proved no more successful. This time Gordon led his men across a stone bridge over the creek. The enemy fire in this quarter, however, was just as vicious. Gordon fell with a wound[1] in his leg, and his men were forced back as before. Gordon fainted from loss of blood and further efforts without him proved vain, so the attempt on Kintang was abandoned.

Gordon's wound was fortunately not severe. It was a flesh

[1] Gordon was wounded on 21 March 1864. The day before, while campaigning in the south supported by d'Arguebelle's Franco-Chinese force, General Ching was mortally wounded.

138

wound just below the knee, although the bullet had passed close to an artery. He was still able to accompany his troops, but he had to remain lying in his boat. Nevertheless no further attempt was made on Kintang which was later evacuated by the rebels when they fell back on their last stronghold at Nanking. Tanyang was similarly abandoned. But in the assault of Changchufu, which Gordon joined in April 1864, he and his force played an important part. It is from his own account that the following description of the last episode is taken. He explains why his force did not take part in the final capture of Nanking, and he describes his last battle. He writes:

The rebels are very much pressed, and three months should finish them. They are in possession of Nanking, which is entirely surrounded, and where a hundredweight of rice fetches £20. Tsêng Kuofan is, and has been, besieging the city for from ten to twelve years. The Imperialists do not want me to go there, as they feel sure of taking it in time, and they feel a sort of shame to let us go in and capture the city before which they have been so long, and if the Tien Wang were to offer to surrender to my force, I should be obliged to refuse to listen, and perhaps be the unwilling witness of a massacre. I have three or four times written to different authorities, to get them to send up British gunboats to prevent any wholesale massacre, but to no avail. The chiefs, however, deserve their fate . . . I am about to attack Changchufu, which is full of refugees from other cities. It is commanded by Hu Wang, a Kwangsi man, and one of the most able of the chiefs. He has lost one eye, and therefore is called ' cock-eye '. The Imperialists here are in great numbers, over thirty thousand, and have been four months *in statu quo*. They have got their stockades one hundred and fifty yards from the wall, and in one place a Frenchman in their employ has bridged over the ditch. They have been making as many as three breaches in the wall, but they have not tried storming. This is the style they go upon: they hammer away with some large guns they have manned with Europeans, and then stop and let the rebels build their defences again. They have their stockades at all the gates except the west, from which the rebels have a good road to Tanyang. It is this road I am on my way to attack and cut off. Changchufu is shaped like a kidney; its walls are rotten and it has four months rice. The next city is Kintang, from which I was repulsed. I should not have fallen back if I had not received the news of the irruption[1] of the rebels into the Imperial districts. Of the men

[1] A rebel counter-attack after the battle of Kintang.

who composed that expedition not two thousand escaped; the captured ponies exceeded five hundred. The numbers slain cannot be stated, for I did not push on when I saw the rebels in flight, but let the Imperialists do their own work. I started them from the stockades, and followed them up, so as to start them again if they made a stand, which they did do more than once. In one village the Imperialists killed over three thousand. I will say this much: the Imperialists did not kill the coolies and boys. The villagers followed up and stripped the fugitives stark naked, so that all over the country there were naked men lying down in the grass. The cruelties these rebels have committed during their raids were frightful; in every village there were from ten to sixty dead, either women, frightfully mutilated, old men, or small children. I do not regret the fate of these rebels, who were able to escape if they had liked to do so. I have no talent for description, but the scenes I have witnessed of misery are something dreadful: and I must say that your wish for me to return with the work incomplete would not be expressed if you saw the state of these poor people. The horrible furtive looks of the wretched inhabitants hovering around one's boats haunts me, and the knowledge of their want of nourishment would sicken anyone; they are like wolves. The dead lie where they fall, and are, in some cases, trodden quite flat by the passers-by. I hope to get the Shanghai people to assist, but they do not see these things; and to read that there are human beings eating human flesh produces less effect than if they saw the corpses from which that flesh was cut.

The Imperialists are not so very contemptible, and it is a mistake to put down everything to the foreign forces. The latter certainly give the Imperialists great confidence and make the rebels fear, but the foreign forces, if left to themselves, could not do much. My leg is all right; the eleventh day after receiving the wound I was up, and by the fifteenth day I could walk well. The ball went through the thick part of the leg just below the knee.

In a later letter he says: ' I have the satisfaction of knowing that the end of this rebellion is at hand, while, had I continued inactive it might have lingered on for years.'

Changchufu was carried on 11 May. The Imperial troops had assaulted in two columns. They met with desperate resistance on the ramparts, and one column began to give way in confusion. At this critical moment, Gordon himself, followed by his 1st Regiment and two hundred volunteers from the remainder of his force, rushed to its support over a bridge still standing in the area; and the place fell. On the same day Gordon wrote to his

Mother, 'Changchufu was carried by assault by the Quinsan Force and the Imperialists at 2 p.m. this day, with little loss. I go back to Quinsan on 13 May, and shall not again take the field. The rebels are done . . . and Nanking will probably fall in about two months . . .'

With the capture of Changchufu ended Gordon's connection with the Chinese Government. He moved his force to Quinsan and disbanded it.

THE VALUE OF THE FOREIGN-TRAINED ARMIES

Nanking fell on 19 July 1864 to the Imperial forces commanded by Tsêng Kuo-fan's brother. They broke down part of the main wall before the Taiping leaders could make their planned breakout. The Tien Wang did not live to see the end. He died in Nanking at the age of fifty after a lingering illness of twenty days possibly after taking poison.

The fall of Nanking led to a terrible slaughter. The bloody process of the occupation of the Taiping capital and the fanatical death of many Taipings in Nanking who refused to surrender can be read in Tsêng Kuo-fan's report to the throne: 'The Imperialists searched through the city for any rebels they could find, and in three days killed over 100,000 men. The Creek was filled with bodies. Half of the false wangs, chief generals, heavenly generals and other heads were killed in battle, and the other half either drowned themselves in the dykes and ditches or else burned themselves. The whole of them numbered about 3,000 men. The fire in the city raged for three days and nights . . . Not one of the 100,000 rebels in Nanking surrendered themselves when the city was taken but in many cases gathered together and burned themselves and passed away without repentance. Such a formidable band of rebels has been rarely known from ancient times to the present.'

This slaughter was the combined result of the fanatical Taiping defiance and of the policy of Tsêng Kuo-fan, who had determined, long before, that the surrender of the old original Taiping group from Kwangsi was not to be accepted. His goal was the extermination of the whole movement through the death of its core of leaders and followers. A policy of encouraging surrender might well have led to an earlier breakup and prevented such slaughter; but it might also have left a residue of potential successors who might have carried on the Taiping ideas and renewed the attack against the traditional order, which Tsêng Kuo-fan wanted to protect. The ruthless extermination of all the original Taiping force virtually ended this chance.

The fall of Nanking meant the end of the Taiping Rebellion. Taiping activity afterwards was scattered and not very effective, although some did fight on after their central government no longer existed. These consisted of two groups, one south of the Yangtze and one north. The southern group was led by Shih Wang; but the Tien Wang's young son, as Young Monarch and last rallying hope of the movement, was captured trying to reach it. The Shih Wang was assassinated by rivals and by February 1866, the group had been broken up. The northern group had as its principal leader Lai Wen-kung and joined up with the Nien rebels of that area. There is some doubt whether the combined forces should be counted as a continuation of the Taiping Rebellion or as the extension of the Nien Rebellion. In any case, the Taiping element was dispersed by January 1868.

There is disagreement of the value of European trained and led forces to the Imperial cause: Macartney's, Bonnefoy's, d'Arguebelle's, and particularly, Gordon's. It has been the custom for many years for European historians to state categorically that Gordon defeated the Taipings. More recent research by groups of American and Chinese scholars working in co-operation has produced a more qualified appraisement. For example Michael writes:

The role that these foreign units played in the defeat of the Taipings has been greatly overrated by a number of writers who have ascribed the Taiping defeat to foreign intervention. Yet the Ever Victorious Army played only a supporting part in the last stage of military affairs, and its theatre of operations was limited to the area around Shanghai. And although in these battles the Ever Victorious Army played a decisive role, the fighting in this area, though it may have speeded up the end for the Taipings, no longer affected the outcome of the war, which had been determined in the battles for the upper Yangtze area and was brought to an end in the attack against Nanking itself, in which the Ever Victorious Army did not participate.

One of the most misleading images of the Ever Victorious Army was created by its name. It was by no means 'ever victorious'. On several occasions, both under Ward and later under Gordon, it was dealt major defeats by Taiping armies, and a high percentage of it was killed in battle. Some others deserted to the Taipings and fought with them, and substantial desertions took place on a number of occasions. Several times the unit was reformed through new recruitment . . . but on the whole the Ever Victorious Army participated successfully in the defeat and destruction of the Taiping units in the towns of the lower Yangtze area until it was disbanded at the end of May 1864.

Another American scholar, Hail, is a shade more appreciative of Gordon's Force. He writes:

In attempting to estimate the place of the army in the suppression of the rebellion we must bear in mind how many important cities were captured through the brilliant strategy of the American, British and French officers. Without their aid the campaign would doubtless have suffered delays, and difficulties and even dangers might have confronted the Imperial cause which were thus obviated. The members were certainly better armed and better drilled than those of the purely Chinese forces co-operating with them. Their intervention added to that of foreign soldiers and sailors saved Shanghai from falling into Taiping hands and this in turn gave Li Hung-chang the revenues to pay his men. When we consider all the facts we cannot deny that their aid was most useful if not indeed vital.

Yet it would be rash to assert or assume that 'Chinese' Gordon put down the Taiping Rebellion. He never commanded a force of more than three thousand men. He was always strengthened by large Chinese armies to whom a share of the praise is due for the victories which their absence might have turned into defeats. And above all, the less spectacular but no less important work of the vast forces placed by Tsêng Kuo-fan and his generals in Anhwei, Kiangsi, and about the Heavenly Capital itself, was causing the Taipings increasing anxiety, while beyond, in Hupeh and Honan, were other forces preventing the Nien and Taipings from joining hands.

It seems fair, therefore, to accept very literally the estimate of Wilson the chief historian of this army, who, in quoting some of the eulogistic and even flattering accounts of Gordon's work, says:

When we come to look carefully at the sweeping statement that it was Colonel Gordon who put an end to the Taiping Rebellion, truth compels me to pause. Though perhaps, Li, the Futai, in the despatch quoted above, takes a good deal too much credit to himself for his share in the operations in Kiangsu, yet there is no doubt that Gordon and his force, unaided, could not have cleared the province. While the brunt of the fighting fell on him, he required Imperialists to hold the places he took; and their forces under General Ching and others, fought along with him so as greatly to contribute to his success.

Yet in another way the attitude of the Western powers was a decisive factor, for their determination to withhold recognition from the Taiping Government in 1853 and 1854 was of service to the Imperial cause . . . In a negative way, then, we may grant that by leaving China alone to subdue the rebels, instead of aiding the Taipings, the cause of the Manchus had its chance to triumph, and the active aid rendered towards the end of the war made assurance doubly sure.

The Taiping Rebellion overlapped the Third China War described in Part Two of this book. It started even before the Second China War, or *Arrow* War, of 1859, with the foundation of the God Worshippers Society in Tzu-ching-shan in 1844; it continued until 1868, eight years after the signing of the Treaty of Peking on 24 October 1860.

By the Treaty of Peking Britain was granted all she desired from China: another treaty port, Tientsin; confirmation of privileges in the old Treaty Ports of Shanghai, Canton, Amoy, Foochow, and Ningpo; a legation in Peking; and the addition of mainland Kowloon to the island colony of Hong Kong.

The new policy of Britain towards China, evolved by the statesmen and diplomats of the time, is indicated in a letter by Sir Frederick Bruce of 2 January 1864. He wrote:

In fact as our interest in China is trade, and as trade is certain to increase provided China enjoys internal and external tranquillity, my opinion of the policy to be pursued here differs materially from the views of the school of headlong progress of which men like Lay and Osborne may be considered as the chief exponents. We do not wish to revolutionize the country for I am convinced that we are more likely to get on with a Manchoo than with a purely Chinese dynasty. We do not wish to turn China into a second India, even if that were possible, and we should not be satisfied were any other foreign government to make the attempt. Projects such as Railways and Telegraphs which would give to foreigners a landed interest in the interior of China would lead to most serious complications unless the Government of China takes the initiative in such enterprises, and

Sepoys of the 1st Sikhs scale the walls of Peking after taking off their boots

(*Top*) The British Legation, Peking in 1900

(*Bottom*) The Tartar Wall with the Ch'ien Men Gate looking from the Chinese City towards the Tartar and Forbidden Cities after the Boxer Rebellion, 1901

(*Top*) Looking south over the Forbidden City. The Lotus Lake can be seen, and the Peitang R.C. Cathedral (Bishop Favier), which was besieged at the time of the siege of the Legations, is on the right

(*Bottom*) The Altar of Heaven, Peking

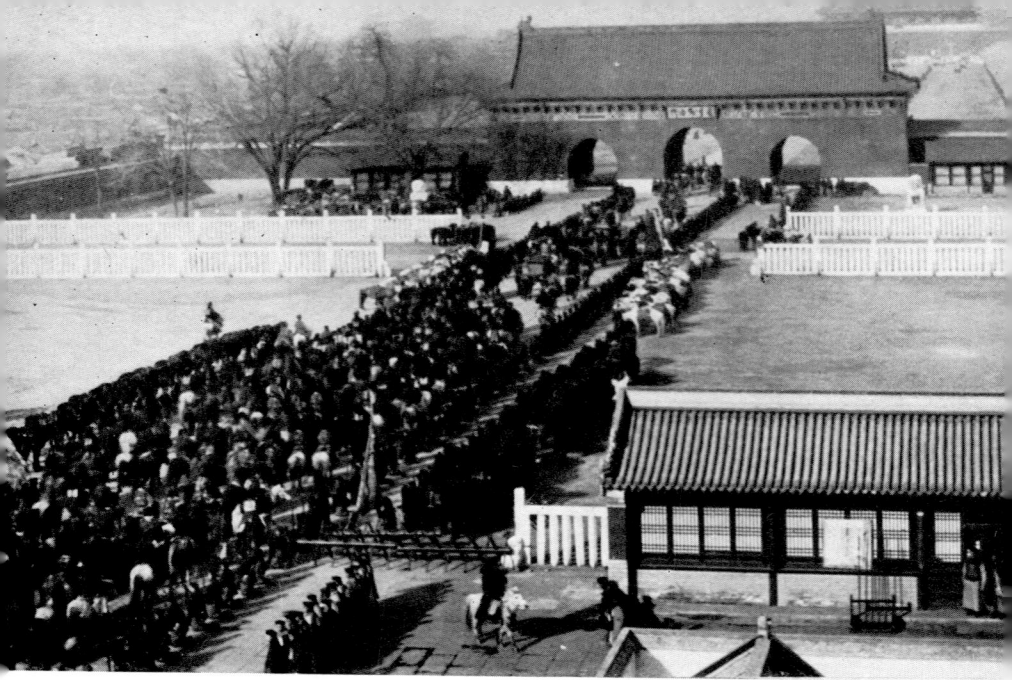

The return of the Emperor and the Dowager Empress into the Forbidden
City, Peking, after the Boxer Rebellion, 1901

unless they are in the main, Chinese concerns, and exclusively within Chinese jurisdiction. I do not look to railways as likely to be of much benefit to foreign trade which is of far more importance to us than putting money into the pockets of foreign speculators. If they are to be constituted in the hands of foreigners, who will be guaranteed their rights of foreign influence, they will imbroil us with the native authorities . . . and their benefits as internal improvements would be outweighed by the obstacles thus created in the way of friendly relations with China. Lay hoped to make China the Vassal of England as representing Western civilization in these waters, and to compel her to adopt the material symbols of progress in the nineteenth century. To suppose that a flotilla of 500 men were a sufficient force for the objects contemplated and that other nations would have long acquiesced in the inferior position allotted to them showed an utter incapacity to comprehend China or realize the susceptibilities of foreign powers. My object is to work with the Chinese Government and not to supersede it on the fallacious assumption that a foreigner is better able to govern China than the natives. I offer them suggestions, I propose novelties: if I can persuade their adoption so much the better; if not, we must trust to time and increasing confidence in us to do what argument and persuasion are unable suddenly to effect.

Progress in the country must be slow in order to be safe: and no course is so calculated to produce a reaction fatal to our interests and to involve England in responsibilities with which no lover of his country would wish to see her burdened as a disregard of the legitimate right of this government to be consulted on questions affecting their interior condition, and the attempt to introduce by pressure, material improvements, which require a continuance of the same foreign pressure, to enable them to subsist. I shall be very glad to see railways and telegraphs established, if the necessity is felt and admitted by the Chinese, but not as the symbol of foreign domination or influence.

In 1853 when the Taiping Rebellion was beginning, part of Shanghai was captured by other rebels from Canton, and the Chinese collector of foreign dues there, a former Hong merchant of Canton, arranged to entrust the collection of foreign dues to a commission of foreigners until order was restored. In carrying out this new arrangement the countries concerned, Britain, America and France, nominated one person each to take charge of the new department. Mr T. Wade, whom we have met before, was the first British representative, and as he spoke Chinese, he took charge; but within a year he was replaced by Mr H. N. Lay. In 1856, Lay used six armoured revenue vessels in the Customs' service, and later visited England to contract for the construction of a steam fleet and secure the services of a number of British naval officers.

Initially, Lay was successful in his endeavours. The eight gunboats, one or two of them powerful vessels capable of carrying two hundred men or more, arrived in China early in 1863 under the command of Captain Sherard Osborne, RN. But the local governors and generals would not allow such a powerful force to remain in the sole command of a foreigner, and at their insistence, Prince Kung and the Peking authorities refused to ratify the arrangement.

Lay had imagined himself commanding directly the fleet as a foreigner engaged by the central Chinese Government to perform certain work for them, *not* under them, and considered that the notion of a gentleman acting under an Asiatic barbarian was preposterous. He could not, as Bruce did, understand that for Britain, at any rate, the days of coercion had passed away, and that time should be allowed for the Chinese to learn gradually in their own way how to rise in the scale of nations.

China's refusal to buy and finance the fleet meant the end of Lay's scheme. The flotilla was taken over by Bruce for the British Government, and Lay was replaced by Robert Hart as the chief of Chinese Maritime Customs, a position he held most successfully for over forty years, becoming the friendly adviser of successive Chinese rulers. Lay, blinded by his own egotism and ambition, ascribed his failure to the ill will of Sir Frederick Bruce, but it is doubtful whether Lay's fleet, under the leadership of such a domineering man, would have been of much use to China.

This incident shows the great power possessed by local authorities and provincial public opinion in China. As has been shown in the study of the Taiping Rebellion, it was largely the militia forces under the command of Chinese gentry or local magistrates, operating under governors of provinces, and commanded loosely by the Generalissimo Tsêng Kuo-fan, which finally quelled that rebellion. Only in the Shanghai area was it achieved with the help of the foreign-led and foreign-trained armies; not elsewhere.

These militia forces have been both a strength and weakness

to China throughout the ages. In the nineteenth and twentieth centuries their influence varied. They were patriotic, rebellious and internecine in turn. The armies of the warlords of the twentieth appear to be direct descendants of these gentry-led bands, both the terms ' gentry ' and ' warlord ' having a different political significance.

An Imperial decree from Peking on the Militia Corps in the Provinces shows how the central government tried to get the bands under the local mandarins instead of leaving them to be led by unattached local gentry. Dated 5 January 1864 and translated from the *Peking Gazette*, it reads:

I have the honour to enclose the translation of an Imperial decree taken from the *Peking Gazette*, detailing the abuses that have arisen from the want of proper control over the local militia stating that these bodies in Chihli and Shantung have been placed under the command of the local magistrates and directing the same course to be pursued in Honan and in other districts where tranquillity is restored. I have had frequent occasion with reference to the province of Moukden and other places, to draw attention of His Excellency Wensiag to the bad effects of allowing the formation of these independent bodies of ' braves '. They took rise in the inability of the government to protect the people from banditti, but gradually they have become a scourge to the industrious and peaceable, and a standing menace to the authority of the government.

The Grand Secretariat has received the following Imperial Edict – the local militia organized in the different provinces was originally established with a view to afford mutual assistance and protection, to repress brigandages and robbery, and to take the place of regular soldiery where these were deficient in number. While there have been, no doubt, numerous cases in which they have assisted the Government troops in the protection of their homesteads, there have been on the other hand degenerate leaders of militia, who, relying upon their stockades have set at nought the constituted authorities, have taken upon themselves the administration of the law, have banded together to oppose the collection of taxes and have settled their private enmities by force of arms; and still worse there have been those, who after deliberation, have entered upon illegal courses, have captured cities, and have murdered officers, like for instance Liu Te-sh'en in Shantung, Li Chan in Honan, and Miao P'ei-lin in Anhwei, who have one after another been at the head of disturbances all of which have been organized among the local militia. Although these men, like grasshoppers opposing their arms to the progress of a cart, have been completely crushed, they have nevertheless occasioned considerable annoyance to the Government troops.

There are no doubt good as well as bad men among those who manage the affairs of the militia, but the consequence of there being one or two among the militia leaders who, relying upon their power, have disregarded the laws, has been that the Government has found itself with an unmanageable affair on its hands (like the tail that has become too large for turning). The increasing evils resulting from the mismanagement of the militia completely oppose the ideas which the Government held in allowing the people to protect themselves viz: the protection of the country and the repression of disorder in its very commencement.

The militia of Chihli and Shantung have already been placed under the command of the local magistrates, and as the rebellion (Taiping) is being gradually extinguished, his Majesty, with a view to concentrating the military authority, commands that the affairs of the different bodies of militia in Honan be in like manner put into the hands of the Government officials.

If the local authorities conscientiously discharge their duty in this affair and act in perfect harmony with the people, the people will trust in them for the protection of their homes and there will be no further resistance of authority.

The Governor of Honan, Chang Chi-wei, is hereby to instruct the different local magistrates to discharge this business with all their heart and strength that there may not be a mere name of making such a change without a reality.

For the organization of militia in the other provinces, officers of character and ability should be chosen to manage the affair with care and success so that good results may be obtained causing the people to receive the benefit of this scheme for mutual protection and assistance, of avoiding cases of contempt of the law and resistance to the authorities, of affording protection against robbery, and inaugurating a system for the prevention of disturbances. Let this Edict be published in the different provinces. Respect this.

In the First China War there occurred an incident in May 1841 relating to these gentry-led bands, which the communist historians of today represent as an early patriotic response to foreign intervention. As has been described, after Gough called off his assault on Canton on hearing of Captain Elliot's armistice, a group of gentry-led Chinese from the villages around massed at San-Yuan-li, and threatened to continue the struggle.

This San-Yuan-li incident has been blown up and distorted out of all recognition. The present day communist version of it is described by Frederic Wakeman Jr of the University of California, mainly from Chinese sources, and the following account is a précis of his description: By military standards the troops behaved exceptionally well – as Gough had exhorted them to do – and there was little rowdiness or drunkenness. But there was no question that the British did some looting. The word loot was of Indian origin and first used in this war, and San-Yuan-li was subject to these raids: gates and fences were broken down, livestock seized, and clothes stolen; graves were opened and plundered by the Chinese camp followers from the South; and what was most offensive, women were raped by Sepoys in the town. These incidents caused the local braves, composed of males between sixteen and sixty, to gather up swords and spears, and what arms they could, and assemble menacingly on the hill in front of the British camp.

Then occurred the skirmish already described on page 33 of this book, when, in a storm which made their muskets unusable, the Sepoy company was relieved by Royal Marines with percussion weapons, and the Chinese driven back for the loss of one private killed. The prefect of Canton was sent for to disperse the bands which still hung around, and when the prefect arrived, he, two local Chinese magistrates and Captain Moore representing the British, walked across the ridge towards the militia. When they reached the braves, the Chinese soldiers refused to let Captain Moore through their ranks, and the three Chinese officials went on alone. The officials told the gentry leading the braves that peace had already been signed, and warned them that they would be responsible for any incidents. While the peasants grumbled and threatened the gentry slipped quietly out of the crowd and returned to their own homes. Leaderless, the irregular braves slowly and grudgingly dispersed. By the afternoon of 1 June 1841 the British had re-embarked, and Canton was left again to itself.

To the British San-Yuan-li was only a skirmish, and not reported in either Elliot's or Gough's official correspondence, but the Chinese turned it into a great popular victory. Tales of Chinese heroism circulated after the affair. It was said that the gongs of San-Yuan-li had been sounded, and 25,000 men from

103 villages had rushed, with mattocks and hoes as weapons, into battle. They broke the British ranks and killed one hundred of them (actually one British private was killed). The British, it was said, offered 10,000 silver dollars to ransom their many dead. Thus, the official records became distorted, and a generation of Cantonese firmly believed that peasant troops had smashed the British attacking force. Finally, the Chinese Communist historians have enshrined this incident. Out of the humiliating defeats of the Opium War they have been able to extract a great popular victory blemished only by the cowardice of the Manchu officials. Today, in Red China, every child's history book contains an account of this battle. Every tablet, every shrine to the dead of San-Yuan-li has been carefully preserved by the local history bureau of the province, and the skirmish has been turned into the first popular movement against foreign imperialism.

Thus, in the period covered so far, the militia is shown in 1841, at least in Chinese eyes, as a patriotic national force capable of leading resistance to foreigners, and in the Taiping Rebellion, as an important body loyal to the Manchus, and one which played the major role in finally defeating that long outbreak in 1864, by the capture of Nanking.

Besides the physical force which well-led militia could provide, it has also been shown that high-ranking officials could persuade the Peking authorities on occasions to change their policy. But lesser officials could also make their opinions felt in China at this time. Three major power groups affected the decision-making process – the Imperial throne, high officials civilian and military, and the lesser officials. All officials had the traditional right to send memorials expressing their views to the Emperor, and these were carefully studied and, at times, acted upon. Thus ' literati opinion ' or *ch'ing-i*[1] influenced Imperial policy. The influence appears to have been in the direction of the maintenance of the *status quo*: it encouraged resistance to French territorial expansion in Vietnam; it advocated the withholding of rights to countries like the United States to extend missionary work; it added its voice in the discouragement of Germany's covetous aims; and supported official resistance to railway and mining concessions.

During the forty years following the signing of Lord Elgin's

[1] *ch'ing-i* means pure discussion, and some scholars object to the freer translation to imply literati opinion, as used above.

Treaty in 1860, China and Britain remained on friendly terms. It was with other countries that China was now in conflict: at war with France in Indo-China; at enmity with Russia over the violation of China's frontiers by Russian gold prospectors in the 1880s; and finally fighting hopelessly against Japan to retain Korea.

# 5 Wars with France and Japan

Since the reign of Louis XIV Frenchmen had aspired to establish an empire in South-East Asia. Lacking merchants to serve as their vanguard for imperial expansion, France initially made use of missionaries instead.

In 1787 a missionary bishop supported, with ships and war materials, the exiled ruler of Annam, and helped him to reconquer his dominions. In return the sovereign, who now assumed the dignity of Emperor, gave certain privileges to French and Spanish missionaries, and hired French engineers to fortify his chief cities.

His successors, however, persecuted the missionaries and their converts and in 1858 and 1861 French expeditions were sent out to Annam to protect them and extend French influence. The 1858 expedition captured Saigon in the south, but very little had been learnt about that part of Asia, and it came as a surprise that the people there resisted foreign occupation, and that France would have been better advised to have seized Hanoi in the north. The south had been chosen because it was hoped that, by controlling the Mekong delta, access could be had to the fertile inland districts up river. It was found, however, that the Mekong was unnavigable, and a better route lay through Hanoi and the Red River.

In 1873 Lieutenant Garnier with a handful of soldiers was sent up from Saigon to Hanoi ostensibly to investigate pirates. On arrival, he demanded a treaty giving the French control of the delta, and within five days he had stormed the citadel of Hanoi. Then followed the capture of nearly all the strong places between Hanoi and the sea. ' Within a month after his arrival the whole of lower Tongking lay at the mercy of the young lieutenant and some two hundred Frenchmen '; and the Annamese in their plight, called upon the suzerain state of China for protection.

The policy of China towards its vassals was to expect as little as possible from them in the hope that they would seldom ask for help. Yet when a subject state was menaced by a foreign power, she did not fail in her duties.

The piracy which Garnier had been initially looking into was being carried out by bands of outlaws known as the Black Flags. These were originally scattered remnants of rebels who had fled into the wild regions along the southern borders of China after the capture of Nanking in 1864. Besides appealing to China for aid, the Annamese also asked for help from the Black Flags; and these were the first to respond, swarming down from their strongholds upon Garnier's detachments.

The Black Flags provide a link with the previous chapter on the Taiping Rebellion. Liu Yung-fu, their commander, was a Hakka like Hung Hsiu-ch'uan, the Heavenly King of the Taipings. He joined the Triad Society and was an ally of the Taipings in their struggle against the Central Government. Because of this, when the Chinese Government prevailed, he became an outlaw and moved with his followers, including some Taipings, into Vietnam, where he helped subdue Miao tribesmen hostile to the Annamese. In this struggle, Liu's band, which had risen to over 2,000, fought with distinction, and was rewarded by having its control confirmed over the northern reaches of the Red River. It was said here that he was so independent of the capital at Hué that 'people know only him and know not the Vietnamese king.'

The Black Flags on this occasion, after a succession of skirmishes, lured Garnier to his death in an ambush. But his successor, on agreeing to withdraw the French from some of the fortified towns, obtained by this concession a great deal for France in the north. This was embodied in a treaty signed with the Annamese in 1874, which was the basis for the future presence of the French in Vietnam. It gave France a virtual protectorate over Tongking, opened Hanoi to trade, and allowed the establishment of a consul at Hanoi as well as a French resident at the Annamese capital of Hué.

Nevertheless, French influence in the north remained shadowy, and China did not withdraw her claim to suzerainty over Annam.

In 1876 the usual tribute-bearing embassy left Annam for Peking, and in 1879 Chinese troops suppressed a rebellion in Tongking without the Annamese calling upon the French for help. Thus, although the Emperor of Annam had been persuaded to sign peace treaties recognizing a protectorate by France in 1874 and again in 1883, China refused to recognize their validity. China sent troops to Vietnam, and when these were badly defeated in open battle with the French, decided to attempt mediation to maintain her rights.

For these negotiations the Peking authorities chose Li Hung-chang who had been governor of Kiangsu in Gordon's operations, and was now vicerory of the province of Chihli in which Peking lay. Li's negotiations were very prolonged, and the pattern of events followed closely that between China and Britain in the 1840s and 1850s, agreements being arrived at by the plenipotentiaries only to be disallowed by the central governments at Peking or Paris, and military operations being carried on without the open declaration of war by either side. For example, a convention was agreed upon by Frédéric Albert Bourée, French Minister to China, and Li Hung-chang. This was known as the Bourée Convention and seemed to settle the differences between the two countries. But there followed a series of petitions from Chinese provincial officials protesting at the terms. This appears to have been an example of the power of *ch'ing-i* or literati opinion already discussed. On this occasion the Chinese officials were against it, but so was the government at Paris. Having first shown themselves favourable to the terms of Bourée's convention a change of ministry led to the reversal of the decision. It was rejected by the French on 5 March 1883.

Meanwhile, reinforcements from France arrived in the China Sea under Commandant Rivière and were sent to reinforce the consular guard at Hanoi, which had been shut up there. Rivière occupied the city by force, and after a year spent chiefly in Hanoi during which time the Black Flags again swarmed around the city, cutting off stragglers and harassing the garrison, he decided to make a demonstration against them. 'But on 19 May 1883, he lost his life in this sortie, a victim of the same contempt of the enemy that had ended the career of Garnier.' French popular sentiment was given a fillip by this incident. Rivière, who had been a national hero after his occupation of Hanoi, was reported to have been ' vilely beheaded '. The French public let out a cry for revenge. By mid-May 1883, both nations had taken long strides in the direction of war.

Some officials in both camps were, however, dragging their feet. The Quai d'Orsay still hoped to attain its aims in Vietnam without provoking a war with the Chinese Empire, and was solicitous that Peking realize that the rejection of the Bourée agreement ' does not imply hostile intentions '.

In China, Li Hung-chang, hero of many operations against the Taipings, whose presence in Tongking was expected to transform the fighting quality of the Imperial armies, was as anxious as the Quai d'Orsay to avoid a fight. After receiving orders to assume command in the south, Li sent a memorial stating reasons against fighting France and for the termination of his appointment as generalissimo. He argued that the French would not be willing to brave the dangers of malaria and difficulties of terrain to take much territory, and would only try to occupy areas in the reach of their navy – which the Chinese could not stop them doing – and not the whole of Vietnam. Li believed that China should not interfere just because Vietnam failed to ask China's permission to sign the 1874 treaty. As for himself, he was willing to negotiate, but he did not want to take command of the Chinese armies and then be beaten. He thought that his appointment to command in the south was a plot by his enemies to remove him from the position of viceroy in the key province of Chihli. His certain defeat by the French in the south would, he believed, ruin his career.

Li was overruled in his plea for peace, although oddly enough he was still entrusted with the general conduct of the campaign against the French. On land, the Chinese gave such a good account of themselves, that the French government, after a spectacular defeat of their troops at Langson, was forced to resign. At sea, however, it was quite another story, and a Chinese fleet together with the naval arsenal at Foochow was destroyed by French bombardment. Meanwhile, the French had occupied the Vietnamese capital of Hué and had imposed a treaty by which Vietnam withdrew from Chinese suzerainty and a French protectorate was established over the whole country. Li thought the Chinese victory at Langson gave a favourable opportunity for making peace; and terms were agreed at Paris in June 1885, which acquiesced in the French conquest of Vietnam. This treaty was drawn up with the help on the Chinese side of one of Sir Robert Hart's customs officials.

Sir Robert Hart's position in China from 1863-1909 was a most important one, for the Maritime Customs, of which he was head, became an outstanding instrument of indirect British political control of Imperial China. The origin of Hart's position was mentioned on page 146. In 1853, when the Taipings occupied the native quarter of Shanghai, British, American and French representatives were invited to control the Shanghai customs on behalf of the Manchu authorities. After Lord Elgin's Anglo-Chinese Treaty signed in Peking in 1860, this system was extended and consolidated. Sir Robert Hart was made Inspector-General of the Imperial Maritime Customs, and in theory was subordinated to the Tsungli Yamen, the new office dealing with foreign affairs; but in effect he became the agent of Britain and other foreign powers. By this means he was able to uphold the Manchu régime with the customs revenues, to neutralize provincial movements towards rebellion or partition, and at the same time to lay down favourable trade and tariff regulations. Also, unlike land, salt and pawnshops, which were static as sources of revenue, the customs expanded with the trade, and provided surplus funds available for new Chinese undertakings.[1]

Following the Sino-French War and the treaty in 1885 which ended it, France, as we have seen, consolidated her position in Tongking and Annam at the expense of China's suzerainty. Britain was well established in Hong Kong and the Treaty Ports for trade, and through Sir Robert Hart, had the ear, and control, of the Chinese authorities in Peking. Now it was the turn of other countries to get more deeply involved in China's affairs – America with her scattered Protestant missionaries, Russia with a trans-Siberian railway and mining interests in Mongolia and Manchuria, Germany from territorial claims, later met by her seizure of Kiaochow in Shantung, and Japan in a controversy over Korea.

The Treaty of Peking in 1860, and the similar treaties with France and the United States of America which followed, allowed missionaries to enter the interior of China, and the missionaries

---

[1] There was set up at this time, with the help of these funds, the 'Self Strengthening Movement'. It proved, however, to be far from successful.

made every use of their new privileges, which included the owning of property. By 1889 there were 1,300 Protestant missionaries, mostly American, with 55,000 converts. But the Roman Catholic Fathers had done better, numbering in 1897 some 750 priests, mostly French, with about half a million Christian followers.

This was not a great number in relation to the 500 million people of China, but the impact of the missionaries was nevertheless significant. Each Church aimed at replacing the native religions by their own particular doctrine, a fact which disturbed many Chinese; and as the missionaries enjoyed the support of their consuls, they were powerful enough to protect their followers, who, in turn, could now obtain a special status in law and society. In lawsuits converts were often represented by their missionaries, and the influence of the latter sometimes procured them immunity from taxation.

Under an Imperial decree of 1899, Roman Catholic bishops were declared to be equal in rank and dignity to viceroys and governors, vicars-general and archdeacons equal to prefects of the first and second class, and ordinary priests as ranking with magistrates. Bishop Favier, whose Peitang Cathedral[1] stood in Peking on an eminence overlooking the Imperial Palace, declared that these privileges were given on the initiative of the Chinese Government in an attempt to gain control over its Christian subjects by incorporating their spiritual leaders into the official system of the Empire, a policy which had been successfully adopted with Buddhism throughout China, and with Islam in Yunnan, Shensi, Kansu, and Chinese Turkestan.

There were British Protestant missionaries besides the American, and with strong moral and financial backing from the Evangelicals of Britain; but their activities did not altogether escape criticism. For example, in 1869 in a debate in the House of Lords, the Duke of Somerset asked, 'What right have we to be trying to convert the Chinese in the middle of their country?' and Lord Grey, referring to the number of British gunboats in Chinese waters, remarked that 'force could not help in religion'.

After the Sino-French War there were more cordial relations

---

[1] Its erection wounded the susceptibilities and suspicions of the court and people alike. It was besieged with the legations in 1900 during the Boxer Rising.

between China and the Western Powers under the influence of the liberal statesman Li Hung-chang supported by the resolute old Dowager Empress Tz'u and Prince Chun, the Emperor's father. Emperor Kuang Hsu assumed the reins of government on 7 February 1887, having succeeded Tz'u's son, Tung Chih, in 1875 as a minor, and he reigned until the end of the century when the old Empress took over again. Prince Kung was dismissed because of the Chinese failures in the Sino-French war.

At this time the Peking authorities planned to bring in Western improvements and reform. Officials were sent abroad to study European civilization; mathematics and other Western studies were recognized as subjects for the civil service examinations; the Imperial Tungwan College at Peking was founded to educate some of the scholar-gentry in Western learning; railways[1] were constructed at the instigation of Li Hung-chang – the Russians were allowed to construct their trans-Siberia railway across Manchuria – and ninety miles of roadway were built from Tientsin to beyond Taku. A move was also made to reorganize arsenals and naval yards on European lines.

All these progressive activities upset the main body of the scholar-gentry in whose hands the government of China had long been. In some of the reforms of the period their prestige and profit were both affected. Sir Robert Hart's Maritime Customs had long taken a lucrative source of gain from the clutches of the sea-board officials. In 1876 *likin,* or internal local transit dues on opium, was abolished in favour of a stipulated tariff of £30 per chest at the port combined with not more than £80 per chest for internal transit, and *likin* profits for local mandarins ended. Projected railways threatened further to curtail the transit dues on roads and rivers, which enriched local officials, especially in the business of transporting the tribute rice to the capital, a source of large illicit profit to those concerned. One by one their old privileges were being denied them, and in each case the origin of their grievances could be traced to un-Asiatic foreign influence.

Spurred on by fear, the jealousy and the hatred of the scholar-gentry for foreigners materialized into a policy of resistance to all measures that traced their origin to the outside world, and of concerted movements against any foreigners living

---

[1] A line to the Kaiping coal mines was constructed in 1883.

in the country who could be safely and conveniently attacked. It was middle-piece officials who appear to have been responsible for the anti-foreign riots; the peasants and mobs were always under direction even in the worst disorders. The upper echelon of the mandarins, at any rate until the end of the century, were not affected to the same degree. In the Boxer Rebellion of 1900, however, the Dowager Empress and some viceroys and governors were supporting the anti-foreign movement clandestinely.

To start with, the vengeance of the anti-foreign mandarins was wreaked chiefly upon missionaries living in the interior, and the disturbances which followed have, in consequence, been called the anti-missionary riots. It does not appear, however, that the missionaries were set on because of their creed, but on account of their race. They had to face the fiercest attacks involving enormous loss of property and some loss of life because as a class they were more isolated and exposed than other foreigners. In the 1840s, 1850s and 1860s, the entire educated class in China was opposed to the coming of Europeans. Later, when European strength proved irresistible, the literati seem to have contented themselves with the reflection that their country was large, and that foreigners were at least confined to the Treaty Ports. Then the French were allowed to send people inland. Concessions granted to Catholics were demanded by other missions; and after this the merchants required, and were allowed to do the same. But few foreigners realized the consternation all this caused throughout China. It meant to the ruling class the invasion of their private preserves for squeezing and taxing the people, to the Chinese merchants the unrestricted competition of foreign rivals, to the multitude of boatmen, carriers, and pedlars, the extinction of their means of livelihood by the introduction of steamers, railways and Western inventions. ' The missionaries themselves had been regarded as comparatively harmless, but used as an argument for the invasion of China, they became a menace to the country '; therefore disturbances began to make the homes of the missionaries no longer safe, and drove them back to the Treaty Ports.

The following accounts of riots are taken from contemporary reports. One of the first occurred at Tientsin on 21 June 1870. It was caused by Chinese suspicions of what was happening at a French Roman Catholic foundling hospital where bounties were paid for children in the last stages of illness so that they might not die without Christian baptism. The report got around that the Sisters were killing the children to get their eyes and hearts to make some sort of medical specific. A mob formed outside the hospital and eventually turned on the French consulate as well. The French consul was thoroughly alarmed and rushed off to find some official who would quell the angry mob. But the officials were as helpless as he was, and merely advised him to go back to his compound and stay there until things quietened down. The consul seems to have been cut down and killed on his way back, after firing into the angry mob to clear a passage. The mob then turned on the orphanage, butchered the defenceless Sisters, and set the place on fire after taking away the children. A Russian with his young bride and a friend were killed in mistake for French people as they tried to escape to a settlement two miles away. Nothing serious was done to the Protestant buildings in the vicinity. The total number of victims in the massacre amounted to twenty Europeans and as many more Chinese servants and converts.

The seven foreign ministers in Peking sent a joint note calling for immediate and vigorous measures. Prince Kung replied that the authorities had been ordered to suppress the riot and arrest the lawbreakers, and punish the mandarins at Tientsin who had allowed it to happen.

In a few weeks the naval forces of the leading Powers reached Tientsin, and the French demanded the execution of the prefect and magistrate of Tientsin for having instigated the riot. The Chinese refused to do this until a trial had established their guilt, and the whole matter of retribution was conducted in a dilatory manner. The Chinese were not much concerned at the wrath of the Powers because two of them, France and Germany, had just begun a war against each other. The Europeans were upset to find that thousands of fans containing pictures of the riot and the murdering of foreigners were being sold in Tientsin. When accused by the British of allowing this, and thus showing support to the perpetrators of a horrible crime, the Chinese minister replied: ' These fans are made to suit the taste of the people, and the fact that such engravings will cause a better sale for the fans is a conclusive argument that there is no sentiment of regret or sorrow among the people over the result of the riot. There is, undoubtedly greater unanimity of opinion in Tientsin in favour of the rioters than in Ireland among the peasantry in favour of one of their number who shoots his landlord. If this feeling in Ireland is strong enough to baffle all attempts of the English government to bring to justice by the ordinary forms of law a peasant accused of injuring the person or property of his landlord, is it surprising that this feeble central government should find it difficult to ascertain and punish the rioters in a city of four hundred thousand inhabitants, all of whom either aided in the massacre or sympathized with the rioters.'

In spite of these excuses, however, action was eventually taken. The prefect and magistrate were banished to Manchuria, and sixteen Chinese who were proved to have killed foreigners were decapitated in the presence of the foreign consuls, and an indemnity was paid to the French for loss of life and property.

Over the years there were periods of outbreaks and violence, interspersed with periods of calm. In 1883-4 a series of riots resulted in the destruction of eighteen Christian chapels in Kwangtung. Between 1885 and 1890 there were continual troubles in Shantung where a German consul sent to investigate found the chief firebrand to be a member of the Chinese Foreign Office. Other troubles arose in Kiangsi; and Szechwan in the middle-west was one of the worst areas. Here a series of riots attended by looting occurred during the years 1886-90, when Catholic and Protestant missionary posts in many places were destroyed and converts persecuted, while the rioters surged about the countryside proclaiming that they had orders from the Emperor and the magistrates to root out and destroy Christianity. The government at Peking, when appealed to, compensated the missionaries for the loss of their houses, and acknowledged their right under treaty to rebuild. But as new chapels and schools were erected, angry gangs again sprang up to burn them, in one place the premises being destroyed three times in four years. An ominous feature was the persistence of the mobs which seemed to be always on hand to persecute the Christians.

In Wuhu, a treaty port on the Yangtze, a riot occurred in May 1891. This led to a series of riots up and down the river. It started when two Sisters of the Jesuit Mission were accosted in the street by some child beggars seeking alms. They stopped to pat the two urchins on the head and ask what they wanted, when,

F

with a cry that the foreign devils were bewitching them, a furious multitude suddenly sprung up from nowhere, hurled themselves upon the women and carried them off to the magistrate. He succeeded in appeasing the people for the moment, but two days later the mob broke down the gates of the Jesuit Mission and, digging up the bodies of some foundlings recently buried in the compound, declared that they saw evidence of their having been cut up for surgical experiments. In an hour the whole buildings were in flames, and by nightfall the crowd was attacking the British Consulate, the Imperial Customs buildings, and other houses occupied by foreigners. Fortunately their inmates managed to find refuge on a steamer. The Customs house was successfully defended against the mob until three Chinese gunboats luckily steamed up the river next day and drove the rioters off by firing a broadside or two. Quiet was then restored.

Here the notable feature of the rising was the violence shown towards the Roman Catholics, all of whose buildings (including a fine cathedral) were looted and destroyed, and also attacks on Consulate and Customs posts, which had no connection with missionary work. The accusations against the Catholics were a repetition of those heard at Tientsin.

Similar convulsions took place during this summer at several places in the Yangtze valley – none of them, however, attended with loss of life. One at Ichang, a port on the river west of Hankow, involved the ruin of every missionary building in the city. Here, too, the local authorities seemed strangely incapable of dealing with the rioters, although there were not very many concerned. In several places, including Ichang, Chinese soldiers were recognized among the most active incendiaries. Their methodical work showed that they were under orders to destroy.

The climax of foreign feeling was reached in 1895 in two outbreaks in the widely separated provinces of Szechwan and Fukien. At Chengtu, the capital of Szechwan, a riot broke out on the day of the Dragon boat festival, ending on the following day with the razing of every missionary post in the city. The foreigners' lives were spared, but some were maltreated, and several who went off to the magistrates to seek protection were ignored. Official connivance was patent. In Fukien, murder was added to destruction when an armed party attacked a group of missionaries in a hill village and massacred ten of them. The village, situated about a hundred miles north-west of Foochow, had been used as a hot weather station by Protestants of various denominations in the province. As was usually the case, the missionaries were very popular among the people of the district, and by trusting them were taken by surprise. This time it was the work of a secret society called the 'Vegetation Society' who called up the riffraff of the people to terrorize parts of Fukien, including some of the magistrates there. The society has been compared to the Mafia in Sicily, and when the prefect of the region called for troops, the influence of the society managed to delay their arrival. After indignant protests from the foreign consuls at Foochow two hundred regulars did arrive, but they came too late to save the missionaries. It had been rumoured that they had contributed money to bring in the troops. To avenge this two hundred Vegetarians fell on the missionaries, killed ten of them, wounded several others, destroyed the foreigners' houses, and then disappeared as swiftly and silently as they had come.

The Chinese authorities were half-hearted in dealing with the disturbances, but they did at least offer monetary compensation for the loss of foreigners' property. They were less willing to punish the officials in the provinces concerned. In 1895, however, the concerted action of the American, British and French Ministers forced the authorities to agree to a commission to investigate the responsibility of the viceroy of Szechwan for continued disturbances in that province. The American Minister proposed the commission, and the British stepped in with an ultimatum that the officials should be punished. A fleet was sent up river, and finally France intervened to explain to China that to avoid trouble she must punish the officials. The Viceroy was degraded from office and, as a warning to others, never employed again. The *taotais* (prefects) and other officers concerned were punished in various ways.

## JAPAN

By 1894 it was not only with the European nations that China was in conflict. Japan now entered the scene in earnest, in a dispute with China over Korea.

Korea was nominally a vassal state of China. But Japan also

put forward claims, and tribute embassies were sent to Japan as well as to Peking, though with greater regularity and continuity to the latter. The Korean monarch, indeed, received his reign-name from the Chinese Emperor, accepted their calendar – a marked sign of vassalage – from his hands, and personally had to welcome any Chinese ambassadors outside his capital Seoul.

There were a series of internal troubles in Korea at the end of the nineteenth century owing to a struggle for power between two court factions – the Mins, mostly members of the clan to which the Queen belonged, and the Anti-Mins headed by the King's father and regent, who had usurped power during his son's minority, who ruled with great severity, and was bitterly anti-foreign. At times, Japanese consular and diplomatic officials were ill-used, and Japan was much inclined to send a force to protect her interests there. The misrule also led to a rebellion by a Korean sect called the *Tong Haks,* who followed a few Christian principles mingled with their mixed oriental doctrine, and are sometimes compared with the Taipings. The *Tong Haks* having established themselves in the southern provinces of Korea, marched in 1893 on the palace at Seoul to demand redress for their grievances.

An appeal from the Korean king for help to deal with the *Tong Haks* led to both China and Japan sending troops. But Japan, glad of a chance of taking control of Korea, sent a much larger detachment, and through the presence of this powerful force browbeat the Korean king into agreeing to her suzerainty there. China thereupon attempted to reassert her sovereignty, and war between China was not far off.

The fighting began before war was declared. On 23 July 1894 three fast cruisers sent from Japan to intercept Chinese rein-forcements on their way to Korea clashed with, and disabled two Chinese men-of-war, and sank the escorted transport with 1,200 aboard.

In Korea, Chinese forces were pressing towards Japanese-held Seoul from the north and the south. The Chinese northern force, reinforced by more Chinese troops from across the Yalu in Man-churia, and comprising 13,000 men, was concentrated at Pyong-yang, the key to North Korea. This Chinese position was attacked by 14,000 Japanese on 15 September 1894. The Japanese made a right hook round the Chinese eastern flank with part of their force and then attacked from all sides. Although the Pyongyang position was a strong one, incorporating 27 individual forts, Chinese resistance was feeble. Surprised and disheartened at the unexpected appearance of the Japanese all around, only one Chinese general showed much spirit, and his death was the end of all real resistance. The Japanese victory at Pyongyang was followed by a general Chinese retreat across the Yalu where, in spite of meeting up with reinforcements, they made no stand. The result was that Korea was swept clear of Chinese.

On the day following the Battle of Pyongyang a naval engagement took place in the Bay of Korea. In early September, Chinese transports carrying reinforcements had crossed the bay from Talien-wan near Port Arthur. As they were returning, they met the Japanese fleet. The two fleets were nearly equal in strength, with twelve vessels on either side. But the skill and efficiency of the gunners and seamen was almost wholly on the Japanese side. In the battle China's best ships were badly damaged, and although losses in men and material could be made good, the Chinese had not the will to replace them, and the Japanese were left in control of the seas around Korea. This naval victory together with the victory on land at Pyongyang meant the end of the war in Korea, and hostilities now moved to China proper.

Japan's objectives were the fortresses of Port Arthur and Wei-hai-wei, guarding, on either side, the entrance to the Gulf of Pechili which opened up the way to Taku, and the traditional route[1] up the Peiho River to Peking. The Japanese plan was to reduce each of these fortresses in turn while their other army crossed the Yalu into Manchuria and captured the ancient Manchu capital at Moukden before moving south-west on Peking likewise.

The attack and capture of Port Arthur was an important operation of the war. The Chinese made the mistake of lining up the ships they still possessed in fixed positions underneath the fortress. This meant that the Japanese landings on the neck of the Liaotung Peninsula, 100 miles to the north, were uncontested. The Japanese next marched down on the 22 supporting forts of Port Arthur. They approached the dockyard by converging roads, expecting opposition, but meeting none. Then on 20 November, after a skirmish, the Chinese garrison was driven out of

[1] The route of General Hope Grant's expedition in 1860.

the first fort reached. It was the same story with each of the other forts in succession. By noon on the following day, the whole land defences had succumbed, and in the evening, the Japanese, at the cost of 288 casualties, were possessors of one of the strongest places and best equipped dockyards in Eastern Asia. The *China Gazette* of December 1894 describes the feebleness of the Chinese resistance:

A first-class fortress, splendidly armed and garrisoned by 20,000 troops is stormed and taken in a few hours by an inferior force. It is a pitiable spectacle. In 1860, one of the Taku forts was cannonaded by a park of 11 siege guns, 36 field cannon, and a battery of rockets, which succeeded in blowing up the principal magazine, an incident calculated to demoralize the stoutest troops. When assaulted, and finally captured by nearly 3,000 French and British, the garrison were found to number but 500, of whom but 100 escaped alive, while the attacking party had 22 killed and 179 wounded. That was a sample of the kind of defence the Chinese could make a generation ago against the best troops in the world. Every one of the Port Arthur forts might have done as well. They were proportionally better armed, better disposed for defence, better fortified, more numerously garrisoned. Yet the total loss inflicted by them upon their assailants did not greatly exceed the loss suffered by the allies in capturing a single fort guarded by five hundred Chinamen. How such an extraordinary discrepancy of results is to be explained it is impossible to say. The Chinese appear to have been totally demoralized. The cruel lesson they received may be for their nation's good, but it is difficult not to be moved to some sentiment of compassion by the spectacle of a great nation put to such signal shame.

Upon entering Port Arthur the Japanese found the heads and mutilated bodies of some of their captured comrades suspended near the gates, Although, as at Pyongyang, notices had been posted in Chinese saying that all who surrendered would be kindly treated, the murder of Japanese prisoners led to a collapse of discipline among the victors. For four or five days the Japanese officers were quite unable to control their soldiery, and the inhabitants and garrison of Port Arthur were massacred without mercy.

Port Arthur and Talien-wan nearby became bases for further Japanese operations; and when Wei-hai-wei fell in its turn, the Japanese army in Korea moved north to take Moukden, the old home of the reigning dynasty,[1] and the burial place of its earlier sovereigns, whose capture would have involved a loss of prestige among their Chinese subjects quite out of keeping with its strategic importance.

But the Japanese never did capture Moukden. Considering that China had taken sufficient punishment for her to accept any terms, Japan agreed to consider China's wish for negotiations for the suspension of hostilities. After some abortive Chinese attempts to negotiate through the medium of American officials, the Empress sent Li Hung-chang for talks with the Japanese at Shimonoseki; and an attempt at assassination of the old viceroy by a fanatic having failed, armistice terms were signed on 17 April 1895.

The terms of the Treaty of Shimonoseki were severe. The Chinese were forced to surrender their age-old suzerainty over Korea, to pay a large indemnity, and to cede to Japan the Pescadores, Formosa, and the Liaotung Peninsula – the last, however, by the triple intervention of Russia, France and Germany, was returned to China.

China's crushing defeat by her small neighbour revived European interest in China; for the disclosure of her weakness served as an invitation to the colonizing powers to compete for spheres of interest in the crumbling Chinese Empire. By 1895 most of the outlying dependencies of the Empire had been lopped off: Britain had taken Burma, France the countries of Indo-China, Russia the territories north of the Amur River and part of Chinese Turkestan, and Japan had received the fruits of her victory of 1894 mentioned above. Now Germany played her part in the story. In 1897, the murder of two German missionaries in Shantung led her to seize Kiaochow, a port of that province, in retaliation. She also gained extensive railway and mining concessions in Shantung. Cordier considers this action by Germany in 1897 to have been a major cause of the next great anti-foreign movement. Certainly it was only a few months later that riots and disturbances, the burning of mission houses and the persecution of converts began again. In May 1898 it was reported that there were associations organized along the border of Shantung and Chihli, declaring hostility against the Christians. The Imperial Court ordered the Governor of Shantung to investigate and to

[1] Ch'ing (Manchu).

maintain order. The Governor reported that the associations were called I Ho T'uan, who were of the I Ho sect and practised I Ho boxing, but there were no riots. This was the first time that the Boxers were reported in the Chinese documents. The Governor apparently wanted to minimize the matter, for the bills which the Boxers distributed actually declared their intention to kill the Christians. In October the Boxers began to act both in Chihli and Shantung. They set fire to over a hundred houses of the Christians, burned chapels and killed at least two Christians.

# 6 The Boxer Uprising

THE BOXERS

All secret societies,[1] ranging from the Masonic Order to the Ku Klux Klan, tend to shun publicity. In general, they usually have some religious or quasi-religious basis; they protect their 'mysteries' from curious outsiders, and regard a mutual self-help among members, and in some cases external charitable works, as sufficient justification for their existence. Chinese secret societies share these characteristics in varying degrees, although their particular significance in the nineteenth century derived from the considerable political influence they exercised. In China they stimulated a growing opposition to the Manchu dynasty as well as anti-foreign influences within the Empire.

There is evidence of the existence of secret societies in China for the last two thousand years, and throughout the centuries they have been associated with rebellions against successive Emperors. Even though the Chinese have shown themselves more tolerant than any other people in matters of religion, from earliest times Imperial tolerance did not extend to the *hui* or secret societies despite their frequent claims to be adhering to Buddhist or Taoist doctrines. Anti-dynastic risings were associated with the Ch'ih-mu or 'Red Eyebrows' in AD 18; with the Huang-chin or 'Yellow Turbans' in AD 184; with the 'White Lotus Sect' at the end of the Yuan dynasty in 1360; and with the 'Roaming Bandits' at the end of the Ming dynasty in 1644. Although they were often inspired by religious beliefs of one sort or another, the rebels sometimes concentrated their attention on land tax and land reform and frequently expressed a racial prejudice, too –

---

[1] The author is indebted to Mr K. W. Walker for this section on Chinese secret societies. Mr Walker spent many years in the Far East and recently delivered a paper on Chinese secret societies at Sandhurst.

thus the White Lotus condemned the Yuan dynasty because it was Mongol, and the secret societies of the Manchu dynasty also used this anti-foreign issue to advantage.

When the Manchus assumed power in China in 1644, they established a penal code to apply to the secret sects: their leaders were to be strangled and their accomplices sentenced to 100 blows with the long stick followed by lifelong banishment to a distance of 300 miles from their homes.

Nevertheless, risings by numerous sects continued throughout the years of the dynasty, and in 1794 there began a series of rebellions inspired by the White Lotus which lasted until 1815. They all put up Pretenders to the throne who invariably claimed to be reincarnations of Buddha and to be descended from the previous Ming dynasty. The repression of these rebellions revealed a defect of Manchu power. The standing army, comprising the Army of the Eight Banners and the Army of the Green Standard, often proved to be hopelessly inefficient, and the suppression of the risings devolved upon the local militia. The militia, as was seen, also played a large part in suppressing the Taiping Rebellion.

Other Chinese secret societies were the Vegetarian Society, Big Sword, Golden Bell, Eight Diagram Sects and Red Fist Society; but probably the most important was the Triad, or Three in Accord, or more simply the Hung Society. The Triad had a common origin with the White Lotus of north, central and west China, but developed its own characteristics as it flourished in a non-Mandarin-speaking part of China, in the three southern provinces of Kwang tung, Kwang si and Fukien, where dialects such as Cantonese, Hakka and Hokkien were spoken.

Records of the Triads appear in China about 1674. Members of the society formed a sworn brotherhood with the traditional aim embodied in the slogan. '*Sao Ch'ing Li Ming*', or 'Overthrow the Ch'ing and restore the Ming', a phrase which according to legend, appeared on the hilt of a magic sword which rose out of the earth for the salvation of five surviving monks of the Shao Lin monastery as they fled from the Imperial troops. From its inception, the Triad Society became a powerful force in southern China, and during the eighteenth and nineteenth centuries was associated with a series of rebellions against the Manchu dynasty, the most significant being the Taiping Rebellion from

1844-64 already described. This, as was seen, was not in origin a Triad revolt though there is little doubt that the 'Triads had a hand in it'. Apart from the Taiping Rebellion, the whole of the provinces of Kwang tung and Kwang si were in a ferment in 1850 and 1851 through the risings of authentic Triad groups. Canton was invested for a time, and the Pearl River – the main artery of trade – was under Triad control. Dissension among Triad leaders, however, led to piecemeal defeat. For once the Imperial troops showed initiative and efficiency. They rounded up the rebels, took them to Canton, and there beheaded them at the rate of 7,000 to 8,000 a day until almost 100,000 had been killed. It is estimated that in Kwan tung province alone, during this period of the Triad suppression, one million people were executed.

In 1853, the Chinese quarter of Shanghai was occupied by Triad rebels, members of the Small Dagger Society and the Society of Heaven and Earth. They encroached on territory allocated by treaty to foreign use and were only driven away the following year by British and American troops. This was the occasion when for safety's sake the Chinese authorities asked the Powers to take control of the Chinese Customs; and this ushered in Sir Robert Hart's long reign.

It seems probable that the Triads had a hand in the successful revolution which overthrew the Manchu dynasty and established the First Chinese Republic in 1911. Its instigator, Dr Sun Yat-sen, was a member of the society and had enlisted the aid of 20,000 of its fighting men in an attempt to overthrow the Manchu dynasty in 1900. In 1911 he again had Triad support. They did overthrow the Manchu dynasty in that year but instead of restoring the Ming created the First Chinese Republic.

But the most notorious of the secret societies operating during the Manchu dynasty were the Boxers and even less is known about them than about the others already mentioned. The first official mention of this sect occurs in 1727 when they are charged in an edict of that year with gathering crowds and stirring up 'the stupid people' under the pretext of practising their boxing cult. In 1747 Jesuits are said to have been expelled from China owing to their influence; in 1809 Emperor Chia ch'ing made an attempt to suppress them, and by 1815 they were driven underground. But the superstition of magical boxing 'kept the tradition of the sect alive in obscurity' until it revived in 1898 and became the focus of a serious anti-foreign and anti-Christian rising in Shantung and Chihli. In public the Boxers seem to have frequented fair grounds and behaved like ordinary mountebanks – erecting gambling booths, giving exhibitions of sword exercises and jujitsu, swindling people out of money and generally creating disorders. Behind closed doors, on the other hand, they inducted members by a form of religious gymnastics or magical boxing which involved a series of exercises of Taoist origin intended to endow the initiated with supernatural powers and create the superstition of invulnerability in war. The Boxers, in fact, appear to have practised a complicated system of physical and spiritual exercises which European observers oversimplified and called boxing. Finally, because the Boxers were eventually enlisted in the service of the Empress, some observers have classified them as militia. Steiger, for example, calls them volunteer militia and ignores their mystic rites. Certainly, they were unlike other secret societies in one respect: they supported the Manchus and were only anti-foreign. On their banners they wrote: '*Fu Ch'ing Mieh Yang*', or 'Support the Ch'ing, destroy the foreigner'. The Communists favour the classification of the Boxers as militia. By doing so the Boxers can be portrayed as patriots in Communist history books, like the militia of San Yuan-li in 1841 outside Canton, and the bands that helped to suppress the Taipings.

## THE DOWAGER EMPRESS

Yehonada, later Empress Tz'u Hsi, was born in 1836. Accounts of her parentage differ, but it seems probable that her father was an officer in the Army of the Manchu Eight Banners. A striking beauty, she was one of twenty-eight Manchu girls selected for the harem of Emperor Hsien Feng,[1] and began her political career as a third-grade concubine.

Despite formidable competition she became a favourite of the Emperor, who was weak, sickly and vicious, and bore him – or anyhow produced – a son. This gained her promotion to the first

---

[1] The Manchu Emperors of China in the period covered by this book were: Tauking, 1821; Hsien Feng, 1851, husband of the Empress Dowager Tz'u Hsi; Tung Chih, 1862, son of the Empress Dowager; Kuang Hsu, 1875, nephew of the Empress Dowager.

grade. Her personal ascendancy over the Emperor made her, while barely in the twenties, a force to be reckoned with in the tortuous precincts of the Imperial Court. She became Regent on Hsien Feng's death in 1861, continuing in that office until her son, Emperor Tung Chih, was declared to be of age in 1872.

Yehonada surrendered power with bad grace; but it was not long before the young Emperor took sick and died. Then her former authority as a Regent was restored for the reign of her nephew, Emperor Kuang Hsu, who succeeded as a minor. Many crimes have been attributed to the Empress Dowager. It was said that she hastened the end of her son Tung Chih by encouraging him in his debaucheries. When his widow who was pregnant committed suicide, it was said she encouraged and arranged it; it was rumoured that after her co-Regent, the Eastern Dowager, had denounced Li Lien-ying, her favourite eunuch – linked with her for the rest of her life – that she hastened her rival's end by foul play. Then three years later, she got rid of a serious rival for power by blaming the failures of the war with France in Vietnam on Prince Kung and obtaining his dismissal.

The Empress Dowager spent most of her long life behind the walls of the Forbidden City, themselves enclosed by the higher walls of Peking. Waited on by eunuchs, her public life was paved with ceremony and roofed with suspicion. She seems to have been fond of amateur theatricals, water picnics, painting and dogs; and she is said to have expressed a warm admiration for Queen Victoria whose picture she hung in her private apartments. She captivated the ladies of the Corps Diplomatique on the few occasions she received them. But in spite of her charm she could calmly order a wrongdoer to dismemberment and slicing.

By rights, the minority of the Empress Dowager's nephew, Kuang Hsu, should have ended in 1887, but she managed to arrange for it to continue until his marriage. This was not a happy one. But two of his concubines caught his sluggish fancy, and he spent most of his time with them – particularly the one called Pearl Concubine. The Empress Dowager was said to have been provoked because her nephew's concubines accepted bribes for putting in a good word to the Emperor on behalf of ambitious mandarins. On several occasions her own nominees were passed over in favour of candidates enterprising enough to have discovered this alternative road to promotion, and both her vanity and her purse found this affront hard to bear.

For some years the Empress Dowager had been trying to re-build a new Summer Palace near the ruins of the one destroyed by Lord Elgin in 1860. Such an undertaking needed more money than was available from the ordinary revenues of the Court, and it was here that the Empress's eunuch Li Lien-ying proved help-ful. He accompanied Li Hung-chang on a tour of the northern arsenals and won his confidence to such a degree that Li Hung-chang diverted funds meant to improve the navy to the Empress for her palace. The war with Japan drew the Empress and Li Hung-chang even closer together, for whereas the Emperor's party advocated the more vigorous prosecution of the war after early defeats, Li and the Dowager were for peace at any price. Later, Li was involved in accepting bribes for furthering Russian demands on China. This was only suspected at the time, but the publication of Tsarist archives by the Soviets revealed that when Li attended as China's representative the coronation of the new Tsar Nicholas II in Moscow, he signed a secret treaty agreeing to joint resistance to any renewed Japanese aggression, which also gave Russia railway rights through north China. As a reward for the latter concession Li received an enormous sum of money. Later still, Li paid a visit to Britain and the United States. One photograph shows him in England in 1896.

Li Hung-chang had been concerned with the early attempts at naval and military improvements and Westernization. But the efforts made in this direction at the end of the century stemmed from the activities of one Kang Yu-wei, and they brought about such a formidable reaction that the Emperor, who supported re-form, was virtually deposed, and the Court gave its support to the Boxers who were anti-foreign.

Kang Yu-wei had been a reformer for some time. He resolved at one time to strike a blow for reform by leaving his daughter's feet unbound, and in due course an Anti-Footbinding Society came into existence and the movement spread. As has been seen, officials were permitted to submit memorials to the Court giving their views on matters of the state. The feelings of the people were discovered in this manner, and *ch'ing-i* or literati public opinion had its effect on policy. At the end of the nineteenth century, *ch'ing-i* seemed on the side of Kang and the reformers, and Kang submitted memorial after memorial and finally obtained an audience of the Emperor. Although he was only a minor official, soon the Emperor became his principal supporter for Reform.

As early as the sixties, about the time when Japan began her reforms under Emperor Meiji, China had taken tentatively to Western technology. Thirty years of diplomacy and armed conflict with the European Powers convinced the authorities that, in order to defend China against foreign aggression, it was necessary to strengthen the country along Western lines. It was considered time to turn to the West for the secrets of power. Under the direction of Tsêng Kuo-fan, Li Hung-chang, and others, arsenals were established in Shanghai and Tientsin, dockyards were built in Fukien and Port Arthur, warships were bought from foreign countries, the army was trained on Western lines, railroads were introduced, mines were exploited, academies and schools were opened for the study of military and applied sciences, telegraph communications were set up, a shipping bureau was organized, and students were sent abroad to study. But all these changes were confined to military and industrial affairs; nothing was done about institutional or social reforms. Li Hung-chang, according to one of the later reformers, Liang Chi-chao, ' knew only military but not social, affairs; diplomatic, but not political, problems '. The new leader of Reform, Kang Yu-wei, however, concentrated on changing the institutions and laws of the Empire, and, surprisingly, the Emperor was captivated by Kang's ideas.

On 29 January 1898, Kang submitted a comprehensive memorial on his reform plans: all high officials should be required either to pledge themselves to the faithful execution of the reform policies or to resign from their offices; people throughout the country and officials high and low should be permitted to submit their opinions directly to the Throne. A committee of Institutions, consisting of twelve brilliant minds of the Empire, should serve as a consultative body to map out the master plans of reform for the approval of the Emperor; and as the existing boards and ministries were inefficient and hostile to changes, twelve new departments should be established for the administration of the reform measures. The details of the administrative reforms were then outlined. These were approved by the Emperor, and were issued as a series of decrees from June 1898 onwards.

The subjects they touched on included the abolition of the traditional essay form examination; the establishment of an Imperial University; the Westernization of the army; the modernization of the provincial schools; the abolition of superfluous temples and monasteries; the inauguration of a special economic examination; the permission for junior officials and the common people to memorialize or petition the Throne directly; the sending of students to study abroad; the promotion of commerce, agriculture, mining and railways under a national board; and the amalgamation of some sinecure offices and appointments.

With the issue of these Imperial edicts, opposition to the reformers, including the Emperor, began to build up. It came to a head when officials ignored the decrees on reforms. The Emperor abruptly dismissed a number of senior officials who had flouted his wishes – including Li Hung-chang – and in retaliation they and the Dowager Empress began their first moves against him. The way the matter developed depended in the end on one general, Yuan Shih-kai, who Kang and other reformers believed would support the Emperor, when the position had become perilous. This is shown by the following letter the Emperor wrote to Kang:

In view of the present difficulties, I have found that only reforms can save China, and that reforms can only be achieved through the discharge of the conservative and ignorant ministers and the appointment of the brave and intelligent scholars. Her Graceful Majesty, the Empress Dowager, however, did not agree. I have tried again and again to persuade her, only to find Her Majesty more angry. You Kang Yu-wei, Yang Jui, Lin Hsu and Tan Sso-tung should deliberate immediately to find some ways to save me. With extreme worries and earnest hopes. The Emperor.

But General Yuan proved a broken reed. He had under his command only 7,000 troops, and in the north around Peking were ten times as many under generals favouring the Empress. Moreover, in spite of their organization and propaganda, the reform party did not have a large following among the high-ranking officials. Indeed, the poor response became more marked when the reformers undertook to abolish the traditional form of the civil service and to sweep away sinecure offices, thus threatening their careers. The chief support for the reform at the top came from the Emperor, a conscientious ruler trying desperately to save his country. His intelligence saw that the country could only be saved by thorough and radical reforms, but his character lacked the iron will to carry through the transformation. As a politician he was merely a child in comparison with the Empress Dowager, whose cold calculation, quick decision, and unscrupulous manoeuvres found no match in the country.

Anyhow, the risks were too great for General Yuan. He disclosed the plot, and those informed immediately told the Empress. On 19 September 1898 the Empress Dowager, furious and indignant, hurried back into Peking from her new Summer Palace. With characteristic determination she acted quickly. She imprisoned the Emperor in his palace on the lake[1] in the Imperial City, and resumed the government of the Empire. Within about a hundred days the reform movement had ended in dismal failure. There was, of course, a mighty hue and cry for the blood of the innovators. Six of their leaders died on the public execution ground. Kang Yu-wei, who had escaped to Tientsin in time, was conveyed under British protection to the safety of Hong Kong.

This dramatic story goes some way to explain how it came about that the authorities in Peking favoured the Boxers in their anti-foreign campaign. All foreign things and foreign ways were suspect as a reaction to reform, and most of those who had supported Westernization were unable to make their views felt. Not all those in authority, however, supported the Boxers. Li Hung-chang, for example, although a supporter of the Empress, did not like co-operating with the Boxers; and the great Viceroys of the south, and Sheng Hsuan-huai, Director of Railways and Telegraphs and of the China Merchants Steam Navigation, not only kept the war with the Powers from affecting the south, but maintained the trade and economic life of the Empire throughout the struggle. This was the advantage of so much decentralization in China. Only the north and Peking were at war, and in the south the Boxers were subdued by the authorities. In the north, to begin with, the authorities also tried to suppress the Boxers (with the exception of the Governor of Shantung) but later, supporters of the Boxers – and war with the Powers – formed the ruling clique around the Empress in Peking. Policy then towards both the Boxers and the Powers fluctuated according to reactionary influence and the fortunes of war around Peking.

This fluctuation of policy is well brought out in the story of

[1] The Lotus Lake.

the siege of the Legations in Peking which will be related in the next chapter. It is told from the point of view of the besieged, and is based on eye-witness accounts of what happened.

## FIFTY-FIVE DAYS AT PEKING

The Boxers started their campaign by attacking their fellow Chinese who had been converted to the Christian faith, pillaging and burning their homes, and finally resorting to murder. On 31 December 1899 they killed their first foreign missionary, a young Englishman called Brooks. Sir Claude MacDonald, British Minister in Peking, telegraphed the Prime Minister in London (Lord Salisbury) about it as follows: ' It is with great regret that I report to your Lordship the murder by a band of anti-Christian rebels of the English missionary Brooks near the town of Fei-Cheng in Shantung Province, where he was travelling. The other members of the mission are safe. The part of China where the murder took place is very disturbed, and I and my French, American and German colleagues have been making strong representations. Peking, 4 January 1900.'

The day before the Tsungli Yamen (the Chinese Foreign Office) described the capturers of Brooks as ' a band of red turbaned " Boxer " rebels armed with swords ' and added, ' we have the honour to observe that troops have been repeatedly sent to deal with the Boxer rebels . . . the Governor on hearing of his (Brooks') capture, immediately sent a deputy to rescue him, but before the soldiers arrived, the missionary had been killed . . . we have to express our deepest sorrow.'

Towards the end of January Sir Claude was writing to the Tsungli Yamen complaining of the disorders in Shantung and Chihli,

Within the last few weeks I have had occasion to address to your Highness and your Excellencies both by letter and personally with regard to the deplorable state of affairs which exists in northern Shantung and the centre and south of Chihli. This state of affairs, which is a disgrace to any civilized country, has been brought about by the riotous and lawless behaviour of certain ruffians who have banded themselves together into two Societies termed respectively the *Fist of Righteous Harmony* and *Big Sword Society* and by the apathy, and in some instances, the actual connivance and encouragement of these Societies by the local officials. The members of these

Societies go about pillaging the homes of Christian converts, breaking down their Chapels, robbing and ill-treating inoffensive women and children, and it is a fact, to which I would draw the special attention of your Highness and your Excellencies, that on the banners which are carried by these riotous and lawless people are inscribed the words: ' Exterminate the Foreigners '.

In March, Sir Claude is writing again to Lord Salisbury about the Boxers,

On the 10th instant I telegraphed to your Lordship with regard to the Anti-Christian Societies in Shantung. I have now to report that the late Governor (Yu Hsien) of that Province has been appointed Governor of Shansi. There is no doubt that the main cause of the recent outrages in Shantung was this official's sympathy with the anti-Christian Societies.

By July, other British representatives were writing about the Boxers to the British Prime Minister. Acting Consul-General Warren at Shanghai writes:

It appears that the Boxer movement is spreading rapidly. The telegraph wires in Shansi, Shensi and Honan have been cut and orders given to kill foreigners and burn churches . . . I have received news that at Ching-te-chen the Roman Catholic Mission was burnt, native converts killed, and the banks pillaged on 11 July.

It appears that the degree of persecution permitted to the Boxers depended on the attitude of the local governors. In Shantung, Yu Hsien was sympathetic towards the Boxers, and welcomed their help in the struggle against Christians and foreigners. When removed and transferred to Shansi, he continued this support in his new domain, personally supervising the butchery of forty-five European missionaries including a number of women and children. Elsewhere, except in the north around the capital, the viceroys, in spite of pressure at times from the central government, were not willing to allow the Boxers to carry out their atrocities. In this way most of China was kept out of the struggle with the West although it was apparent that the Empress was helping the Boxers.

Not only the poor scattered missionaries and their unhappy converts were threatened by the Boxers; there were also the isolated garrison at Tientsin, Bishop Favier and his flock in the

Roman Catholic cathedral in the Imperial City, and the five hundred Europeans of the foreign Legations of Peking. It is the imprisonment and siege of the last group with which this chapter is mainly concerned.

The Legation Quarter lay in the south-east corner of the northern or Tartar City. It was bounded on the north-west by the walls of the Imperial City and separated from it by the famous Hanlin Library whose eaves projected over the British Legation's walls. To the south was the great Tartar Wall cutting off the Chinese City. As a defence area the Legation Quarter was fairly compact, but not compact enough; it was found necessary to shorten the length of the outer barricades, and in doing so the Austrian, Italian and French Legations to the east, and the Dutch Legation to the west, had to be abandoned. It was also found that the whole of the Tartar Wall in the south could not be manned, and the defence line was pulled back from it in the area of the German Legation. The Fu in the north-east of the Quarter was a parklike area, very difficult to defend. Here the Japanese contingent distinguished themselves by fighting most gallantly and throwing back time and again assaults by Boxers and Imperial troops alike.

There was no outstanding leader at Peking, but Sir Claude MacDonald took the most active part in the defence. At first no real fear was felt of the Boxers. Many of the leading Europeans there had spent long years in China, and from past experience considered the Chinese too feeble to do them much harm. As more and more serious news of Boxer atrocities reached their ears, this mood in the Legations changed. Bishop Favier's Cathedral Compound was filling up with thousands of terrified Catholic converts from the countryside, and he was demanding protection. M. Pichon, the French Minister, always apprehensive, and not waiting for general agreement from all the ministers, or the approval of the Chinese authorities who were nominally protecting the Europeans, sent down a demand for armed guards to be sent up from the foreign warships which were now lying off the Taku forts a hundred miles south-east of Peking.

Before the arrival of the armed guard, the situation at Peking went from bad to worse. First, Boxers attacked nearby railways and railway staff. Engine sheds and workshops, machinery and rolling stock, were looted and burnt; engines were completely destroyed. Next, members of the Legation were openly insulted in the streets of Peking. This caused hasty precautions and arrangements for a defence barricade to be made in the British Legation; while in the French Legation, M. Pichon forbade his staff to leave, and requested all Frenchmen in Peking to take refuge in the Legation compound. The whole city was in a feverish state, people running in all directions, some trying to escape before the storm broke out, others in carts and conveyances leaving their houses to seek safety in the Legations. Messengers kept arriving at the Legations with more and more alarming reports, and towards evening it was rumoured that the Boxers were approaching in great force.

The Boxers were not content with trying to wreck the railway. Along the outside of the ancient walls of Peking a squeaky, jolting electric tramway line had been running for some time. The uprights supporting the overhead cable were pulled down, and the cable itself cut and removed, the rails torn up, and the carriages burnt or destroyed. The Boxers claimed the tram disturbed the peace, not of the living, but of the dead men over whose graves it happened to pass. Moreover, a carriage that went along without being propelled by beast or man must be the work of devils.

At first, although a demand was made by the Ministers, the Chinese officials would not allow any facilities for sailors and marines to come up from Taku to guard the Legations, and the Viceroy of Tientsin – no doubt under instructions – refused to let them have a train. Later they relented, showing that at this stage they were not completely on the side of the Boxers. Mercifully the rails were still intact, and early on the morning of 31 May 1900 the first contingents from the warships arrived at the railway station outside Peking. They numbered 78 British with a Nordenfeldt gun, 75 Russians, 25 Austrians, 50 Americans, 50 Italians, 25 French and 25 Japanese. The Italians brought with them a one-pounder gun, and the American Marines a Colt Automatic machine-gun; but it was a small force to protect not only the Legations but Bishop Favier's Cathedral as well – even with the extra fifty-two Germans and thirty-seven sailors who arrived a few days later.

With the arrival of the guards, the community in the Legations felt somewhat happier, but the Boxer menace was still serious.

On 9 June some young sportsmen, having heard that the grandstand at the racecourse had been wrecked – the first real atrocity for them – rode out to see what had happened. They had hardly gone a mile before they came upon a couple of hundred Boxers who shouted at them '*Sha! sha! sha!*' (Kill! kill! kill!). Turning back they met two more from the Legations on the same errand and explained what had happened. The newcomers took another route and, for what it was worth, were able to view the burnt-out stand. On the way back to Peking, they too were attacked by a party of Boxers and fired their revolvers, killing one Chinese. They then galloped off to safety managing to avoid two swords which were hurled after them.

About this time Sir Claude MacDonald reported as follows to Admiral Seymour down by the coast: 'The situation in Peking is hourly becoming more serious; troops should be landed and all arrangements made for an advance on Peking at once.' In answer to this 2,000 men set out by train for Peking.

On the afternoon of 11 June it was announced, by mistake, that this force was approaching, and fifty carts under a guard went out to the station on the south of the city to meet it. Not only had the expected reinforcements not arrived, there was no news of them at the station. The procession that had started so gaily had to make its way mournfully back again. That same afternoon outside the south gate an unprovoked attack was made on Mr Sujiyama, the Chancellor of the Japanese Legation. He had gone in his cart to see if there was now any sign of the relief expedition, and when just past the gate was dragged out of his conveyance by soldiers, and by the order of one of the officers, murdered and hacked to pieces. His Chinese driver managed to escape and bring an account of the assassination to the Legations. As the murderers were not Boxers but Imperial soldiers, the truly perilous situation of the Europeans in Peking was forcibly brought home to everyone. In fact, not only had Prince Ch'eng, who had tried to protect the Europeans in the Legation, been replaced by Prince Tuan, who supported the Boxers, but a 'foreign-hating' Mohammedan General, Tung Fuhsiang, had arrived in Peking with thousands of well-armed but ill-behaved soldiers.

On 19 June the eleven Ministers in the Legations were told that as the Western Nations had threatened to take the Taku forts by force, their countries were at war with China, and they, their staff and families must leave Peking within twenty-four hours. 'To go or not to go?' that was the question. The whole day and the greater part of the night was spent in arguing and discussing the point. The prospect of being shortly in safety among friends seemed attractive enough, but how to realize it was another matter: the railway had been broken up, navigation by river was unsafe, they were hampered by numbers of women, children, and sick, the country was up in arms against them, and the Imperial troops would, as likely as not, shoot them down the moment they got out of cover into the open. The Ministers asked for an interview at the Foreign Office. When no reply was received to this request, they became impatient. Finally, although it had been suggested by the Russian Ambassador that they should all go and see the Chinese officials, they allowed the excitable German Ambassador, Baron von Ketteler, to go on his own to express their views.

Shortly before eight o'clock on the evening of 20 June, therefore, he and his secretary, Mr Cordes, escorted by a guard of German marines, started on their way to the Foreign Office. On reaching the Legation barricade they found a guard of Imperial troops waiting for them, and their officer explained that he would conduct them safely to the Yamen. Baron von Ketteler, a man of great courage, ordered his German guard to return to the Legation. Soon after this, his Chinese groom, who had been riding behind the Minister's sedan chair, galloped back down Legation Street saying that his master was being murdered. A bit later Mr Cordes struggled back wounded. His master had been attacked just outside the Yamen by the soldiers sent to escort him and they had shot and killed him in his sedan chair where he was boxed in and unable to get out. This is how Sir Claude described the assassination of the German Minister to Lord Salisbury in a despatch of 20 September 1900:

The two sedan chairs had just passed a small police station in the main street when Mr Cordes, who had been watching a cart attended by an escort of lance-bearers a little way in front, glanced to the left, and suddenly became aware of a soldier in full uniform who, with his rifle at his shoulder, was following the movements of the Minister's chair, evidently aiming at the head of the occupant. Mr Cordes had only time to utter a startled shout when the soldier fired, instantly killing Baron von Ketteler. The chairs were dropped at once, and Mr

Cordes sprang up, by this movement saving his life, for a second shot, evidently aimed at his head, took effect instead in the lower part of his body. He managed to effect his escape, though badly hurt, the assassins being apparently content with what they had done.

It is interesting to note that although the assassination took place on 20 June 1900, and the telegraph line out of Peking was cut, the news of his murder appeared in all the European and American papers on 16 June, or four whole days before the murder actually occurred. It seems that either the murder was premeditated, or the Japanese Chancellor's assassination on 11 June was reported wrongly as that of the German Minister. The two crimes showed that the Imperial troops could not be relied on for protection, and all thought of leaving was now abandoned. The siege of Peking had begun. By now the number of people seeking safety in the Legations had greatly increased. The American Mission, lying a little way out to the east, consisting of seventy-six American missionaries and their children, and many Chinese converts, took up their quarters in the British Legation Quarter. As this was the largest and easiest to defend, it became the central redoubt in which supplies were concentrated, and on which the garrisons of the other Legations would fall back if dislodged from their positions.

The Ministers were not at all anxious to become swamped by Chinese converts and did little to help them. Many Europeans, indeed, bitterly opposed allowing these poor wretches to come within the line of defence for fear there might be traitors among them. Dr Morrison, the Peking correspondent of *The Times*, was kinder hearted. On hearing that many Christians and converts were still left at the mercy of the Boxers near the Nan-tang Church, he applied to Sir Claude MacDonald for guards to rescue them. Twenty British with some Americans and Germans were given him and Morrison took them over to the church which was by the Tartar Wall south-west of the Imperial City. The rescuing party found the alleys round the Nan-tang mission church full of Prince Ch'eng's soldiers and these showed no hostility towards the rescuers. All around were terrible scenes – houses burnt or burning, women and children gashed or mutilated in the most horrible manner. One woman was about to be murdered by a Boxer when a bullet from Morrison's revolver saved her. Many of the poor converts were still alive, some were fervently praying

MOAT

TARTAR CITY

(RUSSIAN GATE)

RUSSIANS

CHI HU MEN

JAPANESE

IMPERIAL CITY

BISHOP
FAVIER'S
CATHEDRAL

HANLIN LIBRARY

B
R
US

FU

LEGATIONS

U.S.

NAN-TANG CHURCH

TUNG PIEN MEN

TARTAR WALL

SEWER

SHA KOU MEN

BRITISH

CHINESE CITY

JAPANESE
MURDERED HERE

N

RAILWAY TERMINUS

TO TIENTSIN

LEGATIONS

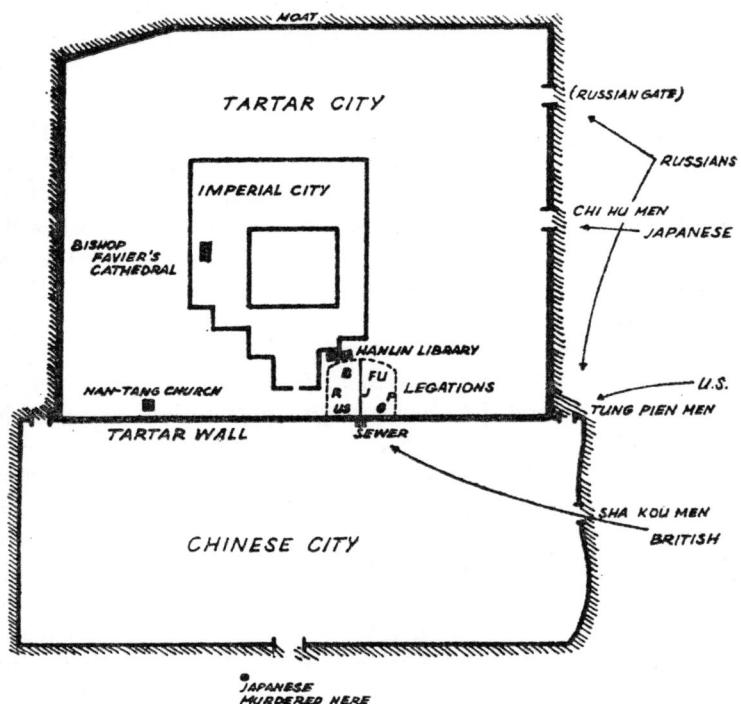

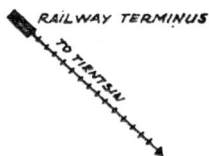

B  BRITISH
R  RUSSIAN
US UNITED STATES
J  JAPANESE
F  FRENCH
G  GERMAN

1        0        1        2

MILES

Map 9   Plan of Peking, 1900

to God for assistance. Messengers were sent in all directions to call the surviving converts together. When no more could be found, they were all safely conveyed back to the Legation's compound. Two hundred in this instance received shelter, and they proved a wonderful help to the garrison, working tirelessly at building the defence barricades.

The fifty-five day siege at Peking had two short respites. These are difficult to account for, but were probably due to Allied successes elsewhere causing the Empress Dowager to pause and have second thoughts in her dangerous design of exterminating the Europeans in the Legations. During the second truce the Empress even sent in carts laden with gifts of melons, vegetables, ice and flour. Most of those who had crowded in to the Legations had given little thought to storing food. They had doubted whether the siege would last more than two or three days, or possibly a week, and they had brought in provisions accordingly. Some had brought nothing, but others had purchased six tons of wheat from a neighbouring Chinese mill, and four huge grindstones to grind it with and had emptied the surrounding foreign shops of tinned provisions and preserves. Several thousand pounds of rice had been brought in from Chinese stores. The Spring race meeting had been held early in May, and the stables were full of ponies. These, numbering about 150, together with a few mules ensured a supply of fresh meat. Thus by the time the attack began there was sufficient food in the Legations to last ten or twelve weeks. The Legation grounds were amply supplied with well water, and as for wines, spirits and beer, there was more than was wanted. The Ministers had made no provision for a siege and it was almost miraculous – the missionaries indeed claimed it to be a miracle – that there was sufficient food to feed more than three thousand people for several weeks.

To begin with the fortifications were very frail, consisting mainly of tipped-up Peking carts. If the Chinese had pressed home their first attacks, they would have been bound to succeed. The building of stronger barricades around the Legations were undertaken by a committee under Mr Gamewell, who had been an engineer before becoming a missionary, and it was said that, more than any other single individual, he secured the safety of the besieged. Fortunately few ever lost heart. This was something to be said for not having any real communication with the outside world. The besieged thought that Admiral Seymour had set out with a substantial relief party, and expected him to arrive any moment. Had they realized that travelling, rather foolishly, by train he had been cut off and forced to retire, they might have been less confident of rescue.

A feature of the early part of the siege were the attempts by the Boxers and Chinese soldiers to burn out the besieged. They had most success with the Hanlin Library, the nearest halls of which almost overhung the walls of the British Legation in the north-west of the Legation compound. The library contained some of the greatest works of Chinese scholars, including the only copy of a hand-written encyclopaedia of the Ming dynasty, completed by a team of 2,000 scholars in 1407, covering history, science, religion and art, and comprising about 27,000 books. The Ministers could not believe that the enemy would sacrifice such a shrine of Chinese scholarship, and could hardly believe their eyes when they saw it ablaze. The British, however, managed to avert the danger. Burrowing a hole in the wall,[1] they moved through water to help extinguish the blaze by means of a long human chain passing buckets, soup tureens, and chamber pots. Even so, it seemed as if nothing could save either the books – some of which Sir Claude had hoped to retrieve in spite of a hail of bullets from the enemy. Then at the last minute the wind veered and the worst of the danger was over. A messenger was sent to the Yamen to ask them to note that thousands of bullets had been fired on Europeans trying to save their priceless books. But it should really have been obvious that the enemy had set fire to the building to destroy the British Legation.

The great Tartar Wall on the south, with the sluice gate cut through it, was a danger point in the Legation defences. As wide as a trunk road on top, the Europeans had breastworks along one edge and the Chinese along the other, with only a few yards separating them. The men hated the task of manning these exposed defences which could only be relieved at night; and on 1 July, the German posts were surprised by the enemy and the Germans driven from the Wall. The Americans seeing the Germans retreating, fell back too, and so for a time the whole Wall

---

[1] During the action Captain L. Halliday won the VC for gallantry while leading 20 marines through the hole in the wall and driving the enemy away; but see appendix for Halliday's own version.

was enemy-held. Then Captain Myers, commanding the US contingent, led two attacks with small mixed forces, stormed the Wall, and drove off the Chinese from most of the American section of it. There was only slight resistance to the first assault, but the second developed into a spirited little battle. They had difficulty in charging and scrambling up the Wall, and there followed some confused fighting in the darkness and rain, in which Captain Myers was wounded. It is considered one of the most important sallies of the siege, and twenty or thirty Chinese were killed and some rifles and bandoliers of ammunition captured.

In the Fu, Prince Su's palace and gardens to the north-east of the Legation compound, the Japanese under Colonel Shiba fought splendidly. Only twenty-four in number – the smallest contingent – it had the unusual distinction of suffering 100 per cent casualties, for every man was wounded at least once. They were supported by thirty-two armed European volunteers and a number of Chinese converts. Although they had to give ground as the siege progressed, and by the end, three-quarters of the garden of the Fu was in Chinese hands, the enemy never got through. Even General Tung Fuhsiang's feared warriors were mown down by the deadly fire of the Japanese sharpshooters when some of the former penetrated the barricade. There is a photograph of this taken at the time. It shows the Japanese, kneeling shoulder to shoulder in their white jackets, pouring fire into the Chinese soldiers from Kansu.

Admiral Seymour's relief force had failed to get through, but, in due course, a larger and mightier one was assembled and moved up towards Peking. It consisted of five main contingents: in order of size, Japanese, Russian, British, American and French; in all about 20,000 men. In getting it moving on Peking, General Gaselee, the British commander, played the leading part, and on 10 August 1900 he managed to send in by runner to the Peking Legations the following encouraging message: ' Strong force of Allies advancing. Twice defeated enemy. Keep up your spirits.'

On approaching Peking it was agreed, on the insistence of the Russians who wanted everyone to have a fair chance of being first into Peking, that all except the French, who had fallen behind, should form up in the neighbourhood of Peking. Then each contingent would attack a different gate of the Peking walls. This arrangement, however, did not quite go according to plan, and it was the Russians themselves who ruined it.

With the Relief Force close at hand the Chinese made one supreme effort to overwhelm the Legations. The extent of this final danger to the besieged was soon apparent when all around the flimsy defences the Chinese were seen massing for an assault, their war trumpets blaring forth, supplemented by threatening yells of ' *Sha! Sha!*' The besieged braced themselves for the worst ordeal of the siege and to good effect. When the fanatical hordes hurled themselves at the frail barricades, they met them with such a withering fire that the Chinese halted in their tracks and recoiled. The first attack was thus held, but the situation remained dangerous in the extreme. The defenders could not hold off many such attacks unless help came, and in spite of General Gaselee's encouraging message about the relieving column, the besieged still waited for it in vain.

The Allies were planning to make their concerted attack on 15 August, and it seemed as if the defenders still had many hours to wait for help to come. In fact, by mistake, it came earlier. The Russians sent forward a scouting party on 13 August, and they reported having approached within two hundred yards of the Tung Pien Men (the American gate) before being fired at, so the Wall there seemed lightly held. The Russian general probably did not realize it was the Americans' gate. He sent forward a battalion of infantry and a troop of guns to secure it at once. The Russian party got over the moat, surprised the occupants of the gate's outer guard-house and killed them all. But they got themselves into terrible trouble. After blasting a way through the wall of the outer gate by gunfire, they met a second gate and wall and were trapped in a courtyard between the two, with fire pouring down on them at point blank range from Chinese marksmen on top of the walls. However, having received reinforcements from outside, in spite of heavy casualties and the slaughter of all the artillery's horses, the Russians made themselves master of the Tung Pien Men before sunrise.

' Owing to the premature advance of the Russians,' wrote General Gaselee in his despatches, ' the intended concentration was abandoned, and the troops were all hurried forward to assault the city of Peking.'

The Japanese got held up badly at their gate, the Chi Hu Men, and did not get through it until nightfall on 14 August, having by then brought up the whole of their artillery and fired a thousand rounds. The Americans were surprised to find the Russians already in possession of their gate but succeeded in scaling the Wall nearby. In the south the British had the most luck of all. Their artillery drilled a hole in the Sha Kou Men, and their troops passed through without much difficulty into the Chinese City of Peking. Turning north, the men saw the ominous great Tartar Wall blocking their view into the American and German Legations in the south of the Legation compound; but they could also see the flags of the nations flying proudly aloft, including the ' Stars and Stripes ' closest at hand. They were in time! As they came nearer a signaller with his blue and white signal flags appeared on the ramparts. ' Come in by the sewer,' he signalled. And that was the way the relief of the Peking Legations was achieved. Led by the Rajputs, followed by the Sikhs, and then the Royal Welch Fusiliers, the rotten ironwork of the sewer grille having been broken down, the troops clambered through the black mud of the sluice into the Legations.

' It was a tremendous score our people being first in,' Sir Claude MacDonald wrote in a letter to the Foreign Office, ' and I nearly burst with pride when I introduced old Gaselee to the Russian, French and Japanese Ministers and their wives.' So ended ' the 55 Days in Peking '.

The relief of the Legations at Peking meant the end of the Boxer Uprising. When the international relief force marched in, the Court fled from Peking by the northern gate towards the south-west, arriving eventually at Sian in Shensi province, and the Boxer Uprising collapsed. The peace imposed by the victorious Allies (the Boxer Protocol) left the Dowager Empress and the reactionaries in power until her death in 1908. But it imposed harsh terms with an indemnity of about £65 million, and the death penalty for some of the leading Chinese officials involved.

In 1904 and 1905 north-east China became the battleground of the war between Russia and Japan, and the effect of the victory of an Asian country like Japan against a European Power stirred Eastern people everywhere to fight for independence, and encouraged revolutionary movements against régimes backed by Great Powers. The Revolution in China began in October 1911 near Hankow on the Yangtze in Hupeh province, and two months later Sun Yat-sen, a Cantonese who had been associated with anti-Manchu secret societies in the south, became its leader. The revolutionary movement soon got a firm hold over the Yangtze region, and Sun was sworn in as first President of the Republic at the new capital of Nanking on 1 January 1912. Sun's first period of power was short-lived, for the traditional antagonism between the North and South already met with in this book asserted itself. Nevertheless, 1912 marks the dissolution of the Paper Dragon, the feeble but likeable old Imperial China of these pages.

# 7 Conclusion

Something of the nature of old China is discernible from the military operations from 1860 to 1900 described in this book. Throughout the period the ineffectiveness of her central administration and the weakness of her armed forces are apparent.

The weakness of the administration is illustrated in the section on the First China War when officials like the Hoppo at Canton obtain excessive 'squeezes' from Anglo-Chinese trade at Canton, and when the officers of the anti-smuggling fleet off that port are recorded as accepting bribes to allow through opium they were supposed to stop entering China. In the same period, the weakness of the armed forces is shown when the British fleet in January 1841 seize the forts of Chuenpi and Tycock guarding the narrow waterway to Canton in a few hours for the loss of thirty-eight British wounded, though killing 500 Chinese. Another illustration of Chinese general feebleness was the speed with which temporary compliance with British demands usually followed the smallest British military success. Commissioner Kishen, on the occasion mentioned above, immediately concluded the Chuenpi Convention and agreed to cede the island and harbour of Hong Kong to the British. Other commissioners of the time, Lin, for example, were of course a great deal more stubborn. But even when commissioners wanted to hold out, they were usually overruled by the Peking authorities as the result of a slight military reverse. The gentry and people, as opposed to the mandarins, are sometimes considered as being made of sterner stuff. The San Yuan-li incident is cited in evidence of this. When the Chinese authorities in Canton sought peace after General Gough's attack, and the regular Tartar garrison had been sent away according to the armistice terms, a group of Chinese patriots under local gentry continued the struggle for a time. This has been enlarged into an affair of great significance in present day Communist literature. But unjustly. The so-called patriots really achieved nothing, and inflicted only a fraction of the casualties claimed. Only one British soldier was killed by them.

The Second China War of 1856-9 illustrates China's pride. China, the Chinese believed, was the centre of the whole world, the fount of learning, culture and civilization. All other countries were lesser states and should bear tribute to the great state of China and the divine Emperor who ruled there. All foreigners were 'barbarians', and no equality of status could be allowed to foreign ambassadors visiting China – a sore point with the British from the earliest days of contact. Even trade, though too vital to be forbidden altogether, was restricted, at first to Canton, later, owing to pressure, to a few other ports as well. To restrict trade for the British in the nineteenth century was to anger and annoy them. The Treaty of Nanking at the end of the First China War in 1842 had conceded to Britain consideration for British nationals, and a similar treaty with France had given religious tolerance. In 1856, the old arrogance reasserted itself, and the British flag was insulted in the *Arrow* incident; while endemic administrative weakness allowed the murder of a French missionary. Again the strong points in Canton were easily taken, and the recalcitrant Commissioner Yeh captured. This time a naval approach to Tientsin up the Peiho was easily accomplished, ending with skilful negotiations by Lord Elgin and Baron Gros. But the next year, the Chinese were too proud to allow the Allied envoys to proceed by the same route to Peking to get the Treaty of Tientsin ratified, and the Third China War of 1860 ensued.

In the Third China War of 1860 resistance was stronger, and (in negotiation) the Chinese were more evasive and tortuous than ever. General Sankolinsin had had two successes, a small one against the Taipings, and a greater one by stopping Admiral Hope from breaking through at Taku in 1859. In 1860, he fought a series of delaying actions from Peh-tang to Taku, and then back up the Peiho into Peking. He combined delays for parleying with his military operations with some skill, though the capture of the British envoys and the murder of some of their staff does not appear to have been sound policy from the Chinese point of view as it brought all the wrath of the Europeans against them. On the way to Peking the Allies were subject to all the usual wiles of

G

Chinese diplomats. At Tientsin, Kweilang, Hang-fu and Hang-ki had no official seal or the power to agree to anything; they were obviously trying to delay the Allies until the winter, when, with the help of the cold weather they could drive the 'barbarians' away. During the march on Peking Lord Elgin received endless letters imploring him to stay the advance of the army, no doubt with the same end in view. Then, around Chanchiawan, it became obvious that General Sankolinsin was setting a trap for the advancing Allied troops. Pretending to agree to a convention, the new Chinese envoy, the Prince of I, began to quibble about the size of Lord Elgin's escort into Peking, and although it was arranged to issue a proclamation telling the Chinese people that peace was made between the Emperor and the Allies, the envoys were kidnapped and the war renewed. At this time, there is also another illustration of the weakness of the Chinese central authorities. In this instance it was because of divided counsels. There were two factions at the Chinese Court, a peace party and a war party, with completely different approaches to foreign policy. In the end the peace party predominated, and the responsible and rational Prince Kung was able to bring about an end to hostilities.

During the long Taiping Rebellion period the militia led by gentry played a valuable part with the General Tsêng Kuo-fan's forces in the suppression of the uprising. Also in this struggle, the European-trained and European-led Chinese armies of Ward, Burgevine, Gordon and others, proved successful in the field, and this is usually taken to show that properly trained and led the Chinese make good soldiers.

The murder of the wangs at Soochow illustrates the barbarity of the Chinese of this period towards their fellow Chinese. But many of the Generals and Commissioners were men of principle, Prince Kung being the prime example. Incidentally, Prince Kung justified Li Hung-chang's murder of the wangs on the plea – and it seems reasonable – that 'by the death of a few dangerous originators of the Taiping Rebellion the death of many was avoided'.

The Taiping Rebellion was an attempt at real revolution – almost the first in the whole long history of China. There had often been changes of dynasty brought about by revolution – a major one every three hundred years, it is said – but always the scholar-gentry educated in Confucian principles, and trying to put those principles into practice, had formed the governing classes, even when the rulers were Mongols like Kublai Khan or Manchus like the Dowager Empress. The Taipings tried, without success, to create a new form of government on Christian communal principles completely at variance with traditional Chinese form of government. They were attempting something closer perhaps to Mao's present China than the China resulting from Sun Yat-sen's revolution of 1911, after which a leader of the traditional type in General Chiang Kai-shek emerged. At the time of the Taiping Rebellion European Powers supported Imperial China, just as in recent years the United States have supported Chiang Kai-shek.

So well formulated were Lord Elgin's terms to Prince Kung after the Third China War of 1860, that until 1900 Britain was not only at peace with China, but, through sage Robert Hart of the Chinese Customs, helping her in her foreign relations. Nevertheless, China continued to fight wars with France and Japan. The French had obtained tolerance for their missionaries only to have them massacred by mobs the Chinese authorities could not control; and they wrested from China the country of Vietnam which, for centuries, had been a part of the Chinese Empire or a tribute bearer to it. In the war against Japan over Korea, another Chinese vassal state, the Chinese armies are shown – for example at Pyongyang – to have been as feeble against Asiatic states as they had been against European.

By the time of the Boxer Uprising the World Powers, European and Asiatic alike, were confident that China must yield to their demands: trade for Britain, development of resources and railways for Germany, Japan and Russia, and the acceptance of missionaries for France and America. For by 1900 the central Government was both weak and divided; there was a progressive party who wished China to adopt Western ways, and a reactionary party, led by the Empress Dowager, who wanted to throw out the foreigners – and were quite willing to support the Boxers who showed some sign of doing just that. But it was not to be. The Great Powers triumphed, and the reactionary faction then in control had to bow to all their demands.

The state of China throughout the period 1840-1900 was well summed up by Lord Elgin when he wrote, 'There must be no

doubt a great deal of wealth in China, but weakness and malad-
ministration has made its Government one of the poorest in the
world.' That wise statesman also seemed to have had a glimpse
of the ultimate repercussions of the high-handedness of military
enforced trade (including opium) and the insistence on all the
trappings of Western international protocol – as the reason for
contemporary Chinese hatred of the West – when he said, ' I
feel that I am earning for myself a place in the Litany immediately after plague, pestilence and famine.' Certainly, however,
modern China is very different from the old. Possessing atomic
weapons, reoccupying old vassal states like Tibet, threatening
others like Vietnam, Korea and Burma, she has become again
the ' Middle Kingdom ', between Russia and the United States,
and is now as much feared as she was once despised.

# Appendix A: Hong Kong

BRITAIN'S PRIZE IN THE CHINA WARS 1840-1900

Although inhabited from primitive times, Hong Kong remained up to the nineteenth century sparsely populated, having only small villages along its coasts like Shek-Pai-wan – now called Aberdeen and noted for its floating fish restaurant. At the time of the Mongol dynasty of Kublai Khan, these fishing villages are recorded as being the haunts of pirates, while in the eleventh century the two main southern Chinese peoples, the Hakka and Cantonese, are shown to have appeared, and in 1278 the Sung Emperor is recorded as being driven back into Kowloon by the Mongols to die there.

In the early days, as has been seen, the British merchants made their headquarters partly in the Factories precinct at Canton and partly in Portuguese Macao on the other side of the estuary of the Canton River from Hong Kong. When Captain Elliot was Superintendent of Trade after the seizure of the Factories in 1836, all the traders and their families, after a short stay in Macao, took refuge in the harbour of Hong Kong and lived in their ships there for a time.

After the First China War, Hong Kong was ceded to Britain (1842) and from then on began to be developed, the name 'Victoria' being conferred on the settlement on Hong Kong island. The first report on population in June 1845 gave the total as 23,817, of whom 595 were Europeans and 363 Indians. Many of the Chinese population lived afloat in the mouths of the rivers, as indeed they still do at Aberdeen and elsewhere.

As a trading centre Hong Kong at first fell behind Shanghai and the Treaty Ports. But when gold was discovered in California in 1849 and in Australia in 1851, it did a good trade in shipping emigrants to those countries, and this stimulated other port activities.

During the Taiping Rebellion the unsettled conditions on the mainland resulted in thousands of Chinese seeking refuge in the Colony, and the population rose by 1861 to 119,321.

During the Third China War the Kowloon peninsula was occupied and used as a camp for the British forces, and Harry Parkes secured from the local Chinese viceroy the perpetual lease of the peninsula as far as Boundary Street and including Stonecutters Island (see map below). Then in 1860 at Peking, Lord Elgin secured Kowloon by outright Chinese cession as part of the terms of the peace treaty at the end of the war.

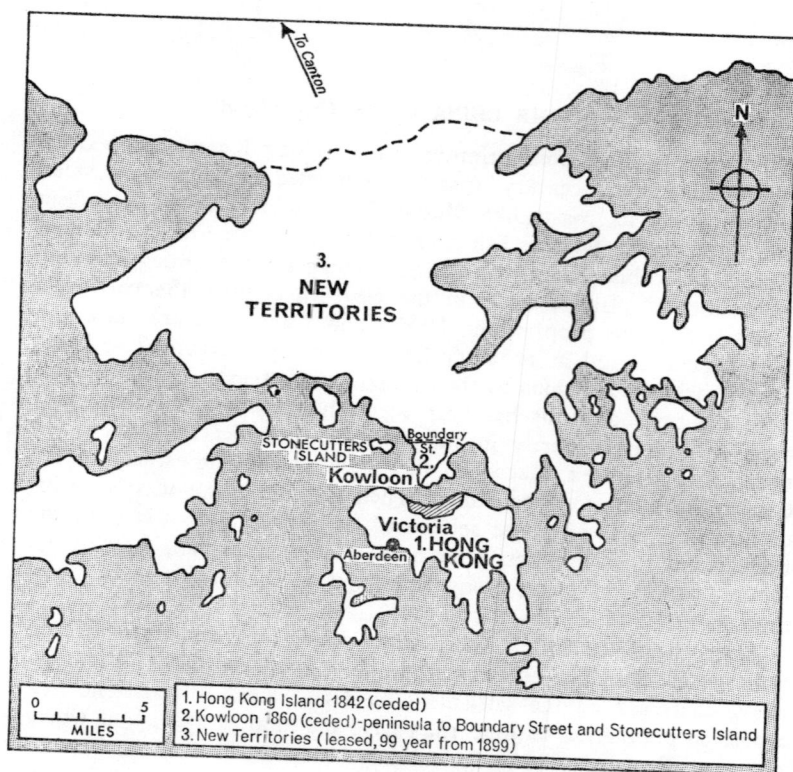

To Canton

N

3.
NEW
TERRITORIES

STONECUTTERS
ISLAND

Boundary
St.
2.

Kowloon

Victoria
1. HONG
KONG

Aberdeen

0 — 5
MILES

1. Hong Kong Island 1842 (ceded)
2. Kowloon 1860 (ceded)-peninsula to Boundary Street and Stonecutters Island
3. New Territories (leased, 99 year from 1899)

Map 10   Hong Kong

Towards the close of the century (1898), just before the Boxer Uprising, France, Germany, Russia and Japan, as well as Britain, were negotiating in rivalry for concessions from the disintegrating Chinese Empire, and at the Convention which resulted from the talks, Hong Kong's boundaries were extended by the 99-year-old[1] lease of rural territory north of Kowloon, an extension which acquired the

[1] Agreed at Convention of Peking 1898; British take-over April 1899 – Hong Kong Annual Report.

name New Territories, and which proved of inestimable value as agricultural land to provide food for the settlements at Kowloon and Victoria.

During the Chinese Revolution of 1911 – led by Sun Yat-sen, a former graduate of Hong Kong's College of Medicine – there followed a long period of unrest in China and again large numbers of refugees found shelter in the Colony.

China's participation in the First World War of 1914-18, along-side the victorious Allies, was followed by strong nationalist and anti-foreign sentiment inspired by disappointment at the little the Ver-sailles peace treaties accorded China. The Chinese now wanted to abolish all foreign treaty privileges. Foreign goods were boycotted, and unrest spread to Hong Kong, where a seamen's strike in 1922 was followed by a general strike in 1925 under pressure from Canton. This petered out, but not before there had been considerable disruption of the life of the Colony. Britain, as the holder of the largest stake in China, was then the main target of this anti-foreign sentiment, but Japan soon replaced her in this position.

Japan's entry into Manchuria in 1931 led to the occupation of most of China's seaboard territories. When Canton was occupied in 1938, a mass of refugees again entered Hong Kong bringing the population at the outbreak of the Second World War to 1,600,000. It was thought that at the height of this influx about half a million were sleeping in the streets, a state of affairs which happened again re-cently.

On 8 December 1941, the same day as the attack on Pearl Har-bour, the Japanese attacked Kowloon. On the night of 18/19 Decem-ber, they overwhelmed Victoria, and on Christmas Day the Colony surrendered.

The war years were bad ones in Hong Kong. British civilians were interned at Stanley in the south-east of the island, and the Chinese population had to suffer steadily deteriorating conditions. Trade vir-tually collapsed, the currency lost its value, food supply was disrupted and government services and public utilities were seriously impaired. Some moved to Macao, the Portuguese Colony hospitably opening its doors to them; and towards the latter part of the occupation the Japanese had to ease the food problem by organizing deportations. In the face of increasing oppression, the bulk of the community remained loyal to the Allied cause; Chinese guerrillas operated in the New Territories, and Allied personnel escaping were assisted by the rural population.

Since World War II Hong Kong has made a spectacular recovery. The Chinese Civil War, and Chiang Kai-shek's defeat by Mao's

Communists, led to another great influx of Chinese refugees into Hong Kong, the population of which reached 3,133,131 by 1961. But the Colony's commercial and industrial activities have been developed greatly in the last few years; and British Hong Kong, although overcrowded, has become a successful small Chinese capitalist state comparable with Chiang Kai-shek's Taiwan.

# Appendix B:
# General Sir Lewis Halliday,
## VC, KCB

General Sir Lewis Halliday, VC, KCB, the oldest surviving holder of the Victoria Cross, died on Wednesday at the age of 95. He was Adjutant-General, Royal Marines, from 1927 to 1930.

He won the VC while serving with the Royal Marine Light Infantry as a member of the guard of the British Legation in Peking in the Boxer uprising of 1900. Last year in a letter published in *Globe and Laurel*, the journal of the Royal Marines, he stated that the official citation recording his exploit was 'wildly incorrect'. The citation described how in June 1900, Boxers and Imperial troops had attacked the west wall of the Legation, set fire to the west gate of the south stable quarters and had taken cover in buildings near by. It went on: 'A hole was made in the Legation wall and Captain Halliday, in command of 20 Marines, led the way into the buildings and . . . engaged a part of the enemy. Before he could use his revolver, however, he was shot through the left shoulder at point blank range, the bullet fracturing the shoulder and carrying away part of the lung.

'Notwithstanding the extremely severe nature of the wound Captain Halliday killed three of his assailants and, telling his men to "carry on and not mind him", walked back unaided to the hospital, refusing escort and aid so as not to diminish the number of men engaged in the sortie.'

In his letter last year Halliday said he felt the citation ought to be corrected. He thought that Captain B. M. Strouts, another RM officer, had been killed before the final draft of the citation had been made. 'Actually,' wrote General Halliday, 'I arrived at the west wall of the Legation to report to Strouts that the Japanese did not need any help. I had been sent to see Colonel Shiba (Colonel G. Shiba, Japanese Military attaché). Strouts had had a hole made in the wall and he told me to make a sortie with five men and a corporal, not twenty men.

'I went down a narrow alley and ran into a group of five Boxers armed with rifles. The first shot was fired without bringing his rifle

to the present. I then shot him and three others. The fifth ran away
. . . I then told the men to carry on and I got back unaided to the
wall. I was helped through the hole and Dr Rooke helped me to the
hospital. Strouts then took out twenty or thirty men and pulled down
the small building and cleared the field of fire.

He told me the next morning that my pistol had had a mis-fired
round so I merely had pressed the trigger at the fifth man and he
had escaped. It will be seen that I was acting under orders and I
think that anyone must have done as I did.'

*The Times* (11 March 1966)

# Bibliography

*Papers*

*Elgin mss, Broomhall,* Fife
*Gordon Papers,* British Museum
*Jardine, Matheson* archives, University Library, Cambridge
*Wolseley Papers,* Hove Public Library

*Foreign Documents*

*Affaires Etrangères et Documents Diplomatiques,* Paris
*Russian Treaties in China 1881-89*
*Senate Executive Documents and Despatches and Correspondence of Ministers,* Washington
*United States Foreign Relations Documents,* Washington

*Despatches and Reports*

*FO Papers,* Public Record Office
*Hong Kong Annual Report*
*Hope Grant Papers,* British Museum
*Official Account of the Military Operations in China 1900-1901,* Major E. W. M. Norrie, Ministry of Defence Library (Army and Central)
*Parliamentary Papers,* Public Record Office, and Ministry of Defence Library
*Parliamentary Papers, China No. 4, 1900,* ' Report on the Siege of the Legations ' by Sir Claude M. MacDonald
*Taiping Documents and Official Publications,* British Museum, Oxford and Cambridge

*Journals and Newspapers*

*Chinese Gazette,* Shanghai
*Chinese Recorder*

*Chinese Repository* (20 volumes and Index, Canton)
This is a journal published in Canton from May 1832 to December

1851 edited by the missionary E. C. Bridgeman and S. Wells Williams and contributed to by the famous German missionary Charles Gutzlaff who also translated the Bible into Chinese, and thereby provided material for Hung for his Taiping religious works. Other contributors were T. Wade, G. T. Lay, J. R. Morrison and Robert Morrison. Articles of note are:

'Description of the Chinese Imperial Army', Sir Thomas Wade (Vol. XX, 250, 300-63)
> (Wade was a junior interpreter and consul in the first part of this book. He became Minister at Peking and later Professor of Chinese in the University of Cambridge 1885-95.)

'Remarks on Chinese Character and Customs', G. T. Lay (Vol. XII, 135)

'History of the Traffic in Opium in China', E. C. Bridgeman (Vol. V, 546)

'Essay on the Opium Trade', S. Wells Williams (Vol. XX, 479)

'Cessation of the East India Company's Rights in China', E. C. Bridgeman (Vol. XI, 48)

'Captain Elliot's letter on leaving China' (Vol. VI, 352)

'Letters from Lin to the Queen of England respecting opium seized by Lin' (Vol. VIII, 321)

'Details of the English leaving Macao', E. C. Bridgeman (Vol. VIII, 222)

'Causes of rupture between England and China', J. R. Morrison (Vol. VIII, 619)

'Bombardment of Canton by Sir Hugh Gough', E. C. Bridgeman (Vol. X, 340)

'Gough's and Senhouse's Despatches detailing the Capture of the Heights of Canton' (Vol. X, 535)

'Treaty of Nanking in Chinese and English' (XIII, 438)


*Hansard*

*History Today,* 1960 – 'The burning of the Summer Palace in 1860', by E. W. R. Lumby

*Illustrated London News* – contains many pictures of the Chinese Wars

*Journal of Army Historical Research*

*Journal of the Royal Artillery,* 1938

*Regimental Histories:*

> Queen's, 2nd Regt of Foot;
> Buffs, 3rd Regt;
> Royal Irish, 18th Regt;

Royal Hampshire Regt, 37th Regt, 67th Regt; Essex, 44th Regt;
Royal Berkshire Regt, 49th Regt
*The Times*
*United Services Institution Journal*
*Japanese Defence Academy's Military History Atlas* (Yokosuka,
1960)


*Books*

Allen, B. M., *Gordon in China* (London, 1933)
Allen, R., *The Siege of the Legations* (London, 1901)
Allgood, G., *Letters on the China War* (London, 1901)
Ashley, *The Life and Correspondence of Palmerston*
Bond, B., editor, *Victorian Military Campaigns* (London, 1967)
Boulger, D. G., *The History of China* (London, 1898)
Bowring, J., *Autobiographical Recollections* (London, 1871)
Bredon, J., *Life of Sir Robert Hart* (London, 1909)
Caillard, Fr. du, *Histoire de l'intervention française* (Paris, 1880)
Chafee, A. R., *Report on Military Operations in China* (Washington,
1901)
Cheng, J. C., *The Taiping Rebellion* (Hong Kong, 1963)
Chung-ti Chang, *The Chinese Gentry* (Seattle, 1965)
Clements, P. H., *The Boxer Rebellion* (New York, 1915)
Collis, M., *Foreign Mud* (London, 1946)
Comber, L., *Secret Societies in Malaya* (New York, 1959)
Cooke, G. W., *China and Lower Bengal* (London, 1861)
Cordier, H., *Histoire Générale de la Chine*, 4 vols (Paris, 1920)
Cordier, H., *L'Expédition de Chine de 1857-58* (Paris, 1905)
Eastman, L. E., *Thrones and Mandarins* (Harvard U.P., 1967)
Fessler, L., *China* (New York, 1963)
Fisher, A., *Personal Narrative of Three Years' Service in China*
(London, 1863)
Fleming, P., *The Siege of Peking* (London, 1959)
Fortescue, *History of the British Army*, Vols XII, XIII
Foster, L. S., *Fifty Years in China* (Nashville, 1909)
Frey, H., *Français et Alliés au Pe'-Tchi-li* (Paris, 1904)
Gautier, H., *Les Français au Tonkin* (Paris, 1884)
Giles, H. A., *A Glossary of Reference of Subjects connected with
the Far East* (London, 1900)
Gordon, H. W., *Events in the Life of Charles George Gordon*
(London, 1884)
Gros, Baron, *Négociations entre France et la Chine en 1860* (Paris,
1863)

Grant, General Sir Hope, ed. H. Knollys, *Incidents in the China War, 1860* (Edinburgh, 1865)

Hake, A. E., *The Story of Chinese Gordon* (London, 1884)

Hall, W. H., *The Nemesis in China* (London, 1846)

Hail, W. J. *Tsêng Kuo-fan and the Taiping Rebellion* (New York, 1927)

Holt, E., *The Opium Wars in China* (London, 1964)

Hoppin, J. M., *Life of Andrew Hull Foote, USN* (New York, 1874)

Hurd, R., *The Arrow War* (London, 1967)

Keppel, Admiral, *A Sailor's Life under Four Sovereigns* (London, 1887)

Knolly, H., *Life of General Sir Hope Grant*, Vol. II (London, 1894)

Kuo, P. C., *A Critical Study of the First Anglo-Chinese War, with documents* (Shanghai, 1935)

Lane-Poole, S., *Life of Sir Harry Parkes*, 2 Vols (London, 1894)

Latourette, K. S., *A History of Christian Missionaries in China* (New York, 1929)

Leavenworth, C. S., *The Arrow War with China* (London, 1901)

Loch, H. B., *Personal Narrative of Lord Elgin's 2nd Embassy in China* (London, 1900)

Liang Chi-chao, *A Critical Study of Li Hung-Chang* (Shanghai, 1936)

Lucy, A., *Lettres intimes sur la Campagne de Chine en 1860* (Paris, 1861)

Martin, W. A. P., *The Siege in Peking* (Edinburgh, 1900)

M'Ghee, G. J. L., *How we got to Peking* (London, 1862)

McAleavy, H., *The Modern History of China* (London, 1967)

Maclellan, J. W., *The Story of Shanghai* (Shanghai, 1889)

McPherson, D., *The War in China 1841-42* (London, 1843)

Michael, F., *The Taiping Rebellion – History and Documents,* 3 Vols (Seattle, 1966)

Morison, J. L., *The 8th Earl of Elgin* (London, 1928)

Morse, H. B., *The International Relations of the Chinese Empire 1834-1900* (London, 1910)

Mossman, S., *General Gordon's Private Diary (China)* (London, 1885)

Murray, A., *Doings in China, 1841-42* (London, 1843)

Neumann, K. F., *Ostasiatischte Geschichte vom ersten chinesischen Krieg bis zu den Vertragen in Peking (1840-1900)* (Berlin 1900)

Oliphant, L., *Episodes in a Life of Adventure* (London, 1861)

Oliphant, L., *Narrative of Lord Elgin's Mission to China and Japan* (London, 1889)

Ping-chia Kuo, *China* (Oxford, 1863)

Purcell, V. W., *China* (London, 1962)

Purcell, V. W., *The Boxer Uprising* (Cambridge, 1863)

Rait, R. S., *The Life and Campaigns of Hugh 1st Viscount Gough,* 2 vols (London, 1893)

Rennie, D. F., *British Arms in China* (London, 1864)

Savage, Lander, A. H., *China and the Allies,* 2 vols (London, 1901)

Selby, John, *Stories of Famous Sieges* (London, 1967)

Sparrow, G., *Gordon, Mandarin and Pasha* (London, 1962)

Spector, S., *Li Hung-chang and the Husi Army* (Seattle, 1964)

Steiger, G. N., *China and the Occident* (Newhaven, 1927)

Swinhoe, R., *Narrative of the North China Campaign of 1860* (London, 1861)

Tan, C. C., *The Boxer Catastrophe* (New York, 1955)

Vladimir, *Russia on the Pacific and the Siberian Railway* (London, 1899)

Wakeman, F. (Jr), *Strangers at the Gate* (University of California, 1966)

Waley, A., *The Opium War through Chinese Eyes* (London, 1958)

Walrond, T., *Letters and Journals of James 8th Earl of Elgin* (London, 1872)

Williams, S. Wells, *A History of China* (London, 1897)

Wilson, A., *The Ever Victorious Army* (Edinburgh, 1868)

Wilson, A. W., *The Story of the Gun* (London, 1944)

Wolseley, G., *The Story of a Soldier's Life,* Vol. II (London, 1903)

Wright, S. F., *Hart in the Chinese Customs* (Belfast, 1950)

# Index

# Index

# Index